Survival

GLOBAL POLITICS AND STRATEGY

Volume 60 Number 4 | August–September 2018

'Under this doctrine, a 159-page document of mind-numbing detail is somehow supposed to have a "spirit" separable from its text that can be violated by its signatories. This spurious neo-Platonism absolves the complainant of any responsibility to prove technical non-compliance.'

Steven Simon, Iran and President Trump: What Is the Endgame?, p. 15.

'In the end, Pierre attempted no grand theory of human nature or international relations, preferring, as he far too modestly put it, "merely [to] observe and describe events" … But he gave us a very rare kind of intellectual nourishment, and left us with questions that we ignore at our peril.'

John L. Harper, Pierre Hassner (1933–2018): An Appreciation, p. 48.

'Overall Alliance cohesion could benefit from the open acknowledgement of allies' diverging threat priorities, and an agreement to allow for a division of labour among them.'

Lucie Béraud-Sudreau and Bastian Giegerich, NATO Defence Spending and European Threat Perceptions, p. 70.

T0332508

Survival

GLOBAL POLITICS AND STRATEGY

Volume 60 Number 4 | August–September 2018

Contents

Survival GLOBAL POLITICS AND STRATEGY

Iran, Korea and President Trump

Steven Simon, James Dobbins, Bruce Bennett, Jeffrey W. Hornung, Andrew Scobell and Mark Fitzpatrick

Cover: Saul Loeb/AFP/Getty

On the cover
US President Donald Trump meets with North Korean leader Kim Jong-un at the start of their historic Singapore Summit, at the Capella Hotel on Sentosa Island in Singapore on 12 June 2018.

On the web
Visit www.iiss.org/publications/survival for brief notices on new books on Politics and International Relations, Russia and Eurasia, and Asia-Pacific.

***Survival* editors' blog**
For ideas and commentary from *Survival* editors and contributors, visit www.iiss.org/blogs/survival-blog.

Survival

GLOBAL POLITICS AND STRATEGY

The International Institute for Strategic Studies

2121 K Street, NW | Suite 801 | Washington DC 20037 | USA
Tel +1 202 659 1490   Fax +1 202 659 1499   E-mail survival@iiss.org   Web www.iiss.org

Arundel House | 6 Temple Place | London | WC2R 2PG | UK
Tel +44 (0)20 7379 7676   Fax +44 (0)20 7836 3108   E-mail iiss@iiss.org

14th Floor, GBCorp Tower | Bahrain Financial Harbour | Manama | Kingdom of Bahrain
Tel +973 1718 1155   Fax +973 1710 0155   E-mail iiss-middleeast@iiss.org

9 Raffles Place | #51-01 Republic Plaza | Singapore 048619
Tel +65 6499 0055   Fax +65 6499 0059   E-mail iiss-asia@iiss.org

Survival Online www.tandfonline.com/survival and www.iiss.org/publications/survival

Aims and Scope *Survival* is one of the world's leading forums for analysis and debate of international and strategic affairs. Shaped by its editors to be both timely and forward thinking, the journal encourages writers to challenge conventional wisdom and bring fresh, often controversial, perspectives to bear on the strategic issues of the moment. With a diverse range of authors, *Survival* aims to be scholarly in depth while vivid, well written and policy-relevant in approach. Through commentary, analytical articles, case studies, forums, review essays, reviews and letters to the editor, the journal promotes lively, critical debate on issues of international politics and strategy.

Editor **Dana Allin**
Managing Editor **Jonathan Stevenson**
Associate Editor **Carolyn West**
Editorial Assistant **Jessica Watson**
Editorial Intern **Daniel Moshashai**
Production and Cartography **John Buck, Kelly Verity**

Contributing Editors

Gilles Andréani	**Bill Emmott**	**Jeffrey Lewis**	**Teresita C. Schaffer**	**David C. Unger**
Ian Bremmer	**John A. Gans, Jr**	**Hanns W. Maull**	**Steven Simon**	**Ruth Wedgwood**
David P. Calleo	**John L. Harper**	**Jeffrey Mazo**	**Angela Stent**	**Lanxin Xiang**
Russell Crandall	**†Pierre Hassner**	**'Funmi Olonisakin**	**Jonathan Stevenson**	
Toby Dodge	**Erik Jones**	**Thomas Rid**	**Ray Takeyh**	

Published for the IISS by
Routledge Journals, an imprint of Taylor & Francis, an Informa business.

About the IISS The IISS, a registered charity with offices in Washington, London, Manama and Singapore, is the world's leading authority on political–military conflict. It is the primary independent source of accurate, objective information on international strategic issues. Publications include *The Military Balance*, an annual reference work on each nation's defence capabilities; *Strategic Survey*, an annual review of world affairs; *Survival*, a bimonthly journal on international affairs; *Strategic Comments*, an online analysis of topical issues in international affairs; and the *Adelphi* series of books on issues of international security.

SUBMISSIONS

To submit an article, authors are advised to follow these guidelines:

- *Survival* articles are around 4,000–10,000 words long including endnotes. A word count should be included with a draft. Length is a consideration in the review process and shorter articles have an advantage.
- All text, including endnotes, should be double-spaced with wide margins.
- Any tables or artwork should be supplied in separate files, ideally not embedded in the document or linked to text around it.
- All *Survival* articles are expected to include endnote references. These should be complete and include first and last names of authors, titles of articles (even from newspapers), place of publication, publisher, exact publication dates, volume and issue number (if from a journal) and page numbers. Web sources should include complete URLs and DOIs if available.
- A summary of up to 150 words should be included with the article. The summary should state the main argument clearly and concisely, not simply say what the article is about.

- A short author's biography of one or two lines should also be included. This information will appear at the foot of the first page of the article.
- *Survival* has a strict policy of listing multiple authors in alphabetical order.

Submissions should be made by email, in Microsoft Word format, to survival@iiss.org. Alternatively, hard copies may be sent to *Survival*, IISS–US, 2121 K Street NW, Suite 801, Washington, DC 20037, USA.

The editorial review process can take up to three months. *Survival*'s acceptance rate for unsolicited manuscripts is less than 20%. *Survival* does not normally provide referees' comments in the event of rejection. Authors are permitted to submit simultaneously elsewhere so long as this is consistent with the policy of the other publication and the Editors of *Survival* are informed of the dual submission.

Readers are encouraged to comment on articles from the previous issue. Letters should be concise, no longer than 750 words and relate directly to the argument or points made in the original article.

ADVERTISING AND PERMISSIONS

For advertising rates and schedules

USA/Canada: The Advertising Manager, Taylor & Francis Inc., 530 Walnut Street, Suite 850, Philadelphia, PA 19106, USA Tel +1 (800) 354 1420 Fax +1 (215) 207 0050.

UK/Europe/Rest of World: The Advertising Manager, Routledge Journals, Taylor & Francis, 4 Park Square, Milton Park, Abingdon, Oxfordshire OX14 4RN, UK Tel +44 (0) 207 017 6000 Fax +44 (0) 207 017 6336.

SUBSCRIPTIONS

Survival is published bi-monthly in February, April, June, August, October and December by Routledge Journals, an imprint of Taylor & Francis, an Informa Business.

Annual Subscription 2018

Institution	£505	$885	€742
Individual	£144	$243	€196
Online only	£442	$774	€649

Taylor & Francis has a flexible approach to subscriptions, enabling us to match individual libraries' requirements. This journal is available via a traditional institutional subscription (either print with online access, or online only at a discount) or as part of our libraries, subject collections or archives. For more information on our sales packages please visit http://www.tandfonline.com/page/librarians.

All current institutional subscriptions include online access for any number of concurrent users across a local area network to the currently available backfile and articles posted online ahead of publication.

Subscriptions purchased at the personal rate are strictly for personal, non-commercial use only. The reselling of personal subscriptions is prohibited. Personal subscriptions must be purchased with a personal cheque or credit card. Proof of personal status may be requested.

Dollar rates apply to all subscribers outside Europe. Euro rates apply to all subscribers in Europe, except the UK and the Republic of Ireland where the pound sterling rate applies. If you are unsure which rate applies to you please contact Customer Services in the UK. All subscriptions are payable in advance and all rates include postage. Journals are sent by air to the USA, Canada, Mexico, India, Japan and Australasia. Subscriptions are entered on an annual basis, i.e. January to December. Payment may be made by sterling cheque, dollar cheque, euro cheque, international money order, National Giro or credit cards (Amex, Visa and Mastercard).

Survival (USPS 013095) is published bimonthly (in Feb, Apr, Jun, Aug, Oct and Dec) by Routledge Journals, Taylor & Francis, 4 Park Square, Milton Park, Abingdon, OX14 4RN, United Kingdom.

The US annual subscription price is $842. Airfreight and mailing in the USA by agent named Air Business Ltd, c/o Worldnet Shipping Inc., 156-15, 146th Avenue, 2nd Floor, Jamaica, NY 11434, USA. Periodicals postage paid at Jamaica NY 11431.

US Postmaster: Send address changes to Survival, C/O Air Business Ltd / 156-15 146th Avenue, Jamaica, New York, NY11434.

Subscription records are maintained at Taylor & Francis Group, 4 Park Square, Milton Park, Abingdon, OX14 4RN, United Kingdom.

ORDERING INFORMATION

Please contact your local Customer Service Department to take out a subscription to the Journal: **USA, Canada:** Taylor & Francis, Inc., 530 Walnut Street, Suite 850, Philadelphia, PA 19106, USA. Tel: +1 800 354 1420; Fax: +1 215 207 0050. **UK/Europe/Rest of World:** T&F Customer Services, Informa UK Ltd, Sheepen Place, Colchester, Essex, CO3 3LP, United Kingdom. Tel: +44 (0) 20 7017 5544; Fax: +44 (0) 20 7017 5198; Email: subscriptions@tandf.co.uk.

Back issues: Taylor & Francis retains a two-year back issue stock of journals. Older volumes are held by our official stockists: Periodicals Service Company, 351 Fairview Ave., Suite 300, Hudson, New York 12534, USA to whom all orders and enquiries should be addressed. *Tel* +1 518 537 4700 *Fax* +1 518 537 5899 *e-mail* psc@periodicals.com *web* http://www.periodicals.com/tandf.html.

The International Institute for Strategic Studies (IISS) and our publisher Taylor & Francis make every effort to ensure the accuracy of all the information (the "Content") contained in our publications. However, the IISS and our publisher Taylor & Francis, our agents, and our licensors make no representations or warranties whatsoever as to the accuracy, completeness, or suitability for any purpose of the Content. Any opinions and views expressed in this publication are the opinions and views of the authors, and are not the views of or endorsed by the IISS and our publisher Taylor & Francis. The accuracy of the Content should not be relied upon and should be independently verified with primary sources of information. The IISS and our publisher Taylor & Francis shall not be liable for any losses, actions, claims, proceedings, demands, costs, expenses, damages, and other liabilities whatsoever or howsoever caused arising directly or indirectly in connection with, in relation to or arising out of the use of the Content. Terms & Conditions of access and use can be found at http://www.tandfonline.com/page/terms-and-conditions.

The issue date is August–September 2018.

The print edition of this journal is printed on ANSI conforming acid free paper.

Adelphi Book

ONCE AND FUTURE PARTNERS

THE UNITED STATES, RUSSIA AND NUCLEAR NON-PROLIFERATION

Edited by William C. Potter and Sarah Bidgood

Adelphi 464–465; published 27 July 2018; 234x156; 96pp; Paperback: 978-1-138-36636-7

Dr William C. Potter directs the James Martin Center for Nonproliferation Studies and is the Sam Nunn and Richard Lugar Professor of Nonproliferation Studies at the Middlebury Institute of International Studies at Monterey. Trained as a Sovietologist, he has participated as a delegate at every NPT meeting since 1995.

Sarah Bidgood is a senior research associate and project manager at the James Martin Center for Nonproliferation Studies at the Middlebury Institute of International Studies at Monterey. Her research interests include US–Russia relations and the international non-proliferation regime.

Relations between the United States and Russia today are beset by rivalry in almost every sphere, and mutual suspicion reigns. Both parties have shunned arms-reduction talks and are pursuing nuclear modernisation programmes; a new nuclear arms race looms. Yet the two leading nuclear powers have shared interests in checking the proliferation of nuclear weapons and related technologies, as did the US and Soviet Union during the Cold War.

This *Adelphi* book reaches back to episodes of US–Soviet cooperation on nuclear non-proliferation to identify factors that permitted successful joint action, even in circumstances of profound geopolitical rivalry. It includes essays on the collaboration that prevented South Africa from conducting a nuclear-weapon test in 1977; Cold-War-era discussions on peaceful nuclear explosions and the developments that led from the Limited Test-Ban Treaty to the Treaty on the Non-Proliferation of Nuclear Weapons (Non-Proliferation Treaty, or NPT); negotiating and sustaining the NPT; the establishment of the London Club and nuclear-export controls; bolstering IAEA safeguards; and negotiating the draft Radiological Weapons Convention. From these case studies, the editors identify seven lessons for contemporary policymakers and three immediate challenges that can only be overcome through bilateral cooperation.

> **" "** *Superb. A must–read for all interested in US–Russia relations and the history of nuclear cooperation. The lessons of close cooperation on nuclear non–proliferation – even during the darkest days of the Cold War – can teach us how to "go back to basics" to rejuvenate such cooperation in the future.*
> Siegfried S. Hecker, Senior Fellow Emeritus, Center for International Security and Cooperation, Stanford University and former director, Los Alamos National Laboratory

> **" "** *Even during the Cold War, the United States and the Soviet Union worked together to limit nuclear arms and build the global regime to stem the spread of nuclear weapons. Today, Washington and Moscow seem to have forgotten these habits of cooperation, and partly as a result, the architecture of nuclear order is in crisis. This critically important book details how the superpowers succeeded in the past – including the central role of personal relationships between experts on each side in finding creative solutions – and offers urgent ideas for rebuilding cooperation to take on today's challenges.*
> Professor Matthew Bunn, Harvard University

AVAILABLE 27th JULY FOR PURCHASE ONLINE: www.iiss.org/publications/adelph

Iran and President Trump: What Is the Endgame?

Steven Simon

The election of President Donald Trump appears to signify the end of an epoch, stretching back to the Second World War, in which Iran and the United States have lurched alternately closer and further apart. There is now a US administration committed not to containing Iranian power but to rolling it back to Iran's territorial borders and ultimately disarming it. These maximal aims would appear to entail regime change. Yet dislodging Iran's government would take a massive effort and likely entail another American war in the Middle East.[2] Whether Trump has the focus, will, and domestic and international support for this quest seems dubious. But he does appear to have the intent.

The annals of American ambivalence toward Iran are long. In the late 1960s and early 1970s, as Britain unwound its empire east of Suez amid economic pressures, and the United States became overextended in Southeast Asia, the US had to deputise protecting powers to secure American interests in the Persian Gulf, which revolved around what a senior official blithely described to the author a few years later as 'our oil'. Iran and Saudi Arabia were the only plausible candidates. Richard Nixon formalised this arrangement as the Twin Pillars policy. But the Nixon administration's push to reverse the oil-price hikes triggered by the Israeli military occupation of Egyptian territory after the 1973 Yom Kippur War ran counter to the shah's need for funds to pay for an

Steven Simon is the John J. McCloy '16 Visiting Professor of History at Amherst College. He served on the National Security Council in the Clinton and Obama administrations and at the US Department of State.

Survival | vol. 60 no. 4 | August–September | pp. 7–20   DOI 10.1080/00396338.2018.1494975 ambitious development programme, as well as the self-indulgence and corruption of his court.

As the Pahlavi regime's domestic legitimacy eroded during Jimmy Carter's administration, the US was lashed to the mast of an ally about which it essentially knew nothing. The CIA station in Tehran was blocked from recruiting assets and sources, and had to rely on reporting by the SAVAK, the shah's domestic-intelligence service. The embassy had just four Farsi speakers.[3] Compounding the problem was a bad case of circular logic among US intelligence analysts and diplomats. If the regime were in trouble it would be acting as though it were – and because it wasn't, the situation was therefore under control. So the revolution took everyone by surprise. With the Carter administration knee-deep in the 1978 Camp David negotiations that ultimately produced a peace agreement between Egypt and Israel, the Pahlavi regime was left to twist in the wind. Although there was little the US could have done to save Pahlavi's authority at that late stage, US preoccupation with Arab–Israeli peace impeded preparations that the US could have made to preserve its interests, and perhaps even to have averted the hostage crisis that destroyed Carter's administration and bounded the future of US–Iran relations.

The following year, while the exiled shah, dying of cancer, wandered the globe in search of a place to lay his head, the Carter administration convinced itself – against the evidence – that the US–Iran relationship was salvageable. Until the embassy hostage-taking in November 1979 shattered this illusion, the CIA kept up a flow of sensitive intelligence on Iraq to the new regime. With occupation of the embassy in Tehran and under pressure from a reinvigorated Republican Party, Carter reversed course, launching *Operation Eagle Claw* to rescue the hostages – a textbook military disaster that reinforced Iranian threat perceptions while showcasing American incapacity and boosting Ronald Reagan's political prospects.

Oscillations

Reagan was a kind of visionary, among other things, and he believed that rapprochement with Iran would be possible if the US took the first step. He approached the Soviet Union in much the same way, trying to initiate a dialogue with one premier after another, but getting frustrated because 'they keep dying on me'. He finally struck gold with Mikhail Gorbachev. (Iran's Gorbachev has yet to appear, assuming he hasn't taken the form of Hassan Rouhani.) The president's conviction that US–Iranian relations could be reconstituted raised eyebrows, given that a proto-Hizbullah had destroyed both the US embassy in Beirut, killing most of the United States' regional intelligence officers, and the US Marine barracks there, killing 241 US military personnel. The Shia militia had also taken a dozen mostly American hostages, tortured to death a CIA station chief as well as a Marine officer attached to a UN peacekeeping force, and assassinated the president of the storied American University of Beirut. Syria, Iran's (and the Soviet Union's) ally, had downed a US bomber, whose surviving crewmember had to be retrieved from Syria by the clergyman and civil-rights activist Jesse Jackson. Eventually surpassing the weirdness of that episode was a secret US–Israeli pilgrimage to Tehran, featuring the Reagan administration's gift to the Iranian clerical regime of a Bible and a cake in the shape of a key.

The Reagan administration's impressive ignorance of conditions in Iran and its blind reliance on Israeli intermediaries pursuing their own interests are hard to overstate. Among the misconceptions at work was the idea that an Iran weakened by the ongoing brutal war with Iraq could be seduced by the Soviets into an anti-American alliance. This anxiety accounted for defense secretary Caspar Weinberger's acquiescence in the scandalous arms deals of the Iran–Contra affair, the result of Reagan's fantasy of a new era in US–Iranian relations and natural sympathy for the hostages.

With the public disclosure in a Lebanese newspaper of US arms deliveries to Iran in exchange for hostages – and the increasingly obvious Iranian and Israeli gaming of the Reagan administration's forlorn desire for rapprochement and release of the hostages – that hope ended. An intelligence team was dispatched to Baghdad where its members pumped targeting information on Iran to their Iraqi hosts. In turn, Iraq rained missiles down on Iranian population centres and ultimately flooded the battlefield with nerve gas, declaring that for every insect there was a proper insecticide.

At the same time, thanks to Kuwait's shrewd manipulation of US fears of Soviet encroachment in the Gulf, Washington agreed to reflag Kuwaiti tankers as American vessels, thereby acquiring the right to defend them against Iranian attack. This brought the US directly into combat with Iran. Iran scored a few successes, most notably the crippling of the USS *Samuel B. Roberts*, a guided-missile frigate escorting tankers. Although a US Navy ship did, mistakenly and tragically, shoot down an Iranian commercial airliner, killing 290 civilians, the Reagan administration abstained from retaliatory strikes into Iranian territory for fear of pushing Iran into the Soviets' embrace. No administration of either party has since responded to Iran's provocations by bringing the war to its territory.

Iraq, of course, was a different matter. The George H.W. Bush administration assembled a mammoth coalition to expel Iraqi forces from Kuwait in 1991. Iran, however, hovered in the background. Competent realists that they were, the Bush team thought in terms of power balances and alliance management and concluded that a fatally wounded Iraq would empower a revolutionary Iran. They anticipated the problems this would cause and elected not to take *Desert Storm* to Baghdad. The Bush team was preoccupied by other, bigger issues at the time, including the challenge of German reunification in the context of a collapsing Soviet empire.

Dual containment, axis of evil, rapprochement

Like the Reagan administration, the Clinton White House oscillated. Typically, an offshore balancer like the United States would side with the weaker state against the stronger, seeking a stable regional-power equilibrium. It is true that the US only rarely seemed to apply this criterion to its management of ties with Iran and Iraq. In the case of the Persian Gulf, Washington had tended to be more concerned with the balance of threat rather than balance of power. Either way, though, the US chose one side or the other.

Clinton's advisers, however, assessed America's post-Cold War preponderance of military power, demonstrated so dramatically by the first Gulf War, to be ample for managing any challenge to the US position in the Gulf. The result was a novel doctrine of 'dual containment', which declared both Iran and Iraq to be enemies. New, inexperienced administrations often experiment if only to differentiate themselves from their predecessors;

perhaps it should not be surprising that the Clinton White House abandoned strategic logic so comprehensively. The resulting collapse of Saddam
Hussein's regime and empowerment of Iran was anticipated quite clearly
in the pages of *Foreign Affairs*, the oracular voice of sober strategic thinking,
but the critique failed to stir self-examination.[4]

In the meantime, the administration – pushed by Congress – signed
a punitive sanctions law against Iran and launched a worldwide diplomatic campaign to pry third countries with commercial ties to Iran from
the regime. Iran responded by attacking temporary US military quarters
at al-Khobar in Saudi Arabia in June 1996, killing 19 men and women and
wounding hundreds more. Saudi fears of involuntary involvement in a war
between the US and Iran precluded an immediate US response, and ultimately set in motion the US military's expulsion from Saudi Arabia at the
turn of the twenty-first century. Qatar, ever eager to provoke the Saudis,
leapt on the opportunity to provide the regional base access and facilities
the US needed. Despite the wedge this development drove between the US
and Saudi Arabia, Iran still faces a robust US military presence on the Arab
side of the Gulf.

The 1997 election of reformist Iranian president Mohammad Khatami,
who endorsed a dialogue of civilisations and pledged to exert control over
the Iranian intelligence service, provided a reluctant US administration
with the pretext for rapprochement rather than reprisal. The secretary of
state, Madeleine Albright, apologised for US complicity in the 1953 coup,
and the administration relaxed restrictions on the import of pistachios and
carpets by executive order. But congressional resistance and the infeasibility
of direct talks precluded further diplomatic advances.

George W. Bush was clearly yet another vacillator. According to James
Dobbins, the senior-most US diplomat involved in the post-2001 reconstruc-
tion of Afghanistan, as the United States and other members of the so-called
'contact group' of countries were trying to assemble a representative Afghan
government, the US and Iran cooperated closely on account of their shared
interest in a stable Afghanistan, potentially signalling a new beginning in
bilateral relations. But an intercepted message of congratulations from a
senior al-Qaeda operative under house arrest in Iran sent to the perpetra-

tors of a bloody assault on a housing compound in Saudi Arabia impelled the Bush administration to renounce Iranian cooperation on Afghanistan. Iran became one of the poles in the axis of evil.

During the subsequent US occupation of Iraq, given that the United States had wiped Iran's most lethal adversary off the map but was now positioned on Iran's border, Tehran's best option was to raise the cost of US intervention without precipitating a premature American withdrawal and the resuscitation of Ba'athist power. So Iran supplied explosively formed projectiles – extremely effective armour-penetrating munitions – to Shia militias, drawing American blood.

The Obama administration shifted gears as well, but in reverse order. It entered office determined to increase multilateral sanctions against Iran. Free of the political burden of his predecessor's unpopular foreign policy, Obama persuaded the United Nations Security Council to impose unprecedentedly heavy sanctions on Iran, including an oil embargo. While these were slowly strangling the Iranian economy, the administration began working with Israel on a cyber campaign, known as Stuxnet, that would eventually disable one-fifth of Iran's uranium-enrichment centrifuges. Economic misery contributed to the election in 2013 of Hassan Rouhani as president of Iran. Rouhani was no saint, having been implicated in post-revolutionary violence, but he appeared open to negotiated limits on Iran's nuclear programme in return for the alleviation of sanctions.

Two years later, the P5+1 and the EU produced an agreement with Iran known as the Joint Comprehensive Plan of Action, or JCPOA. Through limits on nuclear-related infrastructure, access to fissile material, restrictions on enrichment levels and relatively intrusive inspections, the agreement is intended to make it very hard, if not impossible, for Iran to break out and race for a bomb too quickly for the international community to react effectively. Limits on enrichment and stockpiles of low-enriched uranium are to be in place for another 13 years, for a total of 15.

In the meantime, the US had worked steadily to develop the specialised munitions and tactics necessary to destroy Iran's nuclear infrastructure should Tehran decide to sprint for a bomb. There remains some scepticism, especially among Israelis, that Obama would have followed through on his vow to prevent Iran from getting a nuclear weapon by whatever means necessary. Having worked for Obama during this period, my view is that the president was prepared to use force. In any case, as diplomatic efforts gained traction, the Obama administration reportedly curtailed its cooperation with Israel and chose not to facilitate an Israeli attack against Iran's nuclear infrastructure. From the Obama administration's perspective, if war would set back the Iranian programme by two years and a negotiated agreement would block weapons development for 15 years, war did not make a lot of sense.

End of ambivalence?

In Donald Trump, the US may have finally found a president whose views on Iran are both unambiguous and immutable. They are, as social scientists would say, overdetermined.

First among causes, the Iran deal, like the Affordable Care Act, stands as part of a repugnant Obama legacy and is therefore to be repudiated; whether or not Trump has specific, substantive objections to the deal appears politically immaterial. Trump told the UN General Assembly that the JCPOA 'was one of the worst and most one-sided transactions the United States has ever entered into' and 'an embarrassment to the United States'.[5] Secondly, Trump's small cadre of conservative Jewish donors tend to align with the policies of Israel's governing Likud coalition, which regards Iran as an existential danger to Israel, and the JCPOA as aiding and abetting this threat. Thirdly, endorsements of the nuclear deal, even when they are unambiguous, often appear grudging, as when Secretary of Defense James Mattis was compelled to concede in open testimony that the JCPOA was in the national interest. Fourthly, some proponents, presumably to sustain their reputations as hard-nosed analysts (which admittedly is perhaps a necessity in the current political environment), ritually declare the deal to be bad before explaining why it is good. This qualification reinforces perceptions that, as Trump insists, the US was 'ripped off'. Finally, arguments against the JCPOA generally hold that a deal that banned Iranian nuclear enrichment at any level in perpetuity, and permitted no-notice inspections anywhere in Iran, could easily have been negotiated by a gutsier administration.

If these factors were insufficient to explain Trump's vituperation vis-à-vis Iran, there is also his character: eminently biddable, and therefore susceptible to the astute personal flattery unleashed by Saudi and Emirati allies. They have also injected money into a slew of Washington-based advocacy organisations that have flooded Capitol Hill with dire assessments of the Iranian threat, blurring the line between US interests and the interests of its allies.

Given his posture on Iran, Trump's obligation under the Iran Nuclear Agreement Review Act of 2015 (INARA), to certify every 90 days that Iran is in compliance with the JCPOA, clearly annoyed him. The purpose of this cycle, after all, was to wrong-foot Obama and any Democratic successor. Believing firmly that Iran could be relied upon to cheat, the 90-day certification cycle was imposed to saddle Obama

The Iranians have not cheated

with the iterated embarrassment of either certifying despite evidence of Iranian cheating – thus looking like Neville Chamberlain at Munich – or decertifying, and thus proving the deal's critics right. Regrettably for the drafters of the INARA, the Iranians have not cheated, and the president is of their own party. He has therefore been very unhappy with the certification process, which compelled him to acknowledge Iran's compliance twice. The second time, on 15 July 2017, he made it clear that he was not going to certify again. In that episode, then-secretary of state Rex Tillerson told Trump that he had no choice but to certify because there was no evidence that Iran was not in compliance.[6] Reportedly feeling jammed and angry, Trump's reaction was to take the issue away from the State Department and transfer responsibility for the certification process to White House staff. On 11 January 2018, the administration refused to recertify and punted the question of sanctions to Congress. On 8 May 2018, rejecting pleas from European partners, Trump announced the United States' withdrawal from the JCPOA and ordered the imposition of stringent new sanctions 'as expeditiously as possible' within 180 days.

Under the terms of the JCPOA, which has no withdrawal clause, Trump's action constituted a material breach. The grounds both for not certifying and for withdrawing appear to lie in a novel doctrine, per UN Ambassador Nikki Haley in a September 2017 speech at the American Enterprise Institute, that 'judging any international agreement begins and ends with the nature of the government that signed it' and whether 'it can be trusted to abide by its commitments'.[7] Tillerson explicitly linked the viability of the deal to Iran's support of the Syrian regime and its development of ballistic missiles, even though these factors have nothing to do with Iran's nuclear capability and were explicitly delinked from the JCPOA's negotiation.

Moreover, under this doctrine, a 159-page document of mind-numbing detail is somehow supposed to have a 'spirit' separable from its text that can be violated by its signatories. This spurious neo-Platonism absolves the complainant of any responsibility to prove technical non-compliance, or to acknowledge the relevance of International Atomic Energy Agency (IAEA) assessments of compliance. The appeal of the doctrine to a Trump administration that is clearly frustrated by Iran's compliance with the JCPOA is obvious. From the White House's perspective, Iran's technical compliance could even be said to violate the spirit of the agreement by deviously trapping the United States into suspending sanctions despite the regime's bad behaviour.

At the risk of giving the administration undue credit, the closest analogy to its approach toward the nuclear agreement would be Henry Kissinger's 'hard linkage', which he tried to establish in the 1970s between US participation in arms-control talks and trade concessions on the one hand, and Soviet restraint in the Third World on the other, especially in Vietnam, but also in Africa and Latin America, so as to underpin detente. The formula proved to be as unworkable as it was elegant. The Soviets did not have the control over their clients presupposed by effective linkage, and US legislation tying the emigration of Soviet Jews to trade concessions undermined Soviet confidence in the benefits of linkage. Looking back on linkage many years later, Kissinger assessed that the two issues at stake were 'too incommensurable, the outcome of strategic arms discussion was too uncertain, the Hanoi leadership was too intractable, and the time scale required for either negotiation too difficult to synchronize'.[8] Substitute Damascus for Hanoi and the parallel is inescapable.

In a 13 October 2017 fact sheet, the White House recapitulated existing US concerns about Iranian activities in the region and insisted on fixes to oft-cited flaws in the JCPOA: the absent sunset clause, access to military sites, and the failure to address Iran's missile-development programme.[9] Overall, 'The United States' new Iran strategy focuses on neutralizing the Government of Iran's destabilizing influence and constraining its aggression, particularly its support for terrorism and militants.'[10]

A bipartisan majority in the US Congress likely grasps that Trump's withdrawal from the deal and imposition of new sanctions against the wishes of the other signatories have ceded the moral high ground to Iran. The French, Germans and British are making clear that, as long as Iran is in compliance with the agreement, they will not withdraw from it. And they have all indicated that they will resist US attempts to apply secondary sanctions to their countries' firms. (Since 1997, the EU has prohibited companies of member states from complying with US secondary sanctions.) It is possible that the administration is to some extent attempting to generate pressure for a renegotiation of the JCPOA. Given that Iran would no doubt bring its own list of grievances to the table and that the P4+1 would be unenthusiastic about renewed talks, it is unclear where this process could lead.[11] There is a strong possibility that the European signatories will be unable to sustain their resistance to US pressure and that the JCPOA will collapse as a result.

The French, German and British governments, along with various EU officials, have spoken of a potentially catastrophic breach in the transatlantic relationship precipitated by the US withdrawal, and it goes almost without saying that Russia and China will follow the P3's lead. Trump thus appears ready to trade NATO solidarity for a new alliance structure privileging powers like Israel and Saudi Arabia that do not fully subscribe to the established liberal international order. This shift would lead ineluctably to a more multipolar world and the erosion of US influence. That such a development would aggrandise, rather than weaken, Iran is a reality that appears not to trouble Trump.

US regional approach

The paramount question at this stage is not what the United States will do in the nuclear domain but how it will act on Iran's regional violations of the 'spirit' of the agreement. The 13 October statement describes 'Iran's steady expansion of proxy forces and terrorist networks ... in hopes of dominating the greater Middle East ... as they try to establish a bridge from Iran to Lebanon and Syria'. The administration, according to this document, will 'address the totality of these threats from and malign activities by the Government of Iran and will seek to bring about a change in the Iranian regime's behavior'.[12]

During the Eisenhower and Reagan administrations, 'rollback' of Soviet power from Eastern Europe was a cause célèbre for the right. Containment, as advocated by George Kennan, was condemned as immoral in consigning the populations of Eastern Europe to Russian domination. And, with Munich in mind, it was also deplored as a strategic blunder. Rollback was never embraced as policy, however, because Eastern Europe was more important to the Soviets than it was to the United States. Asymmetry of interest virtually guaranteed escalation and Soviet victory.

The rollback of Iran's presence to its territorial borders poses the same difficulty. Proponents of rollback, who include Israeli Prime Minister Benjamin Netanyahu and Saudi Crown Prince Mohammad bin Salman as well as Trump-administration principals, argue that Iran seeks to carve out 'land corridors' to the Levant to embed itself on Israel's borders while sustaining a wounded Syrian regime. Land and naval bases would follow. Land corridors naturally evoke interwar geopolitics; this exaggerates the stakes by creating the impression that we are now in a pre-war crisis that will determine the fate of the West.[13]

Iran, however, has pursued these goals for decades, certainly since 1982. Iran fed Hizbullah's stockpiles of Iranian missiles not through a land corridor, but by flying them in cargo planes to Damascus and then shipping them by road the short distance to Lebanon. Until 2003, when the US removed Iraq as a barrier to Iranian land access to Syria, Tehran did fine without such corridors.

Since a bloodied Reagan administration withdrew from Lebanon, having entered to ensure America's global credibility, successive US administrations have rejected rollback of Iran as infeasible. Israel's forced withdrawal from Lebanon in May 2000 reflected the same calculation. Perhaps there was such a possibility in early 2011, when Syrian President

Bashar al-Assad supposedly agreed to abandon Iran in return for the Golan Heights. The outbreak of civil war that spring eliminated the possibility of any such deal.

According to State Department testimony on 11 January 2018, President Trump's 'strategic judgment' calls for an indeterminate US military presence in the 'crucial north and northeast' of Syria. This continuous deployment is meant to achieve a number of objectives: to foster the political reconstitution of a Syria without the Assad family at the helm; to protect the largely Kurdish Syrian Democratic Forces, who fought 'so valiantly' against the Islamic State (ISIS); to prevent the resurgence of ISIS; to facilitate humanitarian aid; and to ensure the 'diminishment' of Iran's 'malign activities' in Syria.[14] Members of the Senate Committee on Foreign Relations, who were the recipients of this strategic judgment, asked for clarification, given that there was no conceivable scenario in which Iran would not have a role in Syria's future. And if this were indeed the case, then the US presence would necessarily be permanent. Asked to clarify, the witness, a long-serving, customarily punctilious diplomat, initially refused to answer in open session; but his implication that the purpose of US troops in Syria was too secret to reveal didn't fly. Pressed further, he disclosed that the administration was 'deeply concerned with the activities of Iran, with the ability of Iran to enhance those activities through a greater ability to move materiel into Syria'.[15]

Yet this raises additional questions. Iranian land routes through Syria do not pass through the northern areas where US forces are now deployed. The so-called corridor transits southern Syria where the borders of Jordan, Iraq and Syria meet, or central and eastern Syria around the beleaguered city of Deir ez-Zor. The southern flashpoint includes the neighbourhood of al-Tanaf and Al-Bukamal, astride the Baghdad–Damascus highway.

*   *   *

The apparent confusion could signify that the administration's reliance on Iranian corridors as a predicate for a long-term presence in Syria is merely cover for another purpose, such as threatening the Assad regime with attack if, in the fullness of time, Assad doesn't depart. Or it could presage an impending adjustment of the US military presence to interdict the nettlesome corridors. Israel's alleged 18 June airstrikes on Shia fighters on the Syria–Iraq border, reportedly killing 52, reinforced perceptions that momentum towards concerted military action along these lines was building. Or the ambiguity could mean that a coherent strategy was being formulated but was not quite ready for prime time. Or it might simply reflect real confusion. If so, the Trump administration would turn out looking like many of its predecessors for whom neither marriage nor murder was an acceptable resolution to the tensions entailed by the bilateral relationship.

A couple of signs pointed to the latter possibility: the administration's eventual decision to conduct rather limited strikes in response to the Douma chemical attack and its reluctance to engage Iranian forces in eastern Syria. But the subsequent appointment of John Bolton as national security advisor and Mike Pompeo as secretary of state indicated a harder line. Furthermore, the Trump defence budget suggests that the administration is gearing up for a fight. The 2018 request would significantly increase the size of the navy, air force and ground forces. Indeed, it would exceed the last great expansion of America's force structure which began in the last year of the Carter administration and vastly increased in Reagan's first term. Adjusted for inflation, the Trump budget matches Reagan's cataract of cash for the Pentagon. The difference is that Reagan thought that a powerful military was the prerequisite for negotiation with America's adversaries. For Trump, negotiations are valorised but avoided, precluded by unilateral action or undermined, as shown by the withdrawal from the Trans-Pacific Partnership, the Paris climate-change accord and now the JCPOA. A gigantic military seems therefore to be an end in itself.

If the administration is genuinely determined to see the Baghdad–Damascus highway reopen under the control of the United States, a perpetual US occupation of a wasteland amid unreliable tribal coalitions is in the cards. As I have noted previously in this journal, for the Trump administration, this is where rollback begins. But, as in the Cold War, someone needs to be asking where it ends.[16]

Notes

1   *Prizzi's Honor*, directed by John Huston, 1985.

2   Hal Brands, *What Good Is Grand Strategy? Power and Purpose in American Statecraft from Harry S. Truman to George W. Bush* (Ithaca, NY: Cornell University Press, 2014), p. 71.

3   Robert Jervis, *Why Intelligence Fails: Lessons from the Iranian Revolution and the Iraq War* (Ithaca, NY: Cornell University Press, 2010).

4   Gregory Gause, 'The Illogic of Dual Containment', *Foreign Affairs*, March/April 1994.

5   'Remarks by President Trump to the 72nd Session of the United Nations General Assembly', 19 September 2017, https://www.whitehouse.gov/briefings-statements/remarks-president-trump-72nd-session-united-nations-general-assembly/.

6   Peter Baker, 'Trump Recertifies Iran Nuclear Deal, but Only Reluctantly', *New York Times*, 17 July 2017, https://www.nytimes.com/2017/07/17/us/politics/trump-iran-nuclear-deal-recertify.html.

7   Nikki Haley, 'Beyond the Echo Chamber: Considerations on U.S. Policy Toward Iran', remarks at the American Enterprise Institute, New York, 5 September 2017, https://usun.state.gov/remarks/7955.

8   Henry Kissinger, *Diplomacy* (New York: Simon and Schuster, 1994), p. 719.

9   The White House, 'President Donald J. Trump's New Strategy on Iran', 13 October 2017, https://www.whitehouse.gov/briefings-statements/president-donald-j-trumps-new-strategy-iran.

10 *Ibid.*

11 See 'The Future of the JCPOA', IISS *Strategic Comments*, vol. 24, no. 15, May 2018.

12 *Ibid.*

13 Ironically, the corridor in the pre-war years was carved out to allow Poland access to the sea after the First World War, and it was the Germans who regarded it as a *casus belli*.

14 See 'U.S. Policy in Syria After ISIS', C-SPAN, 11 January 2018, https://www.c-span.org/video/?439411-1/foreign-relations-panel-explores-us-policy-post-isis-syria.

15 See 'Satterfield Follow-up on U.S. Presence, Goals in Syria', C-SPAN, 11 January 2018, https://www.c-span.org/video/?c4706676/satterfield-follow-us-presence-goals-syria.

16 Steven Simon, 'Rollback', *Survival*, vol. 59, no. 4, August–September 2017, pp. 209–12.

After the Summit: Prospects for the Korean Peninsula

Bruce Bennett, James Dobbins, Jeffrey W. Hornung and Andrew Scobell

The 12 June summit meeting in Singapore was long on atmosphere but short on specifics. The joint statement issued by President Donald Trump and North Korean leader Kim Jong-un was largely an abbreviated version of promises made by Kim Jong-un's father and grandfather – and those made in more detail by the younger Kim to South Korean President Moon Jae-in less than two months ago.

President Trump's promises in the joint statement were equally general. Although not mentioned in the written document, Trump agreed to halt US–South Korea joint military exercises, while Kim agreed to halt nuclear and long-range missile tests. In substance, therefore, the Trump–Kim meeting has produced the 'freeze for freeze' bargain that China had been long urging. This is a modest result for all the fanfare, but one with some concrete benefit to offset the possible cost in South Korean and US military readiness. As long as the freeze continues, North Korea will probably not be able to complete development of an operational intercontinental ballistic missile (ICBM) capable of delivering nuclear warheads to American cities.

Less noticed was the two leaders' commitment 'to build a lasting and stable peace regime on the Korean Peninsula'. Again, this is a brief and less specific version of the more extensive commitments contained in April's joint declaration between the two Korean leaders, who 'agreed to actively pursue trilateral meetings involving the two Koreas and the United States,

Bruce Bennett is a Senior Defense Analyst, **James Dobbins** a Senior Fellow, **Jeffrey W. Hornung** a Political Scientist, and **Andrew Scobell** a Senior Political Scientist, all at the RAND Corporation.

Survival | vol. 60 no. 4 | August–September | pp. 21–28   DOI 10.1080/00396338.2018.1494976

or quadrilateral meetings involving the two Koreas, the United States and China with a view to declaring an end to the War and establishing a permanent and solid peace regime'. The war referred to was that fought from 1951–53 that ended in a military armistice. Although the Moon–Kim declaration contains no timetable, the two leaders reportedly agreed to complete this process by the end of the year.

Both propositions – denuclearisation and ending the Korean War – have a long history. Kim's father and grandfather made similar promises. The United States has twice negotiated agreements for the dismantlement of North Korea's nuclear programme, and North Korea promised South Korea in 1992 that the North would have no nuclear weapons and no nuclear-weapon production capabilities. There is a growing expectation, encouraged by Moon and Trump, that this time will be different – that the younger Kim means what he says. If that is true, the changes for both Koreas and the American role on the peninsula will be profound. If, on the other hand, expectations are dashed, the resulting confrontation could become even more bitter and dangerous. History suggests that the most likely outcome will be further meetings and agreements that unravel over time.

Denuclearisation

Defining denuclearisation and the steps needed to carry it out has proved immensely complicated, and execution has always fallen short, mostly but not exclusively on the North Korean side. This iteration will prove even more difficult. Previous American negotiations with North Korea, in the 1990s and again in the following decade, have focused on dismantling its nuclear infrastructure. But now such measures, even if faithfully undertaken, would not be enough, because North Korea has an unknown number of actual nuclear weapons and an extensive nuclear programme largely hidden from view. The challenge with long-range missiles is similar. A decade ago it sufficed to halt flight-testing. Now that will not suffice because North Korea has already produced and tested a missile that could reach the United States.

In their 27 April joint statement, Moon and Kim pledged to fully implement 'all existing agreements and declarations between the two sides thus far'. In one of those former agreements, dating back to 1992, both sides agreed not to 'test, manufacture, produce, receive, possess, store, deploy or use nuclear weapons'. They also promised not to possess reprocessing or enrichment facilities. Like his father and grandfather, Kim has joined Trump in a broad statement of intent along these lines, but his officials can now be expected to negotiate tenaciously, resist intrusive verification, seek early sanctions relief, demand substantial economic compensation for the costs involved in dismantling their nuclear facilities, and require a complete and irreversible American guarantee of the North Korean regime's survival.

This is the third time the United States and North Korea have started down the path toward denuclearisation and normalisation of relations. Previous efforts failed not just because the North Koreans cheated, as they did, but because neither side fulfilled its commitments. The Clinton administration promised to provide North Korea with heavy fuel oil and two new proliferation-resistant reactors in exchange for shutting down its old ones. Congress was slow to fund the fuel oil, while Japan and South Korea baulked at paying for and supplying the new reactors. Clinton also procrastinated on the promised normalisation of relations. Under George W. Bush, resistance to moving forward with the Six-Party Agreement came from within his own administration.

Verification has always been the most difficult obstacle and will now be even more so. North Korea is a much more closed society than Iran, and it is difficult to imagine Kim's actually agreeing to a verification regime comparable to the one still in place in the latter country. But even if he did, it would be inadequate. Nuclear reactors and enrichment sites are large, immobile and often observable from space. Nuclear weapons are small, portable and if hidden nearly impossible to locate.

Ending the Korean War

Some 65 years ago, the fighting in Korea was suspended in an armistice signed by an American general on behalf of the United Nations, a Chinese general representing the Chinese 'volunteers' who had entered the war, and a North Korean general. The South Korean leadership had not wanted to stop fighting and did not sign the agreement. Nine months later a peace

conference was convened, but neither North nor South Korea would recognise the other and each wanted to militarily reunify the country on its
own terms. The conference failed, and formally at least the Korean War has
continued ever since.

Ending the Korean War has been an intermittent topic of discussion
over the succeeding decades. The first brief interval of North–South detente
occurred in the early 1970s; it produced a joint declaration in which the two
sides agreed to work toward reunification. There were intense North–South
and US–North Korea negotiations during the Clinton and George W. Bush
administrations. These focused on North Korea's nuclear programme, but
also ranged more widely to include discussions about ending the war. In
the late 1990s, these conversations led to a series of meetings on the topic
among the two Koreas, China and the United States. These talks about a
peace treaty lapsed in 1998 without result.

Efforts to end the war have foundered on a number of substantive
and procedural obstacles. Both North and South Korea have continued to
espouse the goal of reunification and have therefore been reluctant to accept
the indefinite division of the peninsula. North Korea has conditioned any
peace agreement on the withdrawal of American forces, which has been
unacceptable to both Washington and Seoul. Even the question of who
should negotiate and sign a peace agreement has been problematic. North
Korea has wanted to negotiate a bilateral peace agreement with the United
States, whereas Washington has always insisted that South Korea needs to
be involved. China was a reluctant and not very active participant in the
late-1990s discussions.

It has generally been assumed that the Korean War would be ended as the
result of a peace treaty among the main parties. Technically, however, this is
not essential. Harry S. Truman considered the American intervention a 'police
action' and did not seek congressional authorisation. The United States fought
at the head of a United Nations force of 17 countries that was created by the
UN Security Council in the absence of the Soviet Union, which boycotted the
proceedings. This American-led UN Command remains in existence, with the
American commander of US Forces–Korea leading the Command in South
Korea and a UN Command-Rear headquartered in Japan.

Although the Second World War in the Pacific ended with the 1951 signing of the Treaty of San Francisco, the war in Europe did not end in a peace treaty. In 1945, the victorious powers agreed on the provisional division of Europe. In 1975, the United States and the Soviet Union joined 33 other European states in a political accord, the 1975 Final Act of the Conference on Security and Cooperation in Europe (CSCE), in which they declared those post-war boundaries to be 'inviolable'. This, and the agreements surrounding German reunification in 1990, effectively ended the Second World War in Europe.

A joint declaration by the two Korean governments declaring an end to the Korean War would seem unlikely to satisfy the North Korean leadership, which has long regarded the United States as its principal adversary. Yet, an actual peace treaty would in the US case require Senate ratification, which has become an almost insurmountable hurdle in recent decades. The Trump–Kim declaration's commitment to build a 'peace regime' suggests that both sides may be keeping open the option of something short of an actual treaty. Some less formal combination of measures might include a four-power (US, China and the two Koreas) statement declaring the war over, a UN Security Council resolution terminating the conflict and dissolving the United Nations Command, and perhaps some wider regional pact along the lines of the 1975 CSCE Final Act.

Even in the absence of these wider measures, the simple declaration of a peace regime by both Koreas could have a substantial impact on South Korean and international opinion, particularly if endorsed by the United States. Kim has reportedly told Moon that he would not demand the departure of American troops as part of any such agreement. His father once said the same thing. Yet even if he adheres to this position, ending the war could affect the status of American forces and the willingness of both the South Korean and American leaders and people to sustain the current arrangement.

Regional views

Beijing has every reason to be pleased with the outcome of the Singapore Summit – that is, the freeze on North Korean nuclear and long-range missile testing and US–South Korea joint military exercises, both long-advocated Chinese goals. Beijing favours denuclearisation and a negotiated end to the

Korean War, but is uneasy about the prospect of any peace process moving too rapidly and wary of being marginalised. Chinese President Xi Jinping was initially stunned by the fast-moving Korean Peninsula-related events and has scrambled to catch up. Xi's two meetings with Kim Jong-un helped ease concerns that China's interests would be ignored. Kim's first visit to Beijing was remarkable not just because it was the first face-to-face meeting between the two leaders but also because it signalled a sudden thaw in what had been an extremely chilly bilateral relationship since Kim had succeeded his father in December 2011. China is pleased about the dramatic decrease in tensions on the peninsula, and hopeful that making progress on formally ending the Korean War will translate into multiple outcomes desired by Beijing: the denuclearisation of North Korea, the withdrawal of US forces from South Korea, a decline in American influence in the region, and a corresponding rise in China's influence.

The Singapore Summit has done little to assuage Japanese anxieties. Japan badly wants denuclearisation and supports ending the Korean War, but it is sceptical of Kim Jong-un's current charm offensive. Japanese officials are not only doubtful that the current flurry of diplomacy will produce the desired ends, they are also nervous that their interests will be ignored should diplomacy begin to yield results. Japan would be concerned if an agreement on ending the state of war were to lead to a reduction of US forces in Korea, or even in Japan, which still hosts the UN Command-Rear and seven UN-designated bases directly linked to the defence of South Korea. Japan believes it should be at the table in any negotiations with North Korea, whether about peace or nuclear weapons. Neither North Korea nor South Korea favours such participation. Japan is threatened by North Korean medium- and intermediate-range missiles, and fears these will be ignored as the US focuses on eliminating the ICBM threat. Yet Japan would be called upon to help fund and provide technical assistance as part of any package for the North that emerged from a nuclear deal. Finally, Japan is still seeking the return of more than a dozen Japanese citizens abducted by North Korea several decades ago.

*   *   *

Most experts on North Korea do not believe that Kim will actually give up his nuclear arsenal. Even if he agrees to do so, full verification will be virtually impossible. History suggests that the most probable consequence of the Singapore Summit will be difficult and lengthy negotiations followed by slow and eventually inadequate compliance, quite possibly on both sides. If this period is accompanied by a continued pause in testing and other positive steps, such as dismantling some nuclear sites or even turning over some weapons, this outcome may be better than nothing, especially if North Korea can be prevented from fielding hundreds of nuclear weapons in the coming decade or two. But in the end, the nuclear-armed confrontation could well resume.

Kim wants to move forward with an end to the state of war. If this process advances more quickly than denuclearisation, as it easily could, the result could make it much more difficult to sustain the economic, political and military pressures on Kim to complete the denuclearisation process.

Trump and Kim have committed themselves to this effort earlier on and more publicly than did their predecessors. Kim seems politically unassailable at home, and Trump has shown a remarkable ability to reshape long-held views of his party. But sometime fairly early in the process of dismantling the North Korean nuclear infrastructure, Trump will need to go to Congress to fund whatever compensatory assistance he will have promised Kim, at which point Trump may need more than just Republican votes. And the path to denuclearisation is now a lot longer than it was a decade or two ago. Some experts maintain it could take ten to 15 years to dismantle North Korea's nuclear infrastructure,[1] which is much more extensive than it was then. Fully implementing the deal outlined in the Singapore communiqué will therefore require the support of both parties in Congress and perhaps more than one American president. Leadership in South Korea and Japan could also change during that period, perhaps several times.

Maintaining a domestic and international consensus behind whatever actual agreement emerges will prove difficult, particularly as questions arise regarding North Korean implementation, as they will. Of course, Kim might surprise us. No one expected Mikhail Gorbachev to accept German reunification in 1989. Yet by the time the Berlin Wall fell Gorbachev had established a strong record of reform and moderation. Kim's record so far is less encouraging. He is also aware that the Soviet Union did not long survive Gorbachev's opening to the world. The North Korean regime, more repressive and closed than the Soviet Union, would seem even less likely to do so.

Notes

[1] This view is disputed. Nuclear expert David Albright has written: 'If North Korea agrees to denuclearize and to cooperate fully, admittedly big "ifs," then verified dismantlement of the key parts of its nuclear weapons program can happen in parallel and be accomplished in as little as about two years.' See David Albright, 'Technical Note on a Timeline for North Korean Denuclearization', *Institute for Science and International Security*, 29 May 2018, http://isis-online.org/isis-reports/detail/technical-note-on-a-timeline-for-north-korean-denuclearization/.

Kim Jong-un's Singapore Sting

Mark Fitzpatrick

Judged by any metric, the bare-bones agreement reached between US President Donald Trump and North Korean leader Kim Jong-un on 12 June fell short. It did not define 'denuclearisation', it did not provide for meaningful deadlines to meet the goals announced, and it did not address any of the other challenges that the Democratic People's Republic of Korea (DPRK) poses to the world, to the region and to its own people.

In American vernacular, the Singapore Summit was a 'nothing burger'. The short, four-point joint statement said nothing about missiles, chemical and biological weapons, human-rights abuses, abductions or other issues of concern. Even the commitment to 'denuclearisation' was cast in terms of 'working towards' that goal.[1] Without timelines or milestones, this commitment was akin to the aspirational disarmament promise of the Nuclear Non-Proliferation Treaty, something President Barack Obama famously said might not happen in his lifetime.[2]

By talking directly with Kim, Trump did achieve something unprecedented, but it was all in Kim's favour. Successive North Korean leaders have long aspired to meet American counterparts. Until now, that honour had been held in reserve as leverage for inducing significant compromises. In 2000, the North Korean leadership pleaded for president Bill Clinton to visit, but would not agree in advance to details on curbing its missile programme. Although Obama had entered office expressing a willingness to

Mark Fitzpatrick is Executive-Director, IISS–Americas.

Survival | vol. 60 no. 4 | August–September | pp. 29–36   DOI 10.1080/00396338.2018.1494977

talk with enemies, he insisted on not rewarding provocations.[3] Trump, by contrast, did not insist on anything tangible in exchange for meeting with Kim Jong-un.

North Korea's meagre concessions

The 396-word joint statement offered far less than was reached in previous agreements with North Korea. To be fair, it was supposed to mark only the beginning of a negotiation process. It thus should be compared not with final agreements reached with North Korea (such as the 1994 Agreed Framework and the 2005 Joint Statement of the Six-Party Talks), but with statements from similar high-level meetings. But even compared with such statements – usefully summarised by arms-control expert Joshua Pollack[4] – the joint statement was very thin gruel.

In the January 1992 joint declaration of South and North Korea on the denuclearisation of the Korean Peninsula, the two sides committed to 'not test, manufacture, produce, receive, possess, store, deploy or use nuclear weapons', and not to possess nuclear-reprocessing or uranium-enrichment facilities.[5] The first bilateral joint statement by North Korea and the US in June 1993 was only 239 words, but it included reference to verification in the form of a commitment to the 'application of fullscope safeguards'.[6] A US–DPRK joint communiqué issued at the end of a visit to the White House by leader Kim Jong-il's special envoy, Vice Marshal Jo Myong-rok, in October 2000 addressed missiles, not the nuclear programme, but included a DPRK commitment not to launch long-range missiles of any kind while talks continued.[7] Although North Korea has held to such a moratorium for the past six and a half months, the Singapore Joint Statement omitted reference to it. The 2012 'Leap Day Deal' included a moratorium commitment as well as verification of an enrichment moratorium by international inspectors.[8]

The Singapore Summit's joint result also pales against the four-page 'Joint Plan of Action' reached in Geneva on 24 November 2013, which specified limits on Iran's nuclear activity and the means for enhanced International Atomic Energy Agency (IAEA) monitoring, as well as goals for a comprehensive agreement, with a six-month deadline for negotiations (which was subsequently extended twice). That statement, of course, led to the 159-page multiparty Iran nuclear deal, reached after two years of slogging negotiations, from which Trump unilaterally withdrew on 8 May. In contrast to the Singapore statement, the Geneva accord exceeded expectations in terms of specificity and concessions by the other side.[9] For Trump to boast of a 'comprehensive' agreement with North Korea after having condemned and withdrawn from the much more balanced Iran deal is grossly hypocritical.

Other than working toward denuclearisation, Kim's only other commitment was to recover the remains of missing US troops from the Korean War. Trump lauded this as a victory, but, again, it is nothing new. A bilateral undertaking had been in place from 1990 to 2005, recovering 229 sets of remains, before secretary of defense Donald Rumsfeld unilaterally ended the cooperative process. Resuming the recovery of remains, the costs for which have been borne by the US, is more of a concession by the US than one on North Korea's part.

In his post-summit press conference, Trump claimed that Kim had agreed to destroy a 'major missile engine testing site', which was subsequently identified as the Sohae Satellite Launching Ground.[10] Whether this would be done under any type of international verification is unclear. When North Korea collapsed the tunnels at its Punggye-ri nuclear test site on 24 May, it invited foreign journalists to observe the destruction. No outside experts were invited, however. Without verification of the sort that should have been provided by the Comprehensive Nuclear-Test-Ban Treaty Organization, unilateral destruction of nuclear and missile facilities destroys important forensic data and can turn out to be a propaganda stunt. On the basis of the small yield of the explosives used at the test site, US officials judged that the tunnels probably survived and could be reused.[11]

Kim's one other pre-summit concession was to release three American citizens who had been imprisoned on the dubious grounds of engaging in 'hostile acts'. Trump heralded this concession as something Obama had failed to achieve, even though two of the three Americans had been detained on Trump's watch.[12] North Korea's pernicious practice of jailing US citizens to serve as bait included at least ten who were released on Obama's watch, without any compromises on Washington's part other than the dispatch to Pyongyang of current or former senior officials to pick up the prisoners.

America's real concessions

In exchange for these paltry North Korean concessions – a vague commitment to work toward denuclearisation, a moratorium on missile and nuclear tests not pledged in writing, incomplete destruction of the nuclear test site and return of hostages – Trump gave Kim seven substantially more precious prizes.

The first was to confer legitimacy on an odious, outcast regime. Trump accorded world-class status to the despot Kim, giving him exactly what he wanted by treating North Korea as a nuclear-armed state. Successful diplomacy often requires holding one's nose while engaging with murderous thugs, but there was no need for Trump to lavish praise on Kim, improbably calling him 'very talented', 'trustworthy' and 'loved by his people'. Who knew North Korean brainwashing could be so easy?

A second concession was to relieve the economic pressure on North Korea. Before the summit, Trump had said he no longer wanted to use the term 'maximum pressure' to describe US policy.[13] Already, however, the global economic pressure that the US had led against Pyongyang had begun to crumble as China, in particular, saw the US–DPRK rapprochement as reason to relax implementation of UN sanctions that had begun to seriously bite.[14]

The strongest source of leverage over North Korea – the threat of a military strike – was also removed as a result of the rapprochement. Threatening to give Kim a 'bloody nose' was a misguided tactic that could have escalated to nuclear war, so taking it off the table is not a bad outcome. At the same time, doing so has to be counted as a major concession from the Trump administration's standpoint. Beyond that, Trump explicitly committed in the Joint Statement to provide security guarantees to North Korea. The US has offered security assurances before – in 1993, 2005 and 2012 – though what the new one means is unclear.

Trump's last three concessions were made unilaterally in his post-summit press conference. Blindsiding South Korean President Moon Jae-in and even his own secretary of defense, Trump announced that combined US–South Korea military exercises would be suspended while negotiations proceeded.[15] Such a suspension makes sense, and has precedent in the cancellation of the *Team Spirit* major exercise in 1992 and 1994–96. To do so without informing his ally is unforgivable, however, as was Trump's employment of DPRK propaganda to call them 'war games' and 'very provocative'. Kim would have been briefed about Trump's habit of echoing the last person he speaks with, but he must have been surprised to score such an easy goal.

Compounding the error in alliance management, Trump said he wanted to bring home US forces from the Korean Peninsula. A partial drawdown in the US troop presence would be a reasonable quid pro quo for a significant reduction of the North Korean military threat in a final deal. To offer it unilaterally up front, however, was to give away America's strongest card.

Finally, Trump undermined the international campaign to expose and stop North Korea's appalling human-rights abuses. Referring to the 'rough situation over there' concerning human rights, he granted North Korea moral equivalency by saying 'it is rough in a lot of places, not just there'. Let us hope that he is correct that the 100,000 or so prisoners in North Korea's gulag will be the 'great winners' of the Singapore Summit, as Trump claimed. But there was no explanation of how this could happen, only an implied expectation that North Korea would undergo political transformation as the result of a nuclear accord. It was not long ago that Trump repeatedly castigated Obama for holding out a comparable – though less outlandish – hope with respect to the Iran nuclear deal.

Better than nothing

Disappointingly thin though it is, the Singapore Summit outcome is certainly better than the alternative of escalating tensions and provocations that afflicted the Korean Peninsula earlier in the Trump administration. Trump and Kim have reduced the threat of war that each was responsible for heightening last year. Work on a peace treaty and the process of denuclearisation must now begin in earnest.

One ray of hope is to be found in the 42-minute video that North Korea released to its public celebrating Kim's successful summit in Singapore.[16] Narrated with thunderous adoration by Ri Chun-hee, the 'pink-dress' newscaster famed for announcing North Korea's missile and nuclear tests,[17] the video showed Kim receiving massive attention from Singaporean crowds and brotherly affection from the superpower. On the one hand, this reinforced Kim's self-image as an object of adoration. On the other hand, Trump's friendly demeanour and the photos of US and DPRK flags side by side tended to negate North Korea's image of the Yankee devil. The video may be evidence of a real shift in North Korea's posture. Unlike George Orwell's dystopian *Nineteen Eighty-Four*, in which Oceania changes its enemy from Eurasia to Eastasia and reverses its alliances overnight, Kim cannot simply erase 70 years of anti-American hatred. Yet autocracies do have an easier time at shifting gears.

North Korea- and Iran-watcher Barbara Slavin remarked at a 14 June discussion meeting at the IISS–Americas office that the montage of the Singapore Summit displayed in the video also sends a message to the North Korean public that 'there is a better life to be had', and that Kim is trying to give it to them by leveraging his nuclear assets. 'It's a remarkable shift for a country that has emphasized self-sacrifice', Slavin said.[18] Like many other veteran arms-control practitioners and analysts, I have long held that no amount of economic benefit would induce North Korea to give up its nuclear arsenal. Trump may be right in principle to test this theory. In practice, however, he is subverting American alliances, values and bargaining power.

Notes

1   The White House, 'Joint Statement of President Donald J. Trump of the United States of America and Chairman Kim Jong Un of the Democratic People's Republic of Korea at the Singapore Summit', 12 June 2018, https://www.whitehouse.gov/briefings-statements/joint-statement-president-donald-j-trump-united-states-america-chairman-kim-jong-un-democratic-peoples-republic-korea-singapore-summit/.

2   Remarks by President Barack Obama, Hradcany Square, Prague, Czech Republic, 5 April 2009, https://obamawhitehouse.archives.gov/the-press-office/remarks-president-barack-obama-prague-delivered.

3   Stephen Collinson, 'Trump Isn't the First US President to Get a North Korean Invite. But He's the First to Accept', CNN, 10 March 2018, https://www.cnn.com/2018/03/09/politics/north-korea-trump-obama-bush-clinton/index.html/.

4   Joshua Pollack, 'Denuclearization

of the Korean Peninsula: Reviewing the Precedents', *Arms Control Wonk*, 10 June 2018, https://www.armscontrolwonk.com/archive/1205354/denuclearization-of-the-korean-peninsula-reviewing-the-precedents/.

5   'Joint Declaration of the Denuclearization of the Korean Peninsula', signed 20 January 1992, available at https://2001-2009.state.gov/t/ac/rls/or/2004/31011.htm.

6   'Joint Statement of the Democratic People's Republic of Korea and the United States of America', New York, 11 June 1993, available at http://nautilus.org/wp-content/uploads/2011/12/CanKor_VTK_1993_06_11_joint_statement_dprk_usa.pdf.

7   'U.S.–D.P.R.K. Joint Communiqué', released by the Office of the Spokesman, US Department of State, 12 October 2000, https://1997-2001.state.gov/regions/eap/001012_usdprk_jointcom.html.

8   US Department of State, Press Statement, Victoria Nuland, Department Spokesperson, Office of the Spokesperson, 29 February 2012, https://2009-2017.state.gov/r/pa/prs/ps/2012/02/184869.htm.

9   Mark Fitzpatrick, 'The Surprisingly Good Geneva Deal', Politics and Strategy: The Survival Editors' Blog, 25 November 2013.

10   Kylie Atwood, 'Officials Identify North Korean Test Site Kim Committed to Destroy at Summit', CBS News, 20 June 2018, https://www.cbsnews.com/amp/news/officials-identify-north-korean-sohae-test-site-kim-committed-to-destroy-at-summit/?__twitter_impression=true.

11   Barbara Starr and Zachary Cohen, 'Kim's Tunnel Explosions a Goodwill Gesture? Not So Fast', CNN, 1 June 2018, https://www.cnn.com/2018/06/01/politics/north-korea-nuclear-test-tunnel-gesture-propaganda/index.html.

12   Katie Rogers, 'Trump Greets 3 American Detainees Freed from North Korea', *New York Times*, 10 May 2018.

13   Oren Dorell, 'North Korea's Isolation Crumbling as Trump Abandons "Maximum Pressure" Campaign', *USA Today*, 4 June 2018.

14   Josh Rogin, 'Maximum Pressure on North Korea Is Gone, and It Isn't Coming Back', *Washington Post*, 17 May 2018.

15   A spokesman for Moon said, diplomatically, 'we need to try to understand what President Trump said'. David Nakamura, Philip Rucker, Anna Fifield and Anne Gearan, 'Trump–Kim Summit: Trump Says After Historic Meeting, "We Have Developed a Very Special Bond"', *Washington Post*, 12 June 2018.

16   Choe San-hung, 'North Korea Film Glorifies Kim's World Debut, With Trump in Starring Role', *New York Times*, 13 June 2018.

17   Benjamin Haas, 'North Korea's "Pink Lady": The Newscaster Set to Announce the End of the World', *Guardian*, 4 September 2017.

18   'Negotiating Non-proliferation with North Korea and Iran', IISS–Americas discussion meeting, 14 June 2018, https://www.iiss.org/events/2018/06/non-proliferation-north-korea-iran/.

Breakthrough in the Balkans: Macedonia's New Name

Edward P. Joseph and Ognen Vangelov

When and how did Arabs become Palestinians? Why did the Burmese government insist that Pope Francis refrain from calling the country's uprooted Muslim community by their name, Rohingya? What caused Serbian players to become incensed when two members of the Swiss team in the current World Cup made a gesture evoking the Albanian flag? National identity and corresponding aspirations and fears are the common elements in the three examples. Until the Arabs of Palestine cultivated an independent Palestinian identity, their national movement foundered. The Myanmar government's refusal to acknowledge the existence of the Rohingya is integral to its effort to expel and expunge them from its borders. The two Swiss footballers in the June 2018 World Cup match were actually born in Kosovo, and their gesture reflects a bitter, 100-year competing claim to the country between ethnic Serbs and Albanians.

The pernicious, pervasive link between national identity and violent conflict is what makes the final agreement between Greece and Macedonia over the latter's name so significant. By directly and comprehensively tackling all facets of their identity clash, the agreement brings to a close the century-old Macedonian question and dims any prospect of armed conflict. For the first time, Macedonians have obtained explicit recognition of their nationality and language as uniquely Macedonian, not some Slav derivative. In turn, Macedonians have agreed to qualify their name with an adjective,

Edward P. Joseph is an adjunct professor at the Paul H. Nitze School of Advanced International Studies (SAIS), Johns Hopkins University. **Ognen Vangelov** is a teaching fellow in the Department of Political Studies at Queen's University, Canada.

Survival | vol. 60 no. 4 | August–September | pp. 37–44   DOI 10.1080/00396338.2018.1495426

as in 'North Macedonia', a gesture of respect for Greece's own region of Macedonia. The compromise effectively terminates Bulgarian and Serbian challenges to the identity of the Macedonians – the only people among the Balkan nation-states whose very existence has been questioned. If the agreement survives political opposition, Macedonia will soon enter NATO and open membership negotiations with the EU, strengthening Europe's strategic position and impeding Russian machinations in the region.

The Prespa Agreement (named for the lake where it was signed) could inform a wide range of identity disputes. Among other innovations, the agreement brings together historians under official auspices to separate historical truth from nationalist propaganda, a long-overdue step in a region still gripped by battles over battles fought some 600 years ago. The agreement contains four implementation mechanisms, including one designed to tackle offensive narratives, some of which are recorded in textbooks – precisely the kinds of storylines that can fuel bigotry and raise tensions. The agreement also takes the parties beyond typical confidence-building measures straight into a commitment to a strategic relationship involving economics, energy and science.

No joke

Although the Macedonian question is often laughed off as an absurd squabble over ancient history, Greek hostility towards its northern neighbour has been as intensely felt as any other identity clash in the volatile Balkans. Like so many conflicts in the Balkans and the Middle East, the dispute over Macedonia and its identity has its roots in Ottoman rule. In 1912, Serbia, Greece and Bulgaria formed an alliance to drive the Ottomans out of their remaining territories in the Balkans, of which Macedonia was the prize. After succeeding, the allies turned enemies and began fighting over the proceeds. Greece and Serbia divided the bulk of the Macedonian territory between themselves, prompting Sofia to start another war with its former allies to seize more Macedonian territory. The initial partition of Macedonia, formalised in the Treaty of Bucharest in August 1913, left most of the territory to Greece and Serbia, and a small chunk in the east to a disappointed Bulgaria.

Meanwhile, within Macedonia itself, the local Orthodox Slav population increasingly identified itself as 'Macedonian' and mounted its own claims to political autonomy, as well as ethnic and linguistic independence from its neighbours. The array of competing claims among Serbia, Greece and Bulgaria, as well as from within those states by increasingly restive ethnic Macedonians, simmered. The Second World War revived open competition for the territory. After the war, Yugoslavian leader Josip Broz – known as 'Tito' – rewarded Macedonia's partisans by recognising the Macedonian people and language, and establishing Macedonia as a constituent republic of Yugoslavia in what had been the Serbian, 'Vardar' portion of Macedonia. In a first for a communist state, Tito went so far as to establish an independent Orthodox Church in the country.

But claims to national patrimony die hard in the Balkans. After Yugoslavia's bloody collapse in the early 1990s, narratives emerged in all three contending states – Greece, Bulgaria and Serbia – suggesting that Macedonia was merely an artificial construct of Tito's and that the Macedonian people were really Bulgarians, Serbs or simply Slavs. As Bulgarians challenged the existence of the Macedonian language, Serbs chafed at the autocephalous Macedonian Orthodox Church seated in Ohrid. The renewed identity challenges, in other words, subsumed the century-old, competing claims to Macedonian territory.

Macedonia's declaration of independence in 1991 rekindled Greek fears and sparked intense resentment among Greeks across the political spectrum. Seizing on maps of 'Greater Macedonia' produced by irresponsible Macedonian politicians, Athens insisted that the new state harboured claims on Greek Macedonia. That year the most radical position, propagated by then-right-wing renegade Antonis Samaras (who would later become prime minister), became the official, lasting position of the Greek government. Athens demanded that its northern neighbour exclude the term 'Macedonia' from its name if it wanted to be recognised as an independent state. The exclusivist Greek position was adopted by what was then the European Community in July 1991, delaying the international recognition of Macedonia until 1993, when Macedonia entered the United Nations under the provisional title 'the former Yugoslav Republic of Macedonia'. The UN resolution directed Macedonia and Greece to find a permanent solution to the name issue.

Exploiting its advantages in power, politics and geography, Athens isolated Skopje beginning in September 1991, when the former Yugoslav Republic declared independence. Athens claimed exclusivity over the name 'Macedonia' and, setting a durable pattern, cowed its European neighbours and even the United States into delaying international recognition of the fledgling transition country. After Washington belatedly recognised Skopje in February 1994, Athens imposed a punishing, 19-month embargo on Macedonia that ended with the US-brokered 'Interim Agreement'.

In 2008, Greece violated the accord by blocking Macedonia's entry into NATO even under the provisional (and, to Macedonians, humiliating) name. Greece also steadfastly blocked the EU from opening membership negotiations with Macedonia. The NATO and EU blockades inflicted a double penalty on the country, stalling the reform process and thereby opening the door to nearly a decade of corruption, abuse and autocracy under former prime minister Nikola Gruevski. In addition, the denial of NATO membership aggravated relations with the large Albanian minority in Macedonia, which has long resented being kept out of the Alliance over a name dispute that means little to them, and which nearly fought a war of secession to remedy the problem in 2001.

Without the guarantee over its borders that NATO membership confers, Macedonia, along with Kosovo and Bosnia-Herzegovina, remained one of the three open questions in the Balkans, tempting those with territorial designs. One scenario, reportedly discussed between senior Serbian and Kosovar officials, called for splitting Kosovo between Serbs and Albanians, with the latter to be 'compensated' for the loss of territory by a carve-up of Macedonia's Albanian-majority territory. Leaving aside the turmoil and mass movement of populations entailed in such a partition, it would re-ignite competing claims for the rump portion among Bulgaria, Greece and Serbia – the three combatants in the first and second Balkan Wars of 1912 and 1913.

In sum, the name dispute between Greece and Macedonia has been anything but risible. It has kept a small, ethnically mixed Balkan country mired in uncertainty, and helped perpetuate instability in the region. Defying the sporadic efforts of diplomats to resolve the stand-off, the dispute had all the makings of another European frozen conflict like Cyprus's. The only thing missing has been inter-ethnic violence – an omission explained by recent, not ancient, history. In fact, violence had been a staple of the 100-year history of the Macedonian question, and its legacy lingers today.

High hurdles

The atavism over Macedonia was most bitter in Greece's case. Owing to Tito's geopolitical ambitions, Yugoslavia insinuated itself as an active belligerent into the vicious Greek Civil War of 1946–49. Still hoping to realise their national aspirations, the overwhelming majority of Macedonians in Greece sided with the communists. When they lost, Greece expelled thousands of Macedonians, many of whom moved north to today's Macedonia. The ancestral family of Macedonian Foreign Minister Nikola Dimitrov – a key figure in the name negotiations, along with his counterpart, Greek Foreign Minister Nikos Kotzias – was among those forced to leave. The Macedonians who remained in Greece were never acknowledged as a minority. All subsequent Greek governments, terrified of Macedonian irredentism, have claimed that there was no such thing as a Macedonian nation or language, inside or outside of Greece. The Prespa Agreement reflects these deep and persistent Greek anxieties with its extensive prohibitions on irredentist Macedonian claims or statements, and even on intervention to protect the rights of Macedonians in Greece. These and other concessions by the Macedonian side have been assailed by critics in Skopje.

Though signed on 17 June by prime ministers Alexis Tsipras of Greece and Zoran Zaev of Macedonia, the agreement is still tenuous. At Greece's insistence, the new name is *erga omnes* – that is, it must apply in all aspects, including internally. As a result, Macedonia must change its constitution, opening the door to opposition from diehard nationalists, political opportunists and outside spoilers, including Russia. Recent chaos in Macedonia has attracted the attention of Moscow, which has stepped up its efforts to thwart Western strategy in the region, particularly in countries with Orthodox Christian majorities. Even if Zaev manages to run the domestic political gauntlet, including a probable referendum requiring two-thirds approval, Tsipras must still convince the Greek parliament to approve a deal that is deeply unpopular in Greece. According to surveys, almost 70% of Greeks oppose the compromise.

The key to overcoming opposition in Macedonia is advancement towards NATO and European Union membership. Shrewdly, the negotiators front-loaded positive developments in this area. Once Zaev obtained initial parliamentary approval of the agreement, Tsipras promptly communicated his support for North Macedonia's membership in NATO and the EU. While the Alliance quickly announced its readiness to begin accession talks, France has blocked the EU from doing the same. Paris is averse to further enlargement, fearing migration from Eastern Europe and harbouring scepticism about the integrity of the rule of law in Macedonia and neighbouring Albania. This EU roadblock undermines Zaev's ability to sell the name compromise to his people. The French position also vastly underestimates the consequences of the deal's collapse and the significance of what was achieved at Lake Prespa.

Risks meriting reward

Because the dispute inflicted far more pain on Macedonia than on Greece, few Greek prime ministers have dared to take the political risk of opening up the issue. Tsipras is the rare Greek leader who has grasped that the dispute also burdened Greece, marginalising it internationally and undermining its claim to regional leadership. Facing continuing challenges over its massive debt and new challenges from an increasingly autocratic Turkey, Tsipras saw the benefit in striking a deal with his neighbour, and authorised his foreign minister, Kotzias, to negotiate.

Zaev's ascension as Macedonia's prime minister last year buoyed Tsipras and Kotzias. Zaev, an avowed reformist, immediately broke with the provocative tactics of his predecessor, Gruevski, which included erecting an ostentatious, 100-foot-tall statue of Alexander the Great in Skopje's town square. Among other gestures, Zaev promptly renamed the main north–south highway from 'Alexander of Macedon' to 'Friendship'. An entirely unforeseen factor – the migration crisis from the Middle East – also built confidence as it compelled the Greek and Macedonian police and interior ministries to cooperate closely for the first time. Zaev's appointment of Dimitrov as his foreign minister was also crucial. In Dimitrov, Zaev elevated the single most experienced diplomat on the name issue, a formidable negotiator well known to the Greeks, and a political personality with links to Macedonia's nationalist party, the Internal Macedonian Revolutionary Organisation–Democratic Party for Macedonian National Unity (known by its anglicised acronym, VMRO–DPMNE). The fact that Dimitrov's family hails from Greek (or Aegean) Macedonia helps insulate Zaev from charges that he has sold out Macedonians expelled in the aftermath of the Greek Civil War or still living in Greece.

The partnership that Dimitrov and Kotzias forged over several months was crucial. Each diplomat was called upon to settle on exacting formulations over topics long considered off limits. Each had to keep his principal engaged even when the prospects for accord looked bleak and criticism mounted. In this endeavour, the two foreign ministers had the able assistance of long-time UN mediator Matthew Nimetz, as well as the encouragement of senior US officials. But the real credit for the agreement belongs to the four Greek and Macedonian leaders who had the courage, vision and stamina to see it through, particularly Tsipras and Zaev, who have staked their political fortunes on its ultimate success. Unlike the iconic Dayton Agreement or other breakthroughs in the region, the heroes of this accord were not outsiders, but leaders from the region who were determined to do the hard work necessary to make peace. In this, the Prespa Agreement – if it survives – is surely a model for other conflicts.

Pierre Hassner (1933–2018): An Appreciation

John L. Harper

Editor's note:

Pierre Hassner, who passed away in Paris on 26 May 2018 at the age of 85, was a long-standing friend of the IISS and contributor to Survival. *His acclaimed* Adelphi *paper, 'Change and Security in Europe', appeared in 1968. His first book review for* Survival *was published in 1965, and his first original article, 'Eurocommunism and Detente', appeared in 1977. When the journal was relaunched in 2008 he became a Contributing Editor, regularly contributing book reviews and articles until poor health forced him to stop in 2016. We asked John Harper, his student and then colleague at the SAIS Bologna Center of the Johns Hopkins University, to reflect on the man and his work.*

Only in recent days did I run across Raymond Aron's observations on his most brilliant student of philosophy (and later colleague) at the École normale supérieure:

> [He] is at his best when he expresses himself in complete freedom, when his monologue, by itself, encompasses both his arguments and the possible objections of his listeners. His subtlety and his feeling for nuance are so superior to those of others – myself included, of course – that dialogue with him becomes difficult. He has to be left alone to conduct the conversation in his own way; each of his listeners will grasp along the way the nourishment suitable to him (or the pearls thrown out at random by an inexhaustible wealth of invention and analysis).[1]

John L. Harper is Kenneth H. Keller Professor of American Foreign Policy at the Paul H. Nitze School of Advanced International Studies (SAIS), Johns Hopkins University, and a Contributing Editor to *Survival*.

Survival | vol. 60 no. 4 | August–September | pp. 45–49   DOI 10.1080/00396338.2018.1495427

Aron's words perfectly describe what my classmates and I discovered in Pierre Hassner's seminar at the Bologna Center of the Johns Hopkins University in 1976. Pierre's habit, as I vividly recall it, was to circle the table for five or ten minutes, ruminating in his sing-song baritone on the day's subject (be it Daniel Bell's argument about the end of ideology, or Samuel Huntington's on post-industrial politics), then pause for breath – and questions from the brave-hearted – before launching into a new monologue. The nourishment grasped was not in the form of precise information, but of puzzling paradoxes and searching questions. Even more dazzling were his longer, set-piece resumés of the state of East–West relations. Typically, they delved beyond state-to-state political and military relations into the realm of culture and society – focusing, as he put it, on 'the underlying (or sometimes, as in 1968 or 1981, sudden) transformation of societies in Europe, in comparison with the rigidity of the bipolar system'.[2] Always, he was alert to the role of technology as an independent, not easily controllable force favouring 'a permanent weakening of borders … while creating new inequalities, imbalances, differentiations, and barriers inside the borders themselves'.[3] For many years, while happily based at CERI–Sciences Po, he was an essential part of what he called the 'travelling circus', a roving band of scholars and commentators who met frequently to analyse and debate international affairs.

This is not to say he was a distant, Olympian figure outside the classroom – quite the contrary. He was a lively, friendly man who liked nothing more than to trade jokes, stories and gossip over coffee or a meal. The one occasion on which I saw him truly annoyed was when a student had launched into an elaborate, sympathetic presentation of the views of someone whose name didn't yet ring a bell to me: Leo Strauss. As I remember the scene, Pierre cut the presentation short, dismissing Strauss's views as misleading, if not wrong. The incident, though I didn't realise it then, was symptomatic of his relationship with the emergent American neoconservatives and their teachers, some of whom he knew personally, including Strauss, and whose company he enjoyed, for example Allan Bloom. Although he was of Rumanian Jewish origin, unlike many of the American neocons, he had no particular feeling for Zionism or Israel. Aron mentions that Pierre disliked the 'pathos' of a column he (Aron) had written defending Israel on the eve of the 1967 war.[4] He was far more attached emotionally to the cause of the Eastern European dissidents who challenged Soviet control in the 1970s and 1980s. When I became his colleague in Bologna in the early 1980s, he often wore a Solidarność button on his lapel.

Obviously, his personal story was important here: his family survived the Holocaust and arrived in Paris as refugees from communism in 1948. Equally important was the influence of his mentor, Aron. One is tempted to say that Aron's real stock-in-trade, for all his refinement, was common sense, and his greatest gift was exposing double standards and cant. Why, Aron asked in *The Opium of the Intellectuals* (1955), were certain contemporaries 'merciless toward the failings of the democracies but ready to tolerate the worst crimes as long as they are committed in the name of the proper doctrines'? Pierre shared the gift, and posed the same inconvenient question. But like Aron, he also rejected doctrinal anti-communism. If I remember well, he had sympathy for the 'Eurocommunist' Italian Communist Party (PCI) under Enrico Berlinguer, for the same reason that the Soviets loathed it: it might offer the example of liberal communism to the East.

After 1989, his Aronian common sense and scepticism led him to challenge both schematic arguments about the coming clash of civilisations, and neo-Hegelian conceits about the end of history. Of the supposed universal evolution of humanity toward liberal democracy and economic liberalism, he said in 1994:

> It seems to me personally that what the twentieth century has demonstrated is that nothing could be less sure. True there is a sort of inevitability about the market and democratic values, because no possible traditional reference point has survived of an organic or cosmological model, but at the same time human and social factors are potentially much more explosive. Are not democracy and the market, like the European Community, merely fair-weather friends, institutions whose existence is threatened the moment there is an economic, social, political or military crisis of sufficient gravity? Are they not mere islands in a world where it is predominantly chaos and the will to power that prevail? Which is

the mainstream and which the incidental? Which is central and which parenthetical?[5]

One of his finest hours as a public intellectual came in 2002–03, when he took a strong position against what he saw as the George W. Bush administration's delusionary attempt to recast the Middle East and win the 'war on terror' by invading Iraq. In one of many interviews, he spoke of the Americans'

> congenital incapacity to see what is obvious to a European: the weight of resentment or of nationalism against the Israeli occupation and American wealth. They [the Americans] reproach the Europeans for a lack of moral clarity when criticizing American or Israeli policies, or for looking for the reasons for the hostility they encounter. But they give a certificate of morality to anybody who is on their side in the war against terrorism![6]

It should be added that on the eve of the Iraq War, he harshly (and in my view, rather unconvincingly) criticised the Chirac government for dramatically breaking with Washington in the UN Security Council, thus playing into the hands of the Bush-administration hawks who wished to divide Europe and go to war without UN authorisation.[7]

His last collection of essays, published in 2015, is entitled *La Revanche des passions* (The Revenge of Passions).[8] In it, he dwells on what had been richly demonstrated by all sides since 2001: the abiding role of *thymos*, the passionate, choleric element of human nature. Citing Aron, he says, 'anybody who thinks people follow their interests rather than their passions understood nothing about the twentieth century'. 'Nor', he adds, 'the twenty-first.'[9] In the end, Pierre attempted no grand theory of human nature or international relations, preferring, as he far too modestly put it, 'merely [to] observe and describe events'.[10] I think this was because he was simply too independent-minded and eclectic in his interests, too steeped in the classics – Rousseau, Kant, Hegel – to imagine that he could really improve on their insights, and too attached to his role as performer nonpareil. But he gave us a very rare kind of intellectual nourishment, and left us with questions that we ignore at our peril.

Notes

1   Raymond Aron, *Memoirs: Fifty Years of Political Reflection* (London: Holmes & Meier, 1990), p. 237.

2   Pierre Hassner, *Violence and Peace: From the Atomic Bomb to Ethnic Cleansing* (Budapest: Central European University Press, 1997), p. 252.

3   Pierre Hassner, 'Calleo the European', in J.L. Harper (ed.), *A Resolute Faith in the Power of Reasonable Ideas* (Bologna: Paul H. Nitze School of Advanced International Studies, 2012), p. 140.

4   Aron, *Memoirs*, p. 335.

5   Hassner, *Violence and Peace*, p. 247.

6   Patrice de Beer, 'La nouvelle Rome entre Barbares et Etats tributaires', *Le Monde*, 11 September 2002.

7   Hassner, 'Guerre: qui fait le jeu de qui?', *Le Monde*, 24 February 2003.

8   Hassner, *La Revanche des passions: métamorphoses de la violence et crises du politique* (Paris: Fayard, 2015).

9   Alain Frachon, 'La Passion selon Pierre Hassner', *Le Monde*, 5 November 2015.

10 Hassner, *Violence and Peace*, p. 257.

Noteworthy

IISS Shangri-La Dialogue

'I think there are consequences to China ignoring the international community. We firmly believe in the non-coercive aspects of how nations should get along with each other, that they should listen to each other. Nothing wrong with competition, nothing wrong with having strong positions. But when it comes down to introducing what they have done in the South China Sea, there are consequences.'

US Secretary of Defense James Mattis speaks on the challenges of Indo-Pacific security at the IISS Shangri-La Dialogue in Singapore on 2 June 2018.[1]

'North Korea has a new leader now, and I believe that North Korea is looking to change the course of history and is making a decisive action towards that. Just because we have been tricked by North Korea before does not guarantee that we will be tricked in the future. If we start to think like this, then we can never negotiate with them and we can never look to achieve peace with them. Leaders of the two Koreas, the efforts made by them, are looking to open a new era. Please understand this.'

South Korean Minister of National Defense Song Young-moo speaks on de-escalating the North Korean crisis.[2]

50
Litres of water used per person per day in Cape Town, which is experiencing severe water shortages

185
Average litres of water used per person per day around the world[3]

Mark Frankenstein?

'You have to ask yourself how you'll be remembered. As one of the three big internet giants together with Steve Jobs and Bill Gates who have enriched our world? Or a genius who created a digital monster that is destroying our societies and democracies?'

Guy Verhofstadt, a former prime minister of Belgium and now a member of the European Parliament, confronts Facebook founder and CEO Mark Zuckerberg during a hearing on 22 May 2018 in Brussels.[5]

Fanboy

'I am increasingly admiring of Donald Trump. Imagine Trump doing Brexit … He'd go in bloody hard … There'd be all sorts of breakdowns, all sorts of chaos. Everyone would think he'd gone mad. But actually you might get somewhere. It's a very, very good thought.'

British Foreign Secretary Boris Johnson talks to Conservative listeners during a private dinner in June.[4]

85
Percentage of the world's firearms owned by civilians

13
Percentage held in military stockpiles

2
Percentage owned by law-enforcement agencies[6]

Persian gulf

'The fact is this was a horrible, one-sided deal that should have never, ever been made. It didn't bring calm, it didn't bring peace, and it never will.'

US President Donald Trump withdraws from the Joint Comprehensive Plan of Action (JCPOA) on 8 May 2018.[7]

'Let me conclude with a message to the Iranian citizens and leaders, to each and everyone: "Do not let anyone dismantle this agreement. It is one of the biggest achievements diplomacy has ever delivered and we have built this together."'

Federica Mogherini, the EU's high representative for foreign affairs, responds to the news.[8]

'The mischievousness of "one" promise-breaker has been removed. The JCPOA will continue to guarantee the interests of Iran. Iran is more united than ever to neutralise the illegitimate American sanctions.'

Iranian President Hassan Rouhani.[9]

'We said that the issue of the US is not nuclear energy as this is just a pretext. They [pragmatists] refused to see that! Now do you see that you were wrong? We accepted the JCPOA, but the enmity towards the Islamic Republic did not end. Now they [US] bring up our presence in the region and our missiles. If we also accept this, then they will come up with even more issues!'

Iranian Supreme Leader Sayyid Ali Khamenei.[10]

'Many regard the invasion of Iraq as the worst foreign-policy move in the history of the American republic. Now we have a competitor.'

James Dobbins, former US ambassador to the EU.[11]

Pity party

'If they want to worsen their relationships with Russia they can blame all their mortal sins on us and this is actually the case nowadays. Brexit, and Catalonia and the Skripal case, God knows what.'

Russian President Vladimir Putin accuses the United Kingdom of blaming Russia for everything that goes wrong both domestically and internationally.[12]

30
Percentage of the global population living in urban areas in 1950

68
Percentage expected to live in urban areas by 2050, according to the UN's *2018 Revision of World Urbanization Prospects*[13]

Rough trade

'Canadians, we're polite, we're reasonable, but we also will not be pushed around.'

Canadian Prime Minister Justin Trudeau announces retaliatory measures in response to US tariffs at the end of the G7 summit.[14]

'There's a special place in hell for any foreign leader that engages in bad-faith diplomacy with President Donald J. Trump.'

Peter Navarro, a trade adviser to US President Donald Trump, criticises Trudeau.[15]

Sources

1 James Mattis, 'US Leadership and the Challenges of Indo-Pacific Security: Question & Answer Session', IISS Shangri-La Dialogue, Singapore, 2 June 2018, https://www.iiss.org/-/media/images/dialogues/sld/sld-2018/documents/james-mattis-qa-sld18.ashx?la=en&hash=A19ACAB4FA116FFD7EA5269D8AC6785AC19C2D08.

2 Song Young-moo, 'De-Escalating the North Korean Crisis: Question & Answer Session', IISS Shangri-La Dialogue, Singapore, 2 June 2018, https://www.iiss.org/-/media/images/dialogues/sld/sld-2018/documents/deescalating-north-korea-qa-sld18.ashx?la=en&hash=3010D3F9D608F84F52F67243B9391C05F8F551AD.

3 Joseph Cotterill, 'South Africa: How Cape Town Beat the Drought', *Financial Times*, 2 May 2018, https://www.ft.com/content/b9bac89a-4a49-11e8-8ee8-cae73aab7ccb?emailId=5ae9348750cbaf0004315941&segmentId=22011ee7-896a-8c4c-22a0-7603348b7f22.

4 Rick Noack, 'Brexit Needs Some of Trump's "Madness," Boris Johnson Suggests in Leaked Audio', *Washington Post*, 8 June 2018, https://www.washingtonpost.com/news/world/wp/2018/06/08/brexit-needs-some-of-trumps-madness-suggests-boris-johnson-in-leaked-audio/?utm_term=.44c673811cc2.

5 Mehreen Khan and Hannah Kuchler, 'Mark Zuckerberg's Answers Leave Angry EU Politicians Frustrated', *Financial Times*, 22 May 2018, https://www.ft.com/content/007c72ce-5df0-11e8-9334-2218e7146b04?emailId=5b04f05fb6c2250004c21436&segmentId=22011ee7-896a-8c4c-22a0-7603348b7f22.

6 The Small Arms Survey, 'Small Arms Survey Reveals: More than One Billion Firearms in the World', June 2018, http://www.smallarmssurvey.org/about-us/highlights/2018/highlight-bp-firearms-holdings.html.

7 The White House, 'Remarks by President Trump on the Joint Comprehensive Plan of Action', 8 May 2018, https://www.whitehouse.gov/briefings-statements/remarks-president-trump-joint-comprehensive-plan-action/.

8 Saeed Kamali Dehghan and Daniel Boffey, 'Iran Vows to Stick with Deal After "Pesky" Trump's Departure', *Guardian*, 8 May 2018, https://www.theguardian.com/us-news/2018/may/08/europe-denounces-trumps-us-withdrawal-from-iran-nuclear-deal.

9 Hassan Rouhani (@Rouhani_ir), tweet translated from Persian, 8 May 2018, https://twitter.com/Rouhani_ir/status/993936272384282624.

10 Sayyid Ali Khamenei (@Khamenei_fa), tweet translated from Persian, 9 May 2018, https://twitter.com/Khamenei_fa/status/994143177241178112.

11 James Dobbins (@Jim_Dobbins), tweet, 8 May 2018, https://twitter.com/Jim_Dobbins/status/993933254213488640.

12 'Putin Accuses Britain of Blaming "All Their Mortal Sins" on Russia', *Guardian*, 25 May 2018, https://www.theguardian.com/world/2018/may/25/putin-accuses-britain-of-blaming-all-their-mortal-sins-on-russia.

13 UN Department of Public Information, '68% of the World Population Projected to Live in Urban Areas by 2050, Says UN', 18 May 2018, https://esa.un.org/unpd/wup/Publications/Files/WUP2018-PressRelease.pdf.

14 Claudia Rebaza, Duarte Mendonca and Angela Dewan, 'France, Germany Slam Trump's G7 Statement U-Turn', CNN, 10 June 2018, https://edition.cnn.com/2018/06/10/world/trump-g7-communique-reaction-intl/index.html.

15 Oliver Laughland, 'Trudeau "Stabbed Us in Back" on Trade, Says Trump Chief Economic Adviser', *Guardian*, 11 June 2018, https://www.theguardian.com/us-news/2018/jun/10/justin-trudeau-donald-trump-tariffs-g7-north-korea-summit.

NATO Defence Spending and European Threat Perceptions

Lucie Béraud-Sudreau and Bastian Giegerich

'Do you give me credit for that?' This was US President Donald Trump's question to NATO Secretary-General Jens Stoltenberg when they met in Washington in May 2018. The latter had suggested to reporters that European NATO allies were now all spending more on defence.[1] Trump seemed to think that this was in response to his particular kind of leadership. In dealing with NATO, Trump has so far interspersed moments of indifference, bullying over defence-spending levels and carelessness concerning NATO's collective-defence commitments with increases in funding for the European Deterrence Initiative (a US programme to help fund activities of the US European Command in response to a changing security environment in Europe), and in forward-deployed personnel and equipment. The US president has seemed oblivious to the underlying spending trends in Europe as they have been developing since before he came to power.

Following years of defence cuts in response to the end of the Cold War and the 2008 financial crisis, Europe began to reinvest in defence in 2014–15 (Figure 1). Three factors explain this turn of events. Firstly, the economic situation has improved across the continent. Although unemployment remains high in some countries, such as France, Italy and Spain, most states experienced stronger GDP growth rates in 2017, and thus have more fiscal space to increase defence budgets. Secondly, threat perceptions have significantly changed, with some threats from the south and east becoming

Lucie Béraud-Sudreau is a Research Fellow for Defence Economics and Procurement at the IISS. **Bastian Giegerich** is the IISS Director of Defence and Military Analysis.

Survival | vol. 60 no. 4 | August–September | pp. 53–74   DOI 10.1080/00396338.2018.1495429

Figure 1: **Total defence spending of European NATO members in real terms, 2008–2017**

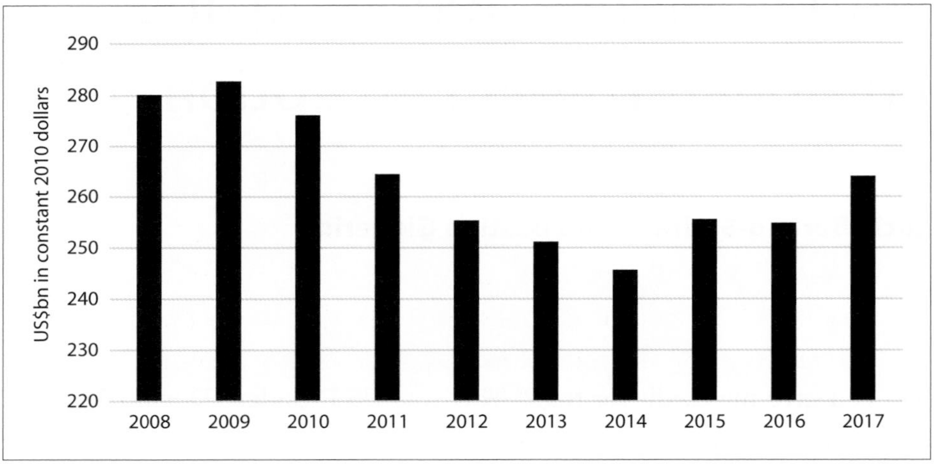

Source: IISS Military Balance+ database

more immediate. In addition, European capitals have come to feel that the world is becoming more unstable and unpredictable, and alliance bonds less certain than before. Thirdly, the effects of two decades of defence cuts are now becoming apparent to many European governments, which face visible readiness and capability shortfalls that put the usability of their armed forces in severe doubt. Thus, Europeans are not spending more to please Trump, but to meet threats.

As European governments have increased their defence budgets, they have stumbled upon budgeting and acquisition processes characterised by inertia. The empirical evidence suggests that European governments are responding to their own analyses of what is required, but are struggling to achieve a pace of adaptation that can keep up with changes in the threat landscape.

This finding is of mixed significance for NATO as it nears its 70th birthday. On the one hand, if defence-investment decisions are based on threats and requirements derived from member-state analysis, they are likely to be more sustainable compared to spending patterns driven primarily by political pressure from the Alliance's most powerful government. On the other hand, the empirical pattern revealed by the data also suggests that burden-sharing will persist as a problem threatening NATO cohesion. Threat perceptions in Europe continue to show some variation, which contributes to different speeds and levels of effort when it comes to adapting to changing requirements. Looking beyond the headline increases, defence-investment trends reflect significant contrasts between countries in the northern and eastern parts of Europe against those in the western and southern parts of the continent. Furthermore, compared to the rapidly changing threat environment, many arms-procurement priorities and deliveries lack urgency. Threat perceptions that are only partially aligned, combined with delayed responses, could be a significant obstacle to a greater European contribution to allied deterrence and defence.[2] This in turn might mean that even the comparatively strong growth in European defence spending might not suffice to prevent a burden-sharing debate of considerable intensity. Simply calling for more money, as the White House seems intent on doing, will do little to address this.[3]

Varying threat perceptions in Europe

While public-opinion polls are occasionally conducted to measure threat perceptions among NATO members,[4] for the purpose of this article we focus on the threat analysis contained in security and defence documents prepared by European NATO members specifically to justify defence-spending decisions. Given that Europe's security environment has changed significantly within the last few years, beginning with the illegal annexation of Crimea by Russia in 2014, it is not surprising that a high number of national strategy documents were published between 2015 and early 2018 by NATO's European members. Some of these documents were triggered by a change in government, but in general they represent an attempt to come to terms with the revived spectre of conventional military conflict on the continent alongside a range of ongoing transnational threats. A deteriorating security environment in Europe, paired with improved economic growth rates and a gradual easing of austerity measures, has encouraged many European governments to raise their defence outlays and to reconsider defence-investment priorities for evolving national force structures. While NATO has attempted to gloss over varying national priorities by arguing that it takes a '360 degree approach' to the analysis of security threats,[5] most member states focus on a smaller range of problems.

The section of the December 2017 US National Security Strategy that deals with Europe portrays Russia as a threat to transatlantic unity, as well as to the sovereignty of European states. It further singles out China's increasing presence in Europe, transnational terrorism, and migration triggered by instability as areas of concern. The strategy commits the US to the collective defence of its NATO allies, but is clear that European NATO members are expected to spend 2% of their GDP on defence and 20% of that spending on capability investment.[6]

Overall, European NATO members share the assessment that the continent's security is deteriorating. Likewise, most national strategy documents by European members share the assumption that governments will have to collaborate in order to meet a variety of threats. Many governments have chosen to identify Russia as a potential source of military aggression and political coercion, and thus as a challenger to Europe's security order. This constitutes a marked shift from the previous generation of strategy documents, including those of many eastern-European countries, which at most pointed to a residual risk stemming from Russia but otherwise stressed the need for some form of partnership with Moscow. Another shared element is a focus on hybrid risks and threats, and hence an emphasis on resilience and whole-of-government approaches to security. Countering terrorist threats is a third priority, although differing constitutional requirements influence the degree to which counter-terrorism is seen by states as primarily a law-enforcement issue, with limited roles for the military. One issue that is not yet fully reflected in most documents is the pressure being generated by migration trends on EU member states, which will require a much more integrated response. The fusion of internal and external security has long been a theme in government and expert circles, but migration is now forcing this trend up the priority list, in part because of the potential link between migrant flows and terrorists seeking to strike European targets. Several countries have begun to reconsider cuts to military personnel that began after the Cold War. For example, Germany announced in 2017 that it would seek to add some 20,000 active personnel to the Bundeswehr by 2024. In 2016, Poland announced that it would set up a 53,000-strong territorial defence force organised into 17 light infantry brigades. While some of these units would be tasked with critical-infrastructure protection, others would be trained in unconventional warfare. Recruitment for the brigades is under way, with the first volunteers having completed their basic training in May 2017. The full force is due to be established by 2019. Other European countries, including France and the United Kingdom, have explored the role of the reserves, attempting to come up with ways in which the contribution of reservists can be strengthened. Overall, there is a sense that a multitude of challenges, including the re-emergence of the spectre of armed conflict on European soil, necessitate somewhat larger forces than Europeans currently have.

While governments have begun to adjust force postures and procurement priorities to achieve a better alignment of threat perceptions, differences regarding national priorities persist. Russia's assertiveness in foreign-policy matters, sustained effort to modernise its armed forces, and support for separatist militias in eastern Ukraine have significantly influenced threat perceptions among defence establishments in central and eastern Europe. For example, Lithuania's 2018 National Threat Assessment bluntly states that 'the major threat to the national security of Lithuania originates from Russia's aggressive intentions and actions'.[7] Poland's 2017 Defence Concept sees Russia as both a national and a systemic problem, arguing that

> the Russian Federation aims at enhancing its position in the global balance of power by using various means. They include breaches of international law, the regular use of force and coercion in relations with other states and various attempts to destabilize Western integrated structures. It poses a threat mainly for Poland and other countries in the region, but also for all other nations desirous of a stable international order.[8]

The 2017 Czech defence strategy and the 2016 Slovak defence White Paper make similar points, with the Czech Republic suggesting that Russia's 'blatant' pursuit of 'its power ambitions, including through use of military force … violates the norms of international law, including the territorial integrity of its neighbouring states'.[9] Slovakia's officials see 'the system of international law, as applied so far, being questioned' by Russia's actions.[10]

Even in Germany, where part of the political spectrum and a fair share of the population remain supportive of Russia, the country's 2016 White Paper argues that

> Russia is openly calling the European peace order into question with its willingness to use force to advance its own interests and to unilaterally redraw borders guaranteed under international law, as it has done in Crimea and eastern Ukraine. This has far-reaching implications for security in Europe and thus for the security of Germany.[11]

In parallel to Russia's re-emergence as a core security problem in Europe, persistent instability across the Mediterranean and Middle East has sent waves of migrants across the borders of Europe's NATO members and produced a heightened tempo of small- to medium-scale terrorist attacks in several of them. Security challenges linked to instability have forced militaries to take on a variety of assistance and support functions otherwise performed by a range of civilian agencies, including patrolling and guard missions, infrastructure protection as counter-terrorism, and border control to help manage migration flows. While mostly acknowledging increasing concerns about Russia, the strategy documents of southern-European members understandably focus on these more southerly problems. Before it was recently voted out of office, the Italian government under Paolo Gentiloni argued that

> the southern shore of the Mediterranean constitutes the 'accumulation point' of the instabilities which, converging from the Middle East, North Africa and sub-Saharan Africa, spread throughout the Mediterranean basin, putting at risk the security, stability, political and socio-economic situation in the region … In particular, the migratory flow that runs through the central Mediterranean route involves us directly.[12]

The newly elected coalition government of Giuseppe Conte can be expected to further de-emphasise Russia as a security challenge, based on coalition member La Liga's position in favour of lifting economic sanctions on Russia.

Meanwhile, the French defence and security review of 2017 suggests that jihadist terrorism represents the most immediate threat to the French people and homeland, noting that even when terrorist organisations disappear, their ideology, and therefore the challenge they pose, endures.[13] Spain's 2017 National Security Strategy notes that, 'as has happened in other European cities, with the August 2017 attacks, Spain became the focus of the terrorist scourge, and the magnitude of this threat for Spain was underlined'.[14]

Hence, while many government documents and speeches by senior leaders cover similar ground, Russia is identified as a threat in much stronger terms by the states of central and eastern Europe. In contrast, southern- and western-European governments, while mostly acknowledging a degree of concern about Russia, place more emphasis on instability arising from transnational challenges, particularly migration and terrorism. It seems reasonable to assume that differences in threat perceptions will cause some variation in policy responses from national governments. This will be the case even in circumstances where a multinational framework like NATO requires a degree of convergence, for example in the form of the 2014 Defence Investment Pledge, which calls on NATO members to focus on a variety of spending goals.[15] These differences in policy output should be visible in spending trends, national procurement activities and force structures.

A two-speed Europe in defence investment

There are two important indicators to suggest that variations in national threat analyses do have an impact on defence-investment trends in Europe: the overall effort allocated to defence spending, and procurement priorities (that is, the kind of equipment bought by governments). These indicators confirm divisions between the northern and central parts of Europe on one side, and western and southern regions on the other.

As noted, a return to defence-spending increases has been a sustained trend since 2015. The defence budgets of NATO's European members increased by 3.6% in real terms in 2017. The largest increases in real-term defence spending were seen in Germany (6.6%), Romania (38.6%) and the Baltic countries (14.4% for the three countries combined). Yet within the

Figure 2: **Pace of defence-spending growth among European NATO members, 2009–2017**

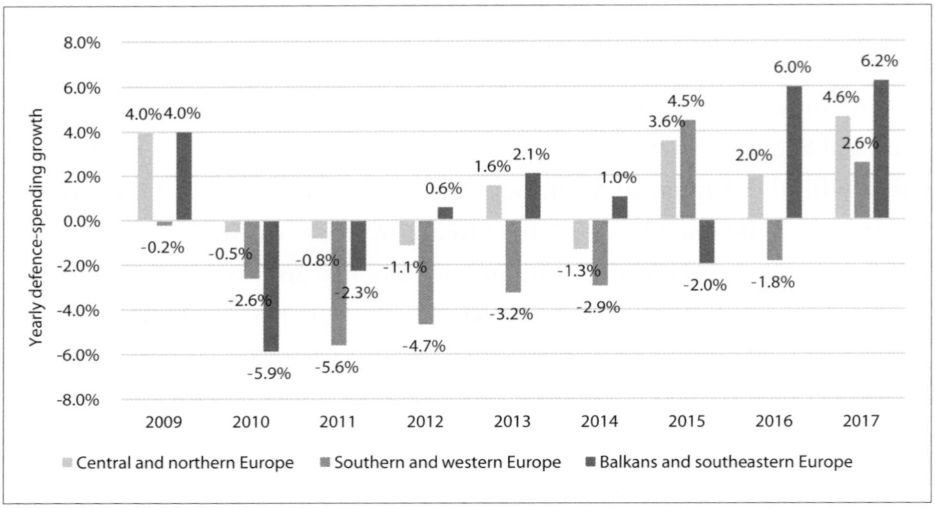

Source: IISS Military Balance+ database

overall trend toward increasing defence spending, some sub-regional variation was still in evidence. Spending in northern and central Europe grew by 5.5%, while in southern and western Europe it grew by 2.5%.[16] This difference can be accounted for by trends going back years. In the aftermath of the 2008 financial crisis, defence spending decreased faster among NATO member states in southern and western Europe, and even as economies recovered, the defence budgets of western and southern countries increased more slowly than in central and northern Europe (except in 2015).[17] In other words, countries located in the west and south of Europe made larger defence cuts after the crisis, and in recent years increased their military expenditure to a smaller degree than their counterparts in the north and centre of the continent (Figure 2). Hence, in post-Crimea Europe, countries in the centre and north of the continent seem to have reacted more quickly to emerging threats on the eastern front, while countries in the west and south have moved more slowly, despite the recovery of their economies.

Beyond headline budget information, a more precise indicator of the different ways in which NATO's European members have reacted to new threats can be found in defence-investment spending. Defence investment encompasses spending on major equipment and research and development

(R&D) for future weapons systems. This category of spending is key for equipping armed forces with the capabilities to meet current and future threats. Procurement of major new weapons systems, or upgrades of existing holdings, allows for both adaptation and innovation in support of the missions that have been defined for a country's armed forces. Likewise, R&D is vital to ensure that innovation and adaptation continue by driving the technological developments of the future. Spending on these expense categories thus provides a useful metric for understanding the degree to which a nation is focused on adapting to threats.

In 2017, NATO Europe's overall real-term defence investments (in constant 2010 US dollars) totalled $58.7 billion, which was higher than the 2011 total of $55.3bn. But here again, NATO members in north and central Europe have increased their defence investments faster than their southern and western allies. With the exceptions of Italy and Luxembourg, all of the countries displaying steady defence-investment growth between 2011 and 2017 are located in northern and central/eastern Europe. This suggests that there were more consistent efforts to increase procurement spending (that is, to modernise inventories) in the eastern parts of Europe compared to the rest of the continent (Figure 3).

Defence-investment spending as a proportion of total defence budgets provides a more direct way of measuring how important this spending category is to governments as compared to, for example, personnel or operating costs. Using the NATO guideline that members devote 20% of defence spending to major new equipment (including R&D) as a point of reference, the number of European NATO members meeting this threshold has grown from eight in 2011 to 13 in 2017, representing close to half of NATO's European membership. Yet once again, significant variation can be seen. Out of ten countries in central and northern Europe, eight (Denmark, Estonia, Hungary, Latvia, Lithuania, Norway, Poland and Slovakia) had increased their share of defence investments by 2017, while two decreased it (Czech Republic and Germany). The situation is more varied in western and southern Europe. Out of ten countries, the proportion of defence investment in relation to overall defence spending declined in six countries (Belgium, France, Greece, the Netherlands, Portugal and Spain[18]), remained

Figure 3: **Defence-investment growth in European NATO members, 2011–2017**

Defence-investment growth
< 0

Defence-investment growth
> 0

Note:

Data for Croatia spans only
2016–17 due to a lack of
data for previous years.

Data for Spain covers
2011–16 due to a change
in reporting methods for
2017.

Data for Slovenia and
Montenegro also covers
2011–16. No 2014 data is
available for Latvia.

Sources: National budget information; IISS communication with governments

stable in one (the United Kingdom) and increased in two countries (Italy and Luxembourg).[19] Thus, there has been greater effort among the northern- and central-European NATO members to increase defence investment as a proportion of overall spending than among their counterparts in the west and south.

Of course, this variation has more than one cause. For example, several northern- and central-European states had some catching up to do, compared to their western and southern counterparts, because their armed forces featured – and in some cases still feature – Soviet legacy equipment in dire need of modernisation. Another explanation is that the threats deemed most important in northern and central Europe have a more direct bearing on territorial- and collective-defence tasks and missions. While the threat posed by Russia to eastern Europe requires modernisation of land-warfare equipment, for instance, the counter-terrorism priorities of western Europe require increased spending in other policy areas, such as homeland security and intelligence.

Procuring for territorial defence vs projection capabilities

The IISS Military Balance+ database currently tracks 186 crew-serviced equipment orders (or intended orders) initiated by Europe's member states since 2010.[20] This covers several categories of major conventional weapons systems, ranging from satellites to artillery systems and combat aircraft to submarines. We assume that the distribution of weapons categories purchased by countries in recent years reflects an attempt to drive up the utility of their armed forces in meeting requirements generated by governments' threat analyses.

Figures 4 and 5 show that countries in northern and central Europe have focused on different types of equipment than countries in the west and south. While central- and northern-European states tend to procure across more equipment categories than do states in western and southern Europe, thus seeming to cover a broader spectrum overall, their orders are actually focused on a small number of categories.

Orders for armoured vehicles, multi-role and transport helicopters, tanker and transport aircraft, and artillery account for more than 50% of the orders placed by NATO members in northern and central Europe. The largest number of purchases in this category deal with armoured vehicles, including main battle tanks (22%). Recent examples include Poland's contracts for *Rosomak* APCs and armoured engineering vehicles. In April 2017, Estonia contracted BAE Systems Hägglunds to upgrade its 44 CV9035 infantry fighting vehicles. Slovakia ordered nine UH-60M *Black Hawk* medium transport helicopters in 2015, the first pair of which arrived in June 2017. In February 2017, Germany contracted Airbus to modernise 26 CH-53 transport helicopters. Work is expected to be completed in 2022. In March 2017, Denmark announced that it had selected Nexter's CAESAR self-propelled artillery system to replace the M109 howitzers it has operated since 1965. In December 2017, Norway announced it had awarded Hanwha Techwin a NOK1.8bn ($213.49 million) contract to supply 24 K9 *Thunder* self-propelled howitzers and associated ammunition vehicles, with an option for 24 more

Figure 4: **Ongoing or completed procurement by category in central and northern Europe, 2010–2017**

Uninhabited aerial vehicles (medium to heavy)
2%

Training aircraft
(fixed and rotary)
4%

Satellites
4%

Multi-role/transport
helicopters
11%

Armoured vehicles
22%

Attack helicopters
2%

Tanker and/or
transport aircraft
11%

**Central and
Northern Europe**

Artillery
9%

Maritime-patrol/anti-
submarine-warfare aircraft
7%

Air defence
4%

Anti-electronic-warfare/
intelligence, surveillance and
reconnaissance aircraft
(fixed and rotary)
2%

Coastal defence missiles
2%

Combat/electronic-
warfare aircraft
4%

Patrol and coastal
combatants
7%

Principal surface
combatants
6%

Submarines
2%

Mine-countermeasures vessels
2%

Source: IISS Military Balance+ database

howitzers. Overall, these orders, particularly those for armoured vehicles and artillery systems, primarily support territorial- and collective-defence tasks, which for the countries concerned would involve some kind of conflict with Russia.

Smaller countries have long needed to be selective in terms of how they spend their procurement funds. For many eastern-European countries, this currently means a focus on territorial defence and on defining a role for themselves within NATO. Since NATO's smaller members have no need to maintain a full-spectrum capability and the associated industries, they might be able to translate political guidance into procurement priorities or modest changes to force posture more quickly than larger states. By contrast, for NATO's larger members, giving up or capping a certain capability

Figure 5: **Ongoing or completed procurement by category in western and southern Europe, 2010–2017**

Uninhabited aerial vehicles
(medium to heavy)
6%

Training aircraft
(fixed and rotary)
2%

Satellites
4%

Armoured vehicles
12%

Multi-role/transport
helicopters
12%

Artillery
1%

Air defence
1%

Attack helicopters
3%

Submarines
6%

Western and Southern Europe

Tanker and/or
transport aircraft
13%

Principal surface
combatants
10%

Maritime-patrol/anti-
submarine-warfare aircraft
(rotary and fixed wing)
7%

Patrol and coastal
combatants
10%

Anti-electronic-warfare/
intelligence, surveillance and
reconnaissance aircraft
(fixed and rotary)
2%

Principal amphibious
vehicles
3%

Combat/electronic-
warfare aircraft
7%

Source: IISS Military Balance+ database

would be a conscious choice, further complicated by their global outlook and perceived international responsibility.

Thus, NATO's members in western and southern Europe display a more balanced procurement pattern across equipment categories. Western- and southern-European governments also procure more uninhabited aerial vehicles (UAVs), including the purchase of MQ-9A *Reaper* UAVs by France and Italy, and place a greater emphasis on maritime capabilities, through deliveries of principal surface combatants, patrol and coastal combatants, and principal amphibious vessels, which together account for 30% of all orders. Examples of such procurements include the United Kingdom's principal surface combatant orders (Type-26 and Type-45), and France's

FTI frigate programmes. These orders would seem to support a somewhat wider set of military tasks, beyond territorial defence.

Overall, defence-investment patterns, as seen in relevant spending and procurement activity, do suggest a link between investment and threat analysis, leading to variations in the policies of European NATO members. Dissimilarities in procurement priorities pose a challenge for Alliance cohesion since they suggest a silent division of labour which might on the one hand create decision-making and inter-operability issues, and on the other argue for a more federated approach to NATO capabilities.

Adapting arms acquisitions to a new threat environment

There will be a lag between changes in the threat environment and any visible response in terms of procurement and acquisitions. Defence procurement often takes many years, and the portion of defence budgets allocated to defence investment is determined several years in advance, meaning that it takes time for new priorities to filter through. The agility of these processes, or rather their lack of agility, has been identified as a problem by several governments and armed forces.

Despite a prevailing political determination among European allies to increase defence budgets, it is difficult for governments to implement stark increases year on year. Budgetary processes favour incremental changes over sharp rises or cuts: the budgets of relevant agencies and departments are decided with reference to the previous year's budget, so that there are usually only limited increases or decreases.[21] In addition, agency leaders will attempt to protect or increase their annual allocations. All this makes it difficult to move significant amounts of money from one programme to another.[22] The decision-making process that underpins budgets further contributes to this incrementalism. The large number of actors that participate from both the executive and legislative branches of government, including finance ministries, cabinet offices and parliamentary committees, all serve to lengthen decision-making time frames, and are all potential sources of resistance that needs to be overcome. A case in point is the ten-year time horizon established by the 2014 Defence Investment Pledge adopted at the NATO summit in Wales. NATO members committed to raising their military expenditure to represent 2% of GDP by 2024, or to at least maintain spending if they were already at this level.[23] According to NATO's own figures, 15 out of 29 allied countries, including the US and Canada, are currently projected to reach the 2% threshold by 2024.[24] In 2014, only three did so.[25]

The incremental nature of budgeting implies that defence spending will not immediately spike in response to changing threats. Budgets can only be expected to radically shift in moments of acute perceived crisis, when new problems enter the political agenda and shake up the usual processes.[26] In this regard, Romania's 38% spending increase between 2016 and 2017, the single largest year-on-year increase in a NATO member's defence budget since 2014, is exceptional.

Military procurement processes, like budgetary processes, have a well-established reputation for incrementalism and a lack of agility, in particular when R&D is required. Developing a weapons programme is a long and complex process. The French *Leclerc* main battle tank, for example, was first conceived of toward the end of the 1960s, but did not begin to enter into service until 1991.[27] Similarly, the UK's HMS *Queen Elizabeth*, an aircraft carrier commissioned in December 2017 and expected to be fully operational in 2020, arguably originated in the country's 1998 Strategic Defence Review.[28] In April 2018, France and Germany launched a cooperative programme for future combat aircraft that are expected to replace current fighter jets between 2035 and 2040.[29]

Arms-acquisition procedures are always tightly regulated, and involve multiple actors from both the state and the private sectors. For instance, the Polish procurement process is divided into four bureaucratic phases: identification, conceptualisation, realisation and exploitation.[30] Moreover, several factors may slow these processes down. For instance, ambitions at the start of the process may be unrealistic given budgetary constraints, generating delays as efforts are made to reconcile desires and costs. As with defence budgets, procurement processes involve a range of actors who will want to have their say, and who may have differing positions and objectives that will also need to be reconciled. The relevant legal procedures can be cumbersome, and any requirement for offsets (compensations or technology transfers required by the client state as part of an arms deal) will further complicate and lengthen the process.

Indeed, it is not unusual for the planned entry into service of major weapons systems to be delayed by several years. For instance, the first Canadian CH-148 *Cyclone* multi-role helicopters were delivered in 2015, instead of 2008 as originally planned.[31] A report from the French audit office in 2010 showed that armament programmes almost systematically slipped in terms of delivery dates.[32] Overcoming technological difficulties can be challenging and therefore take time, as can respecifying weapons-system requirements to match actual development and production capabilities. Such complications are present in all European NATO members.

The slow arms-acquisition process means that, even though governments and armed forces may be aware of a change in the types of threats they face, there will inevitably be a gap between the appearance of new threat assessments and the responses they trigger. This creates a vulnerability for NATO members, which may not be able to adapt with the necessary speed to pressures emanating from a changing threat landscape and the rapid advance of technology, including in sectors that might not be strictly military but have defence-relevant applications, such as artificial intelligence.

NATO countries have begun to recognise this problem. In Germany, the country's defence-procurement agency, BAAINBw, has been criticised for being 'overly bureaucratic' and producing excessively detailed lists of requirements when purchasing military goods.[33] Several recent reports on the country's armed forces have highlighted the need to reform procurement processes, including a Bundestag report published in February 2018,[34] and a German Army paper released the following month. The latter requested that the time lag between the development of new technologies and defence-procurement procedures be reduced.[35]

In France, the deputy president of the Defence Commission at the Assemblée Nationale, Jean-Michel Jacques, has also argued for faster procurement processes. He cited the example of the Islamic State's weaponised drones becoming more lethal every couple of months, while the French Armed Forces had to wait at least six months, and up to three years, to acquire observation drones. He argued that small equipment such as drones and individual weapons should be made available more quickly, with existing acquisition processes continuing to apply to major weapons systems.[36] In response, the French procurement agency (the Direction générale de l'armement or DGA) established an 'Innovation Defence Lab' that was originally focused only on IT systems, but that was extended to cover other domains in 2016.[37] In addition, the Defence Innovation Agency (Agence de l'innovation de défense) was set up in 2018 within the armed-forces ministry to prioritise R&D in the field of artificial intelligence. It will be linked to other mechanisms, including the Def'Investment investment fund and the above-mentioned Innovation Defence Lab.[38] Similarly, the United Kingdom launched in September 2016 the 'Defence Innovation Initiative' in conjunction with the Defence and Security Accelerator for the explicit purpose of increasing 'the pace at which innovation is developed and brought into service'.[39]

*   *   *

The upward trend in European defence spending is likely to continue in the coming years. Many European states, including the top spenders, have announced plans to increase defence budgets in the coming years. German spending is expected to reach $54.9bn (including pensions) in current terms in 2022, and French spending to reach $56.8bn (excluding pensions) in 2023. Similarly, the UK government has committed to increase its defence budget by £1bn ($1.4bn) per year until 2021. Scandinavian states have also unveiled plans to increase spending: Denmark from $3.5bn in 2016 to an estimated $6.3bn in 2023; Norway from $6bn in 2017 to $7.8bn in 2020; and non-NATO-member Sweden from $5.7bn in 2017 to $8.6bn in 2022. The trend also applies further south, with Spain announcing its intention to increase its defence budget to €18bn ($23.2bn) by 2024, up from €10.7bn ($12.1bn) in 2017. Other countries, such as the Baltic states, have made NATO's 2% of GDP target the cornerstone of their defence-spending projections, while Poland announced its ambition to achieve 2.5% of GDP by 2032.[40] It seems clear that, across the continent, defence spending is now widely accepted as a political priority.

Underneath this overall tendency among Europe's NATO members to increase defence spending lie substantial differences in defence-policy objectives. Countries in central and northern Europe, which are comparatively more worried about Russia, have been increasing their spending more quickly, including on defence investments and the procurement of weapons systems directed at territorial defence. Allies in western and southern Europe have also begun to increase their defence spending, but more slowly and with an emphasis on power-projection and maritime-protection systems.

Overall Alliance cohesion could benefit from the open acknowledgement of allies' diverging threat priorities, and an agreement to allow for a division of labour among them. Each country could focus on areas in which it enjoys a competitive advantage, with allies complementing each other, in effect creating federated capabilities. This would require allies to embrace increased interdependence and a new form of burden-sharing, which would of course require strong mutual trust. NATO could also usefully assist member states with recommendations on procurement-process reform, to allow for swifter adaptation to changing threats and technologies. Certainly this would be more helpful than any American hectoring.

Notes

[1]   Quoted in Eli Okun, 'NATO Chief Thanks Trump for Leadership on Military Spending', 17 May 2018, *Politico*, https://www.politico.eu/article/jens-stoltenberg-donald-trump-nato-chief-thanks-trump-for-leadership-on-military-spending/.

[2]   Hugo Meijer and Marco Wyss, 'Beyond CSDP: The Resurgence of National Armed Forces in Europe', in Hugo Meijer and Marco Wyss, *The Handbook of European Defence Policies and Armed Forces* (Oxford: Oxford University Press, 2018), pp. 1–31.

[3]   For the US administration's view, see Martin Banks, 'Newly Confirmed Pompeo Stresses Defense Spending Target at First NATO Meeting', *Defense News*, 27 April 2018, https://www.defensenews.com/global/theamericas/2018/04/27/newly-confirmed-pompeo-stresses-defense-spending-target-at-first-nato-meeting/.

[4]   For a recent comparative poll, see European Commission, 'Special Eurobarometer 464b: Europeans' Attitudes Towards Security', December 2017, http://ec.europa.eu/commfrontoffice/publicopinion/index.cfm/Survey/getSurveyDetail/instruments/SPECIAL/surveyKy/1569.

[5]   North Atlantic Treaty Organisation (NATO), 'Statement by NATO Defence Ministers', 25 June 2015, https://www.

nato.int/cps/en/natohq/news_121133.
htm.

6   The White House, 'National Security
    Strategy of the United States of
    America', December 2017, pp. 47–8,
    https://www.whitehouse.gov/
    wp-content/uploads/2017/12/NSS-
    Final-12-18-2017-0905.pdf.

7   State Security Department of the
    Government of Lithuania, 'National
    Threat Assessment 2018', p. 4, https://
    kam.lt/download/61270/eng.pdf.

8   Ministry of National Defence of the
    Republic of Poland, 'The Defence
    Concept of the Republic of Poland',
    13 June 2017, p. 23, http://en.mon.gov.
    pl/documents/category/dokumenty/
    the-defence-concept-of-the-republic-
    of-poland-j-103276/.

9   Ministry of Defence and Armed
    Forces of the Czech Republic, 'Defence
    Strategy of the Czech Republic', 13
    March 2017, p. 7, available at http://
    www.army.cz/en/ministry-of-defence/
    strategy-and-doctrine/defence-
    strategy-of-the-czech-republic-135549/.

10 Ministry of Defence of the Slovak
    Republic, 'White Paper on Defence,
    2016', p. 33, https://www.mosr.sk/
    white-paper-on-defence-of-the-slovak-
    republic-2016/.

11 Federal Government of Germany,
    'White Paper on German Security
    Policy and the Future of the
    Bundeswehr', 19 September
    2016, p. 31, available at http://
    www.gmfus.org/publications/
    white-paper-german-security-policy-
    and-future-bundeswehr.

12 Defence Ministry of Italy, 'Documento
    Programmatico Pluriennale
    2017–2019', pp. 5–6, https://www.
    difesa.it/Content/Documents/DPP/

    DPP_2017_2019_Approvato_light.pdf.

13 Government of France, 'National
    Defence and Security Review',
    October 2017, p. 37, available at
    https://www.defense.gouv.fr/
    dgris/presentation/evenements/
    revue-strategique-de-defense-et-de-
    securite-nationale-2017.

14 Government of Spain, 'National
    Security Strategy 2017', pp. 56–7,
    http://www.dsn.gob.es/sites/dsn/
    files/2017_Spanish_National_Security_
    Strategy_0.pdf.

15 For the argument that policy diver-
    gence can exist despite multinational
    pressure to converge, see Christoph
    O. Meyer, 'International Terrorism
    as a Force of Homogenization?
    A Constructivist Approach to
    Understanding Cross-National Threat
    Perceptions and Responses', *Cambridge
    Review of International Affairs*, vol. 22,
    no. 4, 2009, pp. 647–66.

16 NATO's European members are
    grouped by region. The Balkans are
    Albania, Croatia, Montenegro and
    Slovenia. Central Europe comprises
    Czech Republic, Germany, Hungary,
    Poland and Slovakia. Northern
    Europe comprises Denmark, Estonia,
    Latvia, Lithuania and Norway.
    Southeastern Europe comprises
    Bulgaria, Romania and Turkey.
    Southern Europe comprises Greece,
    Italy, Portugal and Spain. Western
    Europe comprises Belgium, France,
    Iceland, Luxembourg, the Netherlands
    and the United Kingdom.

17 See the IISS Military Balance+ data-
    base, https://milbalplus.iiss.org/.

18 Data for Spain covers the years 2011 to
    2016. The year 2017 was not taken into
    account due to a change in the way

procurement expenses are reported, which introduces a break in the series.

[19] Iceland is not included in this list because there is no budget-breakdown data available for that country.

[20] See the IISS Military Balance+ database. The total number of arms orders and deliveries was correct as of the end of May 2018. The data consists of a selected record of arms orders that meet the criteria to be included in the IISS *Military Balance*. For example, the IISS does not record small-arms holdings in its entries for individual countries, so these are not included in the dataset. Individual contracts are counted separately, but the exercising of contract options will form part of the same record. The IISS does not capture most orders for missiles because we do not list quantities of air- and ship-launched missiles in the *Military Balance* data. The IISS does capture orders for air-defence systems, ground-launched ballistic- and cruise-missile systems, and certain significant upgrade and development programmes. These include major platforms procurements, deals signed since 2010 or deliveries since 2010. Individual equipment types are counted: for instance, three orders for *Typhoon* combat aircraft by the United Kingdom would be treated as one order, whereas if the UK were to order F-35, F-16 and *Typhoon* aircraft, this would be treated as separate orders.

[21] Aaron Wildavsky, *The Politics of the Budgetary Process* (Boston, MA: Little, Brown, 1964), p. 216.

[22] Joachim Wehner, 'Aaron Wildavsky: The Politics of the Budgetary Process', in Martin Lodge, Edward C. Page and Steven J. Balla (eds), *The Oxford Handbook of Classics in Public Policy and Administration* (Oxford: Oxford University Press, 2015), p. 195, n. 204.

[23] NATO, 'Wales Summit Declaration', 5 September 2014, https://www.nato.int/cps/ic/natohq/official_texts_112964.htm.

[24] NATO, 'NATO Defence Ministers Take Decisions to Strengthen the Alliance', 15 February 2018, https://www.nato.int/cps/ua/natohq/news_152125.htm.

[25] NATO, 'Defence Expenditures of NATO Countries (1995–2015): Financial and Economic Data Relating to NATO Defence', 22 June 2015, https://www.nato.int/nato_static_fl2014/assets/pdf/pdf_2015_06/20150622_PR_CP_2015_093-v2.pdf.

[26] See Christian Breunig, 'The More Things Change, the More Things Stay the Same: A Comparative Analysis of Budget Punctuations', *Journal of European Public Policy*, vol. 13, no. 7, 2006, pp. 1,069–85; and Christoph O. Meyer and Eva Strickmann, 'Solidifying Constructivism: How Material and Ideational Factors Interact in European Defence', *Journal of Common Market Studies*, vol. 49, no. 1, 2012, pp. 61–81.

[27] William Genieys and Laura Michel, 'Au-delà du complexe militaro-industriel: Le rôle d'une élite sectorielle dans le programme du char Leclerc', *Revue française de sociologie*, vol. 47, no. 1, 2006, pp. 117–42.

[28] James Kirkup and Christopher Hope, 'Defence Review: Decision to Build New Aircraft Carriers Made in Labour's 1998 Strategic Defence

Review', *Telegraph*, 20 October 2010, https://www.telegraph.co.uk/news/uknews/defence/8074625/Defence-review-decision-to-build-new-aircraft-carriers-made-in-Labours-1998-Strategic-Defence-Review.html.

29 Dassault Aviation, 'Dassault Aviation and Airbus Join Forces on Future Combat Air System', 25 April 2018, https://www.dassault-aviation.com/en/group/press/press-kits/dassault-aviation-airbus-join-forces-future-combat-air-system/.

30 Wojciech Pawłuszko, 'Polish Ministry of Defence Changes the Procurement Regulations', 13 July 2017, Defence24.com, http://www.defence24.com/polish-ministry-of-defence-changes-the-procurement-regulations-analysis.

31 IISS, 'Figure 4. Canada: Sikorsky CH-148 *Cyclone* Multi-role Helicopter', *The Military Balance 2018* (Abingdon: Routledge for the IISS, 2018), p. 64.

32 Cour des Comptes, 'La conduit des programmes d'armement', annual public report, February 2010, https://www.ccomptes.fr/sites/default/files/EzPublish/1_conduite-des-programmes-armement.pdf.

33 Tobias Buck, 'Germany Struggles to Find Ways of Spending Extra Cash on Defence', *Financial Times*, 18 May 2018, https://www.ft.com/content/43cf404c-59a4-11e8-bdb7-f6677d2e1ce8.

34 Dr Hans-Peter Bartels, 'Unterrichtung durch den Wehrbeauftragten', Deutscher Bundestag, Drucksache 19/700, 20 February 2018, http://dip21.bundestag.de/dip21/btd/19/007/1900700.pdf.

35 Deutsches Heer, 'Thesenpapier II – Digitalisierung von Landoperationen', Thesenpapiere zur Zukunft deutscher Landstreitkräfte, March 2018, p. 8, https://www.dwt-sgw.de/fileadmin/redaktion/SGW-Veranstaltungen/2018/8F7_Landoperationen/Thesenpapier_II_Digitalisierung_Landoperationen.pdf.

36 Jean-Michel Jacques, 'Nos armées doivent acquérir plus rapidement leurs équipements opérationnels', *Le Monde*, 27 March 2018, http://www.lemonde.fr/idees/article/2018/03/27/defense-nos-armees-doivent-acquerir-plus-rapidement-leurs-equipements-operationnels_5277060_3232.html?xtmc=&xtcr=1.

37 French Ministry of Defence, 'Bienvenue au DGA Lab, votre espace dédié à l'innovation de défense', 31 May 2018, https://www.defense.gouv.fr/dga/innovation2/dga-lab.

38 French Ministry of Defence, 'Florence Parly présente son plan en faveur de l'intelligence artificielle, axe d'innovation majeur du ministère des Armées', 22 March 2018, https://www.defense.gouv.fr/dga/actualite/florence-parly-presente-son-plan-en-faveur-de-l-intelligence-artificielle-axe-d-innovation-majeur-du-ministere-des-armees.

39 UK Ministry of Defence, 'Defence Innovation Initiative Information', 10 August 2017, https://www.gov.uk/government/publications/accelerator-themed-competition-revolutionise-the-human-information-relationship-for-defence/defence-innovation-initiative-information.

40 See Bundesministerium der Finanzen (Germany), 'Eckwertebeschluss der Bundesregierung zum

Regierungsentwurf des Bundeshaushalts 2019 und zum Finanzplan 2018 bis 2022', April 2018, https://www.bundesfinanzministerium.de/Content/DE/Pressemitteilungen/Finanzpolitik/2018/05/2018-05-02-PM-Eckwertebeschluss-2019.pdf?__blob=publicationFile&v=2; Assemblée Nationale (France), 'Loi de Programmation militaire 2019–2025', available at http://www.assemblee-nationale.fr/dyn/15/dossiers/programmation_militaire_2019-2025; House of Commons (UK), 'Modernising Defence Programme', *Hansard*, vol. 635, 25 January 2018, https://hansard.parliament.uk/commons/2018-01-25/debates/002ED98B-7B42-424B-8213-7EC5650664BC/ModernisingDefenceProgramme; Danish Ministry of Defence, 'Agreement for Danish Defence 2018–2023', http://www.fmn.dk/eng/allabout/Pages/danish-defence-agreement.aspx; Government Offices of Sweden, 'Försvarsberedningen överlämnar rapport om totalförsvaret', 20 December 2017, http://www.regeringen.se/pressmeddelanden/2017/12/forsvarsberedningen-overlamnar-rapport-om-totalforsvaret/; Miguel González, 'Spain Commits to Boosting Military Spending by 80% up to 2024', *El País*, 28 December 2017, https://elpais.com/elpais/2017/12/27/inenglish/1514369054_282731.html; Ministry of Defence of the Republic of Latvia, 'Strengthening of Latvia's National Defence Capability Will Continue Next Year', http://www.mod.gov.lv/en/Aktualitates/Preses_pazinojumi/2017/10/11-03.aspx; 'Norwegian Government Proposed Significant Boost in Defence Expenditures', 12 October 2017, https://www.regjeringen.no/en/aktuelt/norwegian-government-proposes-significant-boost-in-defence-expenditures/id2575083/; 'Poland About to Increase Its Defence Expenditure up to the Level of 2.5% of GDP', Defence24.com, 24 April 2017, https://www.defence24.com/poland-about-to-increase-its-defence-expenditure-up-to-the-level-of-25-of-gdp-a-new-bill-introduced; and Ministero Della Difesa (Italy), 'Documento Programmatico Pluriennale Difesa', 2017, available at https://www.difesa.it/Content/Pagine/Notaaggiuntiva.aspx.

The Future of Conventional Arms Control in Europe

Łukasz Kulesa

This is not a propitious time for arms control in the Euro-Atlantic area. In both the nuclear and the conventional domain, venerable regimes and treaties are in deep crisis. Some may collapse completely. There has been no successful new arms-control negotiation in Europe since the 1990s. Moreover, the response to the deterioration of the security environment in Europe since Russia's annexation of Crimea has been the build-up of military forces, additional deployments and accelerated modernisation. These developments directly challenge the basic notion underpinning arms control: that greater security can be reached through agreements on mutual restraint and reciprocal limitations, fortified through information exchanges and meaningful verification.

The case for using arms control as a tool for better security in wider Europe remains strong, and a return to conventional arms control, in parallel with strengthening deterrence, is politically feasible. At the same time, the political, strategic and technological challenges to the existing system are profound and cannot be overcome with a mere flurry of diplomatic activity, and a return to the cooperative arms-control atmosphere of the 1990s is impossible. Developing a flexible and multi-pronged arms-control strategy will depend on a newly forged political rationale for engagement in the West and in Russia.

Developments over nuclear arms control – the fate of the US–Russia Intermediate-Range Nuclear Forces (INF) Treaty, its knock-on effects on

Łukasz Kulesa is Research Director at the European Leadership Network (ELN).

Survival | vol. 60 no. 4 | August–September | pp. 75–90   DOI 10.1080/00396338.2018.1495430

New START (Strategic Arms Reduction Treaty) and any successor, and the action–reaction cycle in Russian and US nuclear modernisation – will have an impact on the climate for conventional arms control in Europe. But Europeans have a greater say over conventional arms control, which is more complex and therefore calls for more probing consideration.[1]

The triumph and downfall of European conventional arms control

The European system of conventional arms control was originally developed during the latter stages of the Cold War to minimise the threat of surprise attack and major war on the continent, build trust between the parties and manage the confrontation between NATO and the Warsaw Pact. In the 1990s, arms-control measures proved important in securing a largely peaceful transformation of the European security environment. That included major reductions of conventional weapons stockpiles.

As established and perfected in the 1990s, the system consisted of legally and politically binding instruments and procedures.[2] Two main legal pillars have been the 1990 Treaty on Conventional Armed Forces in Europe (CFE) and the 1992 Treaty on Open Skies. In addition, based on the Dayton Peace Accords Annex 1-B, Article IV, a sub-regional conventional arms-control regime was established in the Balkans, including currently Bosnia-Herzegovina, Croatia, Serbia and Montenegro. The Organisation for Security and Cooperation in Europe (OSCE) states have also been implementing a set of politically binding confidence- and security-building Measures (CSBMs), gathered in the periodically updated Vienna Document, with the aim of increasing military-to-military contacts and transparency of their military postures and activities in Europe.

Yet the positive legacy of European arms control has been overshadowed by the worsening crisis in European security, and in particular in NATO–Russia relations. Once the major weapons reductions were completed in the late 1990s, the rationale for preserving a robust European arms-control regime became less evident, and the issue largely disappeared from political radar screens. The system was not updated to take into account either geopolitical changes such as NATO enlargement (despite the late-1990s attempt to adapt the CFE Treaty) or the development of new weapons and capabilities, and changes in military doctrines and postures. As relations between Russia and the West deteriorated, the arms-control system became one of the first victims. Russia's 'suspension' of CFE implementation in 2007 and the partial 'counter-suspension' of CFE implementation with respect to Russia in 2011 by NATO countries and some partners were important indicators of the depth of the crisis.[3]

Russia's illegal annexation of Crimea and the military confrontation involving Ukraine, separatist forces and Russia in eastern Ukraine seemed to put the final nail in the coffin of European arms control. The only major recent initiative has been the 2016 proposal by Germany, joined by a group of like-minded countries, to 're-launch conventional arms control in Europe'.[4] Yet crucial players, including the US, Russia and a number of Central and Eastern European states, reacted coldly to the 'Steinmeier initiative'. For the United States and others, the 'new opening' suggested by Germany seemed to cut against Western efforts to pressure Moscow towards implementation of Russia's existing obligations. Meanwhile, for Russia, discussing the technicalities of a new arms-control arrangement before agreeing on the political parameters of the European security system did not make sense.

Three challenges to conventional arms control

Pursuing conventional arms control in Europe in the current security setting poses challenges at three levels: political, structural and technical.

The political challenge

At the political level, the rationale for pursuing arms control needs to be reformulated. Before the Ukraine crisis, conventional arms control suffered from a lack of political attention, partly due to its overwhelmingly technical nature and partly because of the small chances of achieving any breakthrough. Ongoing war in eastern Ukraine and the Russian occupation of Crimea, Moscow's dismissive attitude towards arms control as such, its military build-up in Europe and its assertive brinkmanship underline both the need for conventional arms control and the difficulty of advancing it.

One option is to conclude that the days in which conventional arms control played an important role in managing European security are over.

According to this logic, instead of discussing military limitations, the West, primarily through NATO, must re-establish deterrence based on a substantially strengthened set of forces and capabilities. The argument runs that since Russia has broken the letter or spirit of a number of previous arms-control agreements, it is pointless to formulate new proposals or look for new openings, as Russia is likely to exploit such eagerness to divide the West.[5] Only after Moscow fundamentally changes its approach to European security is a return of arms control possible. A somewhat similar logic appears to operate on the Russian side: to Moscow, NATO seems committed to challenging Russia in its neighbourhood and perhaps even to undermining the Russian regime, and will not take Russia seriously unless it vigorously exercises its military capabilities.

Historically, however, arms control in the Euro-Atlantic area has not just been for the good times, and has been pursued in parallel with, and not instead of, strengthening defence. Both the Soviet Union/Russia and the West have embraced it as a means of managing and reducing the risk of confrontation and as a means of pursuing political goals. For example, it has served Russia as a symbol of equivalency with the United States, and the United States as a lever of alliance management. Arms control has also had the incidental benefit of regulating the costs of armaments. Based on such a reading of Cold War history, a quest for security based only on deterrence is likely to lead down a path of action–reaction dynamics and recurrent military crises, with a threat of inadvertent escalation to the level of open hostilities. Russia's moves to strengthen its forces vis-à-vis NATO have already triggered a response from NATO members and other European states that has been used to justify the scope of the next Russian cycle of rearmament and deployments.[6] 'Militarisation' of international relations in Europe is already a fact, but it could reach new levels in the coming years as competitive pressures increase.

On the Russian side, President Vladimir Putin may judge that the risks and costs of confrontation are offset by emerging opportunities to drive wedges into European and transatlantic politics and diminish Western cohesion. But the continued erosion of existing arms-control processes, the related absence of measures to constrain US military modernisation and increased defence spending by European members of NATO are clearly disadvantageous to Russia. Putin craves the great-power recognition that arms control could confer: his reported offer in his first phone conversation with US President Donald Trump to extend New START presumably was not idle. Although manageable, defence spending is a heavy burden on the Russian economy. In this light, managing and limiting the scope of the confrontation should constitute the core of the new political rationale for European conventional arms control.

The structural challenge

With regard to the structure of the arms-control architecture, most discussions about the future of European conventional arms control focus on the rejuvenation of the trinity of the CFE Treaty, the Open Skies Treaty and the Vienna Document.[7] Their historical importance is beyond dispute. The CFE Treaty was instrumental in securing transition from NATO–Warsaw Pact competition to the era of cooperative security of the 1990s. The confidence-building measures included in the Open Skies Treaty and in the Vienna Document represent the most developed and sophisticated set of mechanisms for political-military and military-to-military contacts anywhere in the world. Yet their operation has become so contested and compromised that they are no longer feasible bases for an effective new system.

The CFE Treaty was modified in 1999 to manage – together with the NATO–Russia Founding Act of 1997 – the changes connected with NATO enlargement to the east. But the ratification of the Adapted CFE was never completed. Russia's Western partners expected that Russian forces would be fully withdrawn from Moldova and Georgia, before proceeding with ratification.[8] Russia rejected the linkage and pointed to a number of measures it had taken to reduce its military footprint and the amount of Treaty Limited Equipment (TLE) in both countries. The likelihood of Russia returning to the implementation of the CFE now, after ten years of its unilateral 'suspension', is close to zero, as openly stated by Russian diplomats and experts. While the treaty remains in force between other signatories (including Russian ally Belarus), its practical influence on European security is questionable – especially since the actual TLE holdings of Russia and NATO countries remain far below the thresholds.[9]

The implementation and update of confidence-building measures in the Open Skies Treaty and the Vienna Document also fell victim to Russian political brinkmanship.[10] Adding to the existing Turkish–Cypriot and Russian–Georgian disputes over Open Skies, Russia has limited the possibility of conducting Open Skies overflights over some parts of its territory. In response, there has been discussion in the US on the introduction of parallel limitations for Russian Open Skies overflights over US territory.[11] The Vienna Document's mechanisms are ill-suited to a number of challenges that have emerged since 2014. These include incidents involving Russian and NATO armed forces operating in close proximity; unusual military activities, including the rapid concentration of forces; major military exercises just below the existing thresholds for notification and observation; and unplanned 'snap' drills. Russia has a number of motives for circumventing its obligations and refusing to modernise the confidence-building mechanisms. An important one seems to be pushback against NATO countries which, in the past, have shown limited interest in Russia's proposals to increase the transparency of NATO's operations and military deployments or to discuss the introduction of new confidence-building measures.

Given this accumulated baggage, it could be useful to treat historical arms-control agreements such as the CFE or Open Skies Treaty as sources of inspiration rather than templates. It is natural to think of the future in terms of an ordered, comprehensive architecture and not to dismiss out of hand the possibility of a grand treaty akin to the CFE. But any new arms-control structure ultimately emerging from discussions could well consist of a number of piecemeal arrangements instead of a single comprehensive one, and could be regional rather than pan-European in scope.

The technical level

Further complicating the picture, rapid doctrinal and technological changes in military affairs are quickly diminishing the substantive relevance of the existing European arms-control system. It has been a recurring suggestion of the expert community that in any future update of the system there is a need to expand the CFE's five categories of TLE (battle tanks, armoured combat vehicles, heavy artillery, combat aircraft and attack helicopters) in order to better capture the new capabilities crucial for conducting offensive warfare in Europe.[12] Some degree of continuity is needed here: recent conflicts in the OSCE area (especially fighting in Donbas and skirmishes between Armenia and Azerbaijan), as well as the force-development plans of major European countries, confirm that these categories of weapons will remain important for the foreseeable future.

Nevertheless, certain categories of offensive and defensive weapons that would be highly relevant for major warfighting in Europe are not currently covered by any arms-control regime. These include air- and missile-defence systems, a range of categories of unmanned aerial vehicles (UAVs), tactical ballistic and cruise missiles, major multi-purpose naval platforms, and strategic air- and sea-lift carriers. These systems would have a key role in conducting any major military operations in Europe during an inter-state conflict, and therefore would need to be included in any system that aims to reduce the likelihood of such a conflict. Prompt long-range strike systems may also need to be taken into account, even if they are deployed outside of Europe.

Moreover, the existing arms-control system is now poorly suited to monitoring, let alone restraining, the capabilities of modern armed forces that increase their potential for being used in offensive operations. Issues such as deployability, readiness levels, sustainability, jointness and inter-operability will have as crucial an impact on military stability in Europe as the hardware itself.[13] Assessment of a specific unit's combat capability arguably now needs to be factored into matters such as the quality of training, the quality (as opposed to quantity) of available weapons systems and the availability of supporting infrastructure and logistical systems. Without accounting for these capabilities, any control system designed to increase predictability, limit incentives for surprise attack and thus build confidence is likely to fall short.

Furthermore, some new military capabilities, most notably cyber-warfare and information-warfare assets, but also electronic-warfare systems, cannot be easily incorporated into the existing arms-control framework. For example, measuring and limiting offensive cyberspace tools would require a degree of openness and information exchange about the 'holdings' of every country that would defeat the very purpose of developing these capabilities.[14] It is possible that a humanitarian-law paradigm that introduced limitations as to the targeting of cyber attacks (for example, civilian critical infrastructure as opposed to military targets) and the methods used might be a more useful way of addressing these challenges than using a more traditional arms-control paradigm.

Return to conventional arms control: kick-starting the process

Given the long list of challenges, rejuvenating conventional arms control in Europe may appear hopeless. Especially from the Western perspective, whether initiating a new discussion with Russia on European arms control is worth the time and diplomatic capital is a vexing question. There are legitimate worries that doing so could lead to excessive concessions towards Russia, or effectively absolve Moscow of its actions in Ukraine and previous violations of arms-control arrangements. Yet pursuing the current course – in which the major players have prioritised deterrence and the strengthening of warfighting capacities over arms-control diplomacy – has created a far less stable relationship than most political leaders tend to assume. The Russian leadership in particular seems to believe that it is able to increase or decrease the degree of military confrontation with the West according to the needs of Russia's external and internal policy, without fear of provoking an all-out conflict. What the Kremlin may see as assertive diplomacy backed by force, however, risks being interpreted by outsiders as preparation for a major war or even as the initial stage of a conflict. Given the lack of transparency and absence of confidence regarding Russia's intentions, its neighbours, and NATO itself, have felt compelled to adopt ever-stronger and more responsive deterrence postures. This action–reaction cycle increases the chances of incidents and of inadvertent escalation in any major crisis.[15]

A renewed political rationale for a return to European arms control could take these dangers of confrontation as a point of departure. Avoiding or containing those threats seems to be in the interest of all parties, and can provide a basis for re-engagement. Since neither side is likely to get the

upper hand in the Russia–West confrontation and achieve military superiority, arms-control talks may provide all sides – including Russia – with
a platform for stabilising the relationship. While adjustments to military
postures and modernisation of equipment are unavoidable, engagement
in conventional arms control can offer an avenue towards keeping the confrontation under control and avoiding unnecessary and costly build-ups
of forces.

The chances of Russia's returning to the cooperative security agenda of the
1990s, including the CFE and full range of military-to-military confidence-
building contacts, remain low. But if Moscow decides that stabilising the
relationship with the West is in its interest, arms control and confidence-
building measures might prove a good place to start. There are indications
that this rationale is not completely lost on Moscow. At NATO's prompting,
Russia agreed to make incident prevention, transparency and risk reduction
one of the topics of the ambassadorial-level meetings of the NATO–Russia
Council.[16] Moscow has also apparently begun to use these meetings to table
proposals aimed at confidence-building, including a proposal to activate
transponders on all military aircraft and a suggestion to work towards
reactivation of the Cooperative Airspace Initiative. In addition, Russia has
participated in the work of the International Civil Aviation Organization's
Baltic Sea Project Team, aimed at improving the safety of air traffic and
decreasing the likelihood of civil–military aviation incidents over the Baltic
Sea. These moves may be dismissed as propagandistic stunts aimed at
dividing the Alliance or as serving primarily Russia's own interests, but they
can also be used to test Russia's readiness for more substantive engagement.

Moscow could demonstrate its willingness to re-engage with a decision to
unfreeze the negotiations over the modernisation of the Vienna Document.
This would hardly be a breakthrough. None of the changes to the document
that have already been suggested – including lower exercise-notification
and observation thresholds, more efficient Chapter III measures to deal with
incidents and unusual activities, and prompt procedures to observe 'snap'
exercises – threaten Russian security. Nor do they require major changes to
operations of the Russian armed forces. Moreover, any decision on actual
modernisation of the document would involve a consensual process, during

which Russia could present and promote its own proposals. Even so, as a signal of a change in Moscow's approach, a more positive Russian attitude towards Vienna Document modernisation would be helpful.

A prerequisite for any meaningful progress is a political decision in Moscow on pursuing more constructive diplomacy with the West in general, including a reassessment of the role of CSBMs and conventional arms-control negotiations. In turn, if Western states do not want to play catch-up to any Russian peace offensive, they need to formulate their expectations and objectives for such engagement now, using the full potential of the expert community. The required review would identify short-term priorities for stabilisation of the confrontation, indicate where progress could be made primarily with the use of existing instruments, and outline a longer-term programme of work towards a new system which could provide a foundation for peaceful coexistence in Europe in the coming decades.

A more positive Russian attitude would be helpful

In regard to the first set of priorities, the countries engaged in Russia–West confrontation should focus on the avenues for achieving progress on the specific problems they consider as most likely to lead to accidental or inadvertent escalation. Firstly, to deal with military incidents, the immediate measures could include concluding new and updated bilateral agreements on the prevention of incidents at sea and on the prevention of dangerous military activities between Russia and particular NATO members and partners.[17] Such agreements, modelled on the existing US–Russia or US–China arrangements, would clarify permissible and prohibited behaviour for forces operating in close proximity, stipulate protocols in case of accidents or incidents and establish follow-up procedures.

Secondly, experiences under the European arms-control system should be applied more systematically in existing zones of war and protracted conflict in Europe, especially in eastern Ukraine. Rudimentary measures for disengagement of forces and withdrawal of heavy weapons from the line of control in Donbas, along with monitoring, were agreed as part of the Minsk process.[18] While working towards a full implementation of these measures is a priority, more comprehensive restraint and an arms-control regime need to be developed and submitted for implementation by the parties to the conflict. This regime could involve caps on the number of heavy weapons deployed by all sides in the conflict area and adjacent areas, and limits on exercises and other military activities, as well as a system of information exchange and intrusive verification – most likely with the involvement of external parties such as the OSCE or other third-party inspectors.

Thirdly, the scope of political-military and military-to-military contacts with Russia could be expanded using the existing menu of confidence-building measures. Extra measures could include establishment of emergency hotlines, agreeing to additional reciprocal information exchanges on forces deployed in particular regions (such as in the Baltic and Black seas, or on the Russian–Ukrainian border), beyond-quota visits to military units and bases, and observation of exercises not covered by Vienna Document obligations. These measures could be agreed at the bilateral level, but in some cases also possibly between NATO and Russia. NATO and Russia could also work on a mechanism to provide 'snap' observation of unscheduled military exercises. This could be tested in two small, unannounced exercises (one NATO and one Russian) taking place within a specified time frame. The establishment of a military-to-military crisis-management group as an adjunct to the NATO–Russia Council should also be contemplated, with special attention to responsibility for discussing nuclear, conventional and cyber doctrines and potentially escalatory scenarios. The cumulative effect of these measures would be an increase in predictability and each side's better understanding of the other's capabilities, doctrine and aims.

The longer-term perspective requires looking beyond the stabilisation of the confrontation with Russia and initiating conceptual work on a new European arms-control system. Such an effort, which could take the form of open-ended talks initiated under the auspices of the OSCE in Vienna, would not need to start from scratch. It should utilise the experiences, both positive and negative, of the implementation of existing instruments such as the CFE and the Vienna Document. The OSCE Structured Dialogue and its 'mapping' process could provide a basic shared understanding of the data on military holdings and trends in the development of force postures that could be useful in the work.[19] The participants to the talks would also need to subscribe to the basic principles underpinning European arms control, such as respect for the sovereignty of each participating state, military restraint, predictability, transparency, reciprocity and verifiability.

At the same time, the parameters for such talks should be broad enough to enable discussion of the best arms-control approaches to decrease the likelihood of inter-state war and eliminate the threat of surprise attack in Europe. Talks would thus need to include an open exchange about the categories of weapons systems which would need to be covered, including those utilising new and emerging technologies. Participants would need to work on identifying the military activities and capabilities most relevant for offensive operations and work on establishing meaningful restraint measures on them. And they should discuss a new approach to information-sharing and verification – making use of new technologies and possibly the involvement of international organisations such as the UN, the OSCE, NATO and the Collective Security Treaty Organisation – and a role for non-governmental actors.

Merely convening open-ended talks or consultations on the future of arms control in Europe may play a stabilising role in the current situation, if only by exposing a large group of policymakers, diplomats and military personnel to the complexities of the interplay among strategic stability, deterrence and arms control. On the whole, the process should be seen as a long-term, multi-year investment in stability rather than a sprint towards any new document or an opportunity to score political points. The experience of the Mutual and Balanced Force Reductions (MBFR) talks, proposed by NATO to the Warsaw Pact in the 1970s and conducted until the mid-1980s, may be instructive.[20] While the talks themselves, focusing on ground-forces reductions, proved frustrating and ultimately futile, they offered a moderating diplomatic track of engagement during times of high international tensions. Importantly, once the political interests of the Soviet Union and NATO aligned in the second part of the 1980s, the experience gained in the MBFR talks helped to smooth work on the CFE Treaty.

*　　　*　　　*

European arms control has a future only if it is adapted to contemporary challenges and political realities. In the short term, some elements of the current system can be used to better manage confrontational relations in Europe, with arms control and confidence-building measures customised to specific problems, such as the danger of incidents or the situation within conflict zones, including the Donbas region. Beyond immediate challenges, serious work should begin on a new system that would support a re-established regional order in Europe in the context of doctrinal and technological developments that are likely to change the face of modern warfare. Such work will also need to take into account the increasingly close relationship between conventional, nuclear and emerging cyber capabilities. The overall process is likely to take many years to complete, but may produce sectoral or regional spin-off agreements earlier. For it to bear fruit, all sides involved in the current regional confrontation will have to accept that they should be engaged in arms-control efforts not in spite of that confrontation but because of it.

Notes

[1] This article draws partly on the findings and rich discussion at the conference 'Making Conventional Arms Control Fit for the 21st Century', co-organised by the German Federal Foreign Office and the European Leadership Network in Berlin on 6–7 September 2017. The report for the conference is available at https://www.europeanleadershipnetwork.org/policy-brief/making-conventional-arms-control-fit-for-the-21st-century/.

[2] For an overview, see, for example, Tommi Koivula, 'Conventional Arms Control in Europe and its Current Challenges', in Tommi Koivula and Katariina Simonen, *Arms Control in Europe: Regimes, Trends and Threats* (Helsinki: National Defence University,

2017).

[3] W. Zellner, 'Conventional Arms Control in Europe: Is There a Last Chance?', *Arms Control Today*, March 2012, https://www.armscontrol.org/act/2012_03/Conventional_Arms_Control_in_Europe_Is_There_a_Last_Chance.

[4] See Frank-Walter Steinmeier, 'More Security for Everyone in Europe: A Call for a Re-launch of Arms Control', *Frankfurter Allgemeine Zeitung*, 26 August 2016; and 'Ministerial Declaration by the Foreign Ministers of the Like-minded Group Supporting a Relaunch of Conventional Arms Control in Europe', 25 November 2016; http://www.diplomatie.gouv.fr/en/french-foreign-

policy/european-union/events/article/ministerial-declaration-by-the-foreign-ministers-of-the-like-minded-group.

5   Stephen Blank, 'Pursuing Arms Control with Putin's Russia Is Mission Impossible', Policy Brief (forthcoming), European Leadership Network, 2018.

6   For an overview of the procurement plans of Russia for the next cycle, see Dmitry Gorenburg, 'Russia's Military Modernization Plans: 2018–2027', PONARS Eurasia Policy Memo No. 495, November 2017, http://www.ponarseurasia.org/memo/russias-military-modernization-plans-2018-2027.

7   See, for example, Lucien Kleinjan, 'Conventional Arms Control in Europe: Decline, Disarray, and the Need for Reinvention', *Arms Control Today*, June 2016, https://www.armscontrol.org/ACT/2016_06/Features/Conventional-Arms-Control-In-Europe.

8   For details, see Ulrich Kühn, 'From Capitol Hill to Istanbul: The Origins of the Current CFE Deadlock', Working Paper 19, Centre for OSCE Research, Hamburg, December 2009.

9   See Sergey Oznobishchev and Andrey Zagorski, 'Russia–NATO: A Breakthrough to the Past', in *Revitalizing Nuclear Arms Control and Non-proliferation* (Moscow: National Institute of Corporate Reform, 2017), pp. 37–8.

10   For the record, Russia firmly rejects these accusations and formulates its own counter-accusations against NATO countries. See 'Comment by the MFA of Russia on the US Department of State's Annual Report on Adherence to and Compliance with Arms Control, Nonproliferation, and Disarmament Agreements and Commitments', 29 April 2017, available at the website of the Ministry of Foreign Affairs of the Russian Federation, http://www.mid.ru.

11   George M. Reynolds, 'Taking Stock of the Treaty on Open Skies', Council on Foreign Relations Expert Brief, 3 November 2017, https://www.cfr.org/expert-brief/taking-stock-treaty-open-skies.

12   See, for example, Gregory G. Govan, 'Conventional Arms Control in Europe: Some Thoughts about an Uncertain Future', Deep Cuts Issue Brief no. 5, July 2015, p. 2; and Oleg Shakirov, 'Prospects of Conventional Arms Control in Europe', Note from PIR Center roundtable, May 2017, http://pircenter.org/en/news/6917-prospects-of-conventional-arms-control-in-europe.

13   For an in-depth study on identifying and accounting for military capabilities and intentions in a modified arms-control regime, see Hans-Joachim Schmidt, 'Verified Transparency: New Conceptual Ideas for Conventional Arms Control in Europe', PRIF Report, no. 119, Frankfurt, 2013.

14   Regarding the challenges, see Nigel Inkster, 'Measuring Military Cyber Power', *Survival*, vol. 59, no. 4, August–September 2017, pp. 27–34.

15   See, for example, 'Back from the Brink', Third Report of the Deep Cuts Commission, June 2016, http://deepcuts.org/images/PDF/Third_Report_of_the_Deep_Cuts_Commission_English.pdf.

16   For a Russian position, see press points by Alexander Grushko,

Permanent Representative of Russia to NATO, after a meeting of the NATO–Russia Council, October 2017, https://missiontonato.mid.ru/web/nato-en/-/joint-press-conference-of-russia-s-ambassador-to-nato-alexander-grushko-and-special-representative-of-the-president-of-the-russian-federation-for--afgh?inheritRedirect=true.

17 For details, see Thomas Frear, Denitsa Raynova and Łukasz Kulesa, 'Managing Hazardous Incidents in the Euro-Atlantic Area: A New Plan of Action', ELN Policy Brief, November 2016, https://www.europeanleadershipnetwork.org/wp-content/uploads/2017/10/ELN-Managing-Hazardous-Incidents-November-2016.pdf.

18 See 'Package of Measures for the Implementation of the Minsk Agreements', English version, signed 12 February 2015, https://peacemaker.un.org/sites/peacemaker.un.org/files/UA_150212_MinskAgreement_en.pdf.

19 Thomas Greminger, 'It Is Time to Revitalize Political-Military Dialogue in the OSCE', ELN Commentary, 6 December 2017; https://www.europeanleadershipnetwork.org/commentary/it-is-time-to-revitalize-political-military-dialogue-in-the-osce/.

20 See also the argument made by Ulrich Kuhn in 'With Zapad Over, Is It Time for Conventional Arms Control in Europe?', *War on the Rocks*, 27 September 2017, https://warontherocks.com/2017/09/with-zapad-over-is-it-time-for-conventional-arms-control-in-europe/.

Europe and Israel: Between Conflict and Cooperation

Toby Greene and Jonathan Rynhold

The European Union's policies towards Israel are defined by an internal tension.[1] On the one hand, there is growing friction between Israel and the EU mainly due to the declining confidence in the two-state solution and in public sympathy for Israel. On the other hand, despite claims that Israel's policies towards the Palestinians contravene EU norms and interests, EU pressure on Israel has remained limited, and its attempts to advance the peace process ineffective. Moreover, Europe's own crises and increased instability in the Middle East have led to a reordering of European priorities, which has caused Israel's rising economic and defence capabilities to be viewed as increasingly significant. This situation would appear to suggest, especially to the right-wing Israeli government and its supporters, that Israel can reap increased benefits from the relationship while effectively disregarding European concerns related to the Israeli–Palestinian arena. This, however, would be a mistake. The current Israeli government's failure to maintain a clear commitment to a two-state solution constitutes a self-inflicted wound, inhibiting its ability to seize a window of opportunity to strengthen its position with the EU as a whole. Moreover, if EU unity remains elusive, and if the Trump administration fails to fill the diplomatic vacuum, frustration is likely to lead EU member states, individually or in subgroups, to act beyond EU consensus to advance diplomatic support for the Palestinians and withdraw support from Israel.

Toby Greene is an Israel Institute Post-Doctoral Fellow in the Leonard Davis Institute for International Relations at the Hebrew University of Jerusalem. **Jonathan Rynhold** is a Professor in the Political Studies Department at Bar-Ilan University.

Survival | vol. 60 no. 4 | August–September | pp. 91–112   DOI 10.1080/00396338.2018.1495432

The decline of Israel's standing in Europe

The EU has invested heavily in promoting the two-state solution, not least through substantial aid to the Palestinian Authority (PA). Consequently, the declining credibility of Israel's commitment to a two-state solution since Benjamin Netanyahu came to power in 2009 has been a source of concern and frustration for many European leaders.[2] Taken together with political weakness and internal division on the Palestinian side, many perceive the waning viability of this political goal.

The period 2009–14 saw Netanyahu try to promote a relatively centrist image in Israeli political terms, by including centre-left parties in his coalition and by participating in US-orchestrated negotiations with the Palestinians on the basis of a two-state solution. However, his legacy of opposing the Oslo process and his political partnership with pro-settlement factions exacerbated deep distrust among Palestinians, and also many Europeans. 'I cannot bear Netanyahu, he's a liar,' Nicolas Sarkozy – a leader considered sympathetic to Israel – once hissed to US president Barack Obama, a sentiment echoed across many European capitals.[3] A broad upgrade in EU–Israel relations agreed in June 2008 was shelved in 2009, pending progress towards a resolution on the Israeli–Palestinian conflict.[4]

In 2012, the Palestinians turned to the UN General Assembly to admit Palestine as a non-member state, arguing that attempts to gain statehood through a negotiated agreement with Israel were fruitless.[5] EU members were divided on the issue, a fact that might have constrained its negative political impact on Israel's standing in the EU. However, Israel's reaction – new plans to build settlements in the E1 area east of Jerusalem, which European missions in East Jerusalem warned was vital for a Palestinian state[6] – succeeded in forging unity among the 27 in opposition to Israeli policy.

Subsequently, the Foreign Affairs Council insisted that all EU agreements with Israel explicitly indicate their 'inapplicability to the territories occupied by Israel in 1967', and in 2013, under pressure from the European Parliament, the Commission issued guidance to explicitly ensure EU grants were ineligible to Israelis in the Occupied Territories. The practical implications were limited, but Israeli politicians reacted furiously. Israel temporarily ceased cooperating with the EU in the West Bank, restricting its activities.[7] The demand for a territorial clause excluding the West Bank from the agreement almost derailed Israel's accession to the EU's Horizon 2020 research-funding programme – threatening hundreds of millions of euros in funding to Israeli researchers. As a last-minute compromise, Israel attached an appendix to the agreement specifying its objections to the territorial clause. These were only the first of a long list of opportunities for the EU to force Israel to differentiate between the territory either side of the pre-1967 Green Line, with the hope of pressuring Israel to halt settlement expansion and maintain the viability of the two-state solution.[8]

These moves have been interpreted in Israel, especially by right-wing parties, as legitimising a consumer boycott of settlements, and as the thin end of the wedge of a popular and government-sanctioned boycott of Israel in its entirety. Israel's sensitivity has been heightened by the growing profile of a 'Boycott, Divestment, and Sanctions' (BDS) movement, which aims to generate the kind of pressure put on South Africa in the 1980s. This movement – driven by activists within trade unions, far-left parties, non-governmental organisations (NGOs) and Islamist groups – has not gained the support of a critical mass of European citizens, but it has found a receptive audience among the broader liberal left and European Muslim constituencies.

Yet Israel and the EU continued to sign new trade agreements in agriculture (2009) and pharmaceuticals (2012), and in 2013 inked a major civil-aviation 'Open Skies' agreement. The latter was finalised at a time when there was still a veneer of hope in the Israeli–Palestinian arena, as US secretary of state John Kerry led an intense diplomatic effort.

The year 2014 saw the collapse of Kerry-led negotiations, after PA President Mahmoud Abbas, distrustful and humiliated following repeated Israeli settlement announcements, rejected the United States' proposed framework.[9] Armed conflict between Israel and Hamas in Gaza soon followed. Images of devastation triggered thousands to demonstrate against Israel in Western European cities including London, Berlin, Paris, Dublin and Madrid.

These demonstrations represent the intensification of the negative shift in public attitudes toward Israel that began in the late 1970s,[10] with the waning relevance of the Holocaust in European perceptions of Israel and the reversal of Israel's status from David to Goliath in the Arab–Israeli conflict. Today,

Western European publics are much less sympathetic to Israel than those in North America, although there too, liberals and especially 'millennials' born after 1980 have cooled significantly towards Israel in recent years.[11] Meanwhile, growing Muslim minorities in key states identify with the Palestinians. Universities in some countries, notably the United Kingdom and Ireland, are centres for grassroots campaigns that call for boycotting Israel. Artists and musicians planning to perform in Israel are routinely subjected to high-profile campaigns to cancel their engagements.

The 2014 Gaza conflict increased the impetus in several European states to change the status quo, and led to a movement for recognising the State of Palestine. By the end of 2014, Sweden had extended full recognition, while non-binding resolutions to back recognition were passed by parliaments in France, Ireland, Portugal, Spain, the UK, Belgium and Luxembourg, as well as the European Parliament.[12] An intervention by Conservative Foreign Affairs Select Committee Chair Richard Ottaway in the UK parliamentary debate strikingly illustrated how Israel's policies were alienating formerly well-disposed politicians. Ottaway said:

> I have stood by Israel through thick and thin … I have sat down with Ministers and senior Israeli politicians and urged peaceful negotiations … I thought that they were listening. But … the annexation of the 950 acres of the West Bank just a few months ago has outraged me more than anything else in my political life, mainly because it makes me look a fool.[13]

The 2014 Gaza conflict, as well as provoking widespread public anger against Israel, also led to a surge in anti-Semitic incidents.[14] In light of these events, and deadly attacks on Jewish-community targets in Belgium, France and Denmark by Islamist extremists, Netanyahu declared that European Jews should escape 'terrible anti-Semitism' by coming 'home' to Israel. This call was rejected by politicians in Germany and France,[15] as well as by prominent Jewish-diaspora leaders.[16]

A new phase began in 2015, with elections in Israel resulting in a shift to a hard-right coalition. During the campaign, Netanyahu affirmed that a two-state solution was not in the offing, and he used overtly anti-Arab tropes to rally supporters on election day. Once formed, the government accelerated illiberal legislative moves. A law intended to marginalise human-rights NGOs that receive international funding triggered particular concern from several EU members, being seen as an attack on European support for human-rights groups, and a European External Action Service (EEAS) statement warned Israel it risked undermining its democratic character.[17]

In May 2015 a European Eminent Persons Group including several former European foreign ministers and prime ministers called for a 'fresh examination of EU policy' to include upgrading the status of Palestine and greater accountability on human rights and settlement expansion. Among their concerns was that 'the current financial and political assistance given by Europe and America to the Palestinian Authority achieves little more than the preservation of the Israeli occupation'.[18] In November 2015 the EU Commission announced new guidance that products from Israeli settlements should be labelled as such. It was a move that EU members seeking greater pressure on Israel over settlements had been pushing for since 2013, but was held up so as not to interfere with Kerry's diplomatic initiative.[19] The timing of its emergence was linked to the vacuum in the peace process and renewed settlement announcements.

The election of Donald Trump as US president brought another shift. Pro-settlement Jewish Home Party leader Naftali Bennett – a key coalition partner – pushed for Israel to declare that 'the era of the Palestinian state is over'.[20] Netanyahu himself stopped referring explicitly to the 'two-state solution'. In early December 2016, a bill to legalise some settlements built on private Palestinian land was introduced in the Knesset. This spurred EU members to impose a diplomatic price on Israel. In late December, the UK, France and Spain voted for a stinging UN Security Council resolution condemning settlements that laid a possible foundation for sanctions. This was immediately followed by a French-sponsored conference promoting the two-state solution, which proceeded despite Israel's objections.[21]

In another sign of change, during a visit to Israel in 2017, German foreign minister Sigmar Gabriel met with left-wing Israeli NGOs, thereby foregoing a meeting with Netanyahu, who said he would not see him if he did so. In a subsequent speech in Tel Aviv, Gabriel warned that 'young people in my country are increasingly unwilling to accept unfair treatment of the Palestinians, and it's becoming increasingly difficult for friends like me to explain why we support Israel',[22] underlining concerns expressed on the Israeli centre-left that Israel was losing its friends in its vital European hinterland.

Underlying divides: interests, culture and ideology

Europe derives leverage over Israel from trade, strategic and diplomatic cooperation, and its cultural and scientific ties. The EU is Israel's largest trading partner,[23] and according to a senior EU diplomat, Israel has more favourable agreements with the EU than any other non-member state.[24] The EU also plays an indispensable role as a leading financial supporter of the PA, whose stability and security apparatus in the West Bank is integral to Israeli security.[25] Given the combination of potential leverage and frustration with Israeli policies, one would expect there to be increasing European pressure on Israel. Indeed, to Netanyahu's frustration – as expressed in a recent meeting with leaders from the Visegrad countries[26] – Israel's hardline policies clearly come at some cost, as Europe links the upgrading of bilateral relations to the Israeli–Palestinian issue. An agreement on Israeli cooperation with Europol is stalled because of EU insistence that cooperation not apply over the Green Line.[27] No meetings of the EU–Israel Association Council – the formal ministerial body for agreeing bilateral cooperation – have been held since 2012, as individual EU Council members press for a tougher line on Israel and oppose new EU–Israel agreements.

Unless Israel forces the EU's hand with further steps that undermine the two-state solution, such as formal annexation of territory, however, greater EU-wide pressure is unlikely due to divisions within the European Council and the EU Parliament, and among member states. As a diplomat from a member-state delegation in Brussels explained, 'We [EU members] all agree on the outcomes [of an Israel–Palestinian peace deal] but the moment we touch on how to get there, we fall apart.'[28] France is the leader of a group of states consistently supporting measures to insert the EU into the Israeli–Palestinian agenda, including through diplomatic and EU measures to exert pressure on Israel. This group includes other Mediterranean states like Spain and Portugal, but also northern-European states such as Ireland and Sweden, for which international law and human-rights concerns form an important part of their political culture. A contesting group, more sympathetic to the Israeli position, has customarily countered these initiatives. Germany and the Netherlands – deeply committed to transatlantic relations and influenced by the memory of the Holocaust – used to be at the core of this group. The UK, with its strong historical ties to the Arab world, sought a balanced posture but also typically strove to temper French efforts to compete with US leadership on the Middle East.

Today, however, officials from member-state delegations credit frustration with the policies of the Israeli right for pushing Germany and the Netherlands into a more neutral position. Now this second group is dominated by newer members from the east. While EU Foreign Affairs Council deliberations usually keep this divide behind closed doors, it has been boldly exposed in repeated splits in voting on UN resolutions. The most striking example was the November 2012 vote in the UN on whether to admit Palestine as a non-member state. Of the EU members, 14 voted in favour, and all were Western European except for Greece and Cyprus. The 12 abstaining EU states included almost all the former Eastern bloc countries plus the UK, Germany and the Netherlands. The Czech Republic stood alone in voting against. More recently, EU members Croatia, the Czech Republic, Hungary, Latvia, Poland and Romania were among the 35 states that abstained from the December 2017 UN General Assembly vote of censure following the Trump administration's recognition of Jerusalem as Israel's capital, while all other EU members voted in favour.

Although each state has its own characteristics, in general former Eastern bloc counties joined the EU with an Atlanticist orientation. They lack the legacy of colonialism, the interests in the Arab world and the significant Muslim minorities that are all factors in Western Europe. In many cases their leaders are cognisant of the history of large Jewish communities destroyed in the Holocaust, even while concerns about anti-Semitism on the populist right, and about Holocaust revisionism remain, especially with respect to Poland. In addition, surveys show publics in Hungary and Poland are more hostile to Muslims than those in Britain, France, Germany, the Netherlands or Sweden.[29]

The Visegrad Group of countries – Hungary, Poland, Czech Republic and Slovakia – invited Netanyahu to participate in their 2017 summit and even accepted Netanyahu's invitation to hold their 2018 summit in Israel.[30] The Czech Republic stood out as the only EU state to follow Washington in recognising Jerusalem as Israel's capital in 2017 (though unlike the US it explicitly referred only to West Jerusalem), with its parliament having voted in support of such a move earlier in the year. Meanwhile, Hungary also reportedly moved to block a joint EU Council statement condemning Trump's Jerusalem declaration.[31] An informal breakfast meeting between Netanyahu and the EU foreign ministers in December 2017 was the result of a Lithuanian invitation, which annoyed other members.[32]

A sharp ideological and party-political divide overlays this split at the national level. On both sides of the Atlantic, those identifying as conservatives or on the right are far more likely to be sympathetic to Israel as a nation-state that is part of the West and a front-line ally against common threats. Those identifying as liberals or on the left tend to be more critical of Israeli right-wing policies while sympathising with the Palestinians as victims of Israeli oppression. These ideological splits shape the attitudes of government parties and leaders in the EU Council. They are also clearly visible in the EU Parliament, where centre-left parties led by the Socialists and Democrats (S&D) promote resolutions critical of Israel, and centre-right parties led by the European People's Party (EPP) promote a line more sympathetic to the position of the Israeli government.[33]

Attitudes are also shaped by the fact that for many politicians and their electorates, even in Western Europe, the Palestinians are associated with corruption, internal division and violent extremism. Thus, in opinion surveys in leading Western European countries, the Palestinians are favoured more than the Israelis, but more common still is equivocation or indifference.[34]

As for BDS, several European and American funds have barred cooperation with Israeli firms operating in the occupied territories, and there is evidence that Israeli exports fall during periods of violence.[35] However, BDS has not received wide enough public support to get governments to act. In any case, much of Israel's output consists of high-grade intermediate industrial products that are difficult for bottom-up consumer campaigns to target, and not easily substitutable. Moreover, British and French governments have introduced legal measures against boycotts, and in Germany the notion of a consumer boycott of Israeli products carries an added political weight due to the echo of the Nazi boycott of Jewish businesses.

The rift within the EU Council and the high commitment of many states and leaders to their positions creates a disincentive to securing a formally agreed common stance, especially in the absence of major violence that puts the conflict on the front pages. EU ministers have repeatedly held informal discussions on the Middle East peace process. They held breakfasts with Israeli and Palestinian leaders in late 2017 and early 2018, and EU High Representative for Foreign Affairs and Security Policy Federica Mogherini announced, following the annual informal Gymnich summit in September 2017, that the EU would review 'the modalities of our engagement on the ground'.[36] But aside from a three-paragraph statement in June 2016, there have been no EU Council conclusions formally agreed among the 28 members on the issue since January 2016. No member state has a position calling for sanctions against Israel, nor has any yet followed Sweden in recognising a Palestinian state. Neither did the French-orchestrated international conference in 2017 become a European initiative. All of this reflects the difficulty in reaching consensus.

No EU member has called for sanctions

Even when there is an agreed policy in principle, confronting Israel in practice is hindered by a 'safety in numbers' mentality. As one diplomat from a member-state delegation in Brussels remarked with respect to the labelling of settlement goods, 'It should already have been put into effect by individual member states but we are all too scared to do things by ourselves so we wait for the others. We always want to do things, 28 together.'[37] The characterisation of the EU as a multilateral institution that is singularly hostile to Israel, often heard in Israel, is an exaggeration. The Commission issued guidelines on labelling settlement produce only after repeated requests from numerous member states. EU officials are aware that measures to pressure Israel over settlements feed a narrative of the Israeli right of being victimised by 'anti-Semitic' Europe. Furthermore, EEAS officials stress the importance of maintaining a dialogue with Israel in order to have a meaningful role on the Israeli–Palestinian issue. In response to the labelling guidelines, Israel effectively froze political relations with the EU for a time, and EEAS officials acknowledge that Israel's reaction would make some conclude that it 'wasn't worth the hassle'.[38] Similarly, Israel has acted to marginalise Sweden from any engagement in Israeli–Palestinian diplomacy since Stockholm extended full recognition to Palestine – for example, restricting contact with Foreign Minister Margot Wallström.[39]

There is evidence, however, that individual states, or subgroups within the EU 28, are increasingly inclined to follow Sweden's example and recognise Palestine or extend other forms of diplomatic support. There is strong cross-party and public support for such a move in several countries, including Ireland and Slovenia. In January 2018, the Luxembourg foreign minister said that given the disunity in the EU, France should lead a group of like-minded states in recognising Palestine, which Luxembourg would join.[40] The Labour opposition in Britain made a manifesto commitment in 2017 to recognise Palestine if elected.

While there seems to be insufficient unity for more biting EU-wide measures, the declining credibility of Israel's commitment to a two-state solution is undermining the propensity of several European states to provide diplomatic support to Israel, and increasing motivation for some to apply diplomatic pressure on Israel. At the same time, the variety and complexity of European attitudes towards Israel is increasing due to major shifts in the strategic, political and economic context that are making Israel increasingly significant as an economic and strategic partner in the eyes of many European leaders.

Increased threats from the Middle East

In 2003, the EU's Security Strategy celebrated a 'period of peace and stability unprecedented in European history'.[41] In contrast, its 2016 Global Strategy document was based on the sober assessment that 'we live in times of existential crisis, within and beyond the European Union.'[42] The external dimensions of this crisis stem not only from the Middle East, but also from a strategically aggressive Russia in Eastern Europe and a United States that was retrenching under Obama and whose commitment to the liberal international order has been called into question under Trump. The hope that a democratic Turkey could bridge divides between Islam and the West is now also in tatters, with Turkish President Recep Tayyip Erdogan embracing increasingly Islamist rhetoric and authoritarian policies.[43] In parallel, the dream that the 'Arab Spring' would bring democracy has become a nightmare with the rise of Islamist groups like ISIS, and the collapse of many parts of the region into chaos.[44] All this is affecting a realist turn in EU foreign policy, reflected in additional language in the EU's 2016 Global Strategy document emphasising 'the security of its citizens and territory'. With respect to the southern Mediterranean, this is reflected in the reaffirmation of the 'security–stability nexus' as the 'master frame', whereby stability takes precedence over democracy.[45]

Viewed through this prism, the Israeli–Palestinian arena no longer appears as central to the EU's strategic concerns in the Middle East as it once did. The EU's 2003 Security Strategy stated: 'Resolution of the Arab/Israeli conflict is a strategic priority for Europe. Without this, there will be little chance of dealing with other problems in the Middle East.' In its 2016 Global Strategy document, the issue gets a brief mention in a paragraph on support for 'functional multilateral cooperation' in the Middle East, which itself is just one of five 'lines of action' for the EU's approach to the Mediterranean, Middle East and Africa. By contrast, 'terrorism' gets 32 mentions and 'migration' 26.[46]

The war in the Syrian–Iraqi arena, as well as the chaos in Libya, has had a direct impact on European interests far broader than the Israeli–Palestinian conflict. These interests include the migration wave; the recruitment of Europeans to ISIS and their threatened return; ISIS's efforts to radicalise Muslims in Europe; and the potential spread of instability to other Arab states. As Brando Benifei, a member of the European Parliament's Palestine Delegation, confirmed, 'The Israeli–Palestinian conflict has gone down the agenda in terms of attention by the political sphere because of the insurgence of ISIS.'[47]

Moreover, Israel is a critical security partner for Egypt and Jordan, whose stability is a significant European concern. Israel's role supporting Egypt's fight against jihadists in the Sinai is particularly noteworthy, given Europe's fears that many more Egyptians could join migrant waves from Libya and Syria.[48] Israel is on the same side of key regional struggles as Gulf states with which it has no official relations, especially Saudi Arabia and the UAE.[49] This cooperation has been catalysed by the growing threat from Iran and from Sunni jihadists coupled with US retrenchment, and was enhanced in particular by Obama's outreach to Iran. When Israel went to war with Hamas in 2014, Arab states said little, and Egypt brokered an eventual ceasefire on terms favourable to Israel.[50] According to former British foreign secretary Malcolm Rifkind, one should 'not underestimate the impact of the more thoughtful Europeans saying, "Well I can see how the Saudis and Egyptians, and the Jordanians and the Gulf States are now actually working openly or under the radar screen with Israel, and I draw conclusions from that."'[51] In addition, Europeans and Israelis are equally welcoming of the reform efforts of Saudi Crown Prince Mohammad bin Salman, which includes backing away from promotion of radically anti-Western forms of Islam, and a greater openness to Israel as a potential ally.

Israel supports Egypt in the Sinai

While the occupation and periodic rounds of conflict remain sources of grievance and drivers of radicalisation, the rise of Sunni jihadist threats highlights the security risks involved in a full territorial withdrawal of the Israeli military from the West Bank. Given that every weak or ungoverned space in the Middle East, including the Gaza Strip and southern Lebanon after Israel's withdrawal, has become a base for Islamist extremists, Israel's demands for a special security regime in the West Bank, including Israeli forces along the Jordan River in any future agreement, has greater credibility, with obvious implications for the security of Jordan.

In addition to playing a role in regional stability, Israel has important bilateral security ties with EU members. Israel's intelligence agencies are valued for their expertise. Israel is credited, for example, as the source of the intelligence that ISIS planned to use laptops to bomb airliners.[52] Several politicians and commentators in Europe have responded to terror attacks in their cities by looking to Israel for models on prevention.[53]

There is also a shared interest in containing the spread of Iranian power. Europe and the Netanyahu government have remained at odds on Iran since the signing of the Joint Comprehensive Plan of Action (JCPOA), as the Europeans have defended the deal while Netanyahu has condemned it and supported Trump's decision to withdraw from it. Israel is also concerned about European companies re-entering Iran. Nevertheless, Europe and Israel recognise a shared interest in containing Iran's influence, including Iran's role in Syria where it is allied with Russia, its threat to Western-orientated Arab states, and the risk of its developing nuclear weapons. Iran already has missiles that can hit southern Europe and is continuing to make progress in this area, and European leaders including French President Emmanuel Macron have declared their willingness to work with the US on a new initiative that will limit Iran's missile programme.[54] Israel's intelligence capabilities are of major significance on these issues.

In the eastern Mediterranean, Israel has formed with Greece and Cyprus a defence-orientated 'quasi-alliance' driven primarily by the prospect of cooperating in gas exports to Europe, and by strategic cooperation in the face of Erdogan's Turkey.[55] Some officials[56] involved in EU Council deliberations credit a gas-pipeline proposal signed by Israel, Greece, Cyprus and Italy with shifting those EU members into the Israel-sympathetic group of like-minded states within the Council. Though the potential quantities of gas are small compared to Russian reserves, given Europe's concern to diversify, they are not insignificant.

More broadly, there is readiness to enhance ties with Israel's military across Europe in light of Israel's status as a world leader in various defence-equipment sectors. Last year, European governments bought a record $1.8 billion-worth of defence equipment from Israel, and outlays may increase as EU members face increasing internal and external security challenges, including the Russian threat from the east, and come under US pressure to increase defence budgets. Israeli exports include aircraft and air-defence technology; observation and radar equipment; ammunition; and intelligence and cyber systems.[57] In 2017, Israel Aerospace Industries provided

Italy with its first autonomous earth-observation satellite.[58] In November 2017, France, Germany, Greece, Italy and Poland all participated in an Israeli-hosted air-force exercise.

Europe's internal changes

Positive European attitudes towards Israel turn not only on heightened external security threats but also on internal crises relating to legitimacy, identity, economy and security in the EU. The decade of poor economic performance, which has fuelled support for radical parties on the right and left, and the jihadist threat and Muslim immigration, which have stoked the populist-right resurgence in many European countries, have also warmed perceptions of Israel in parts of Europe.

The chaos that has engulfed Arab states, and the failure of democracy to flourish, further underlines for Europeans the uniqueness of Israel as a democracy and a familiar culture. This is especially significant for those on the right, who tend to embrace a conception of what Thomas Risse has called 'nationalist Europe', which 'emphasizes a (Western) civilization and culture'.[59] This version of European identity excludes 'non-Christian countries such as Turkey, but also non-European immigrants and large parts of the Muslim populations in European cities'. For many mainstream conservatives, Europe's cultural boundaries include Israel, much of whose population originates in Europe.

Meanwhile, further to the right, populist parties and politicians express solidarity with Israel to bolster their anti-Islamic credentials and to resist charges of anti-Semitism.[60] One example is Freedom Party leader and vice-chancellor of Austria Heinz-Christian Strache. While Strache has dismissed his involvement with a neo-Nazi youth movement as a result of being 'stupid, naive and young',[61] his more recent acts, such as posting an anti-Semitic cartoon on Facebook in 2012, have left lingering suspicions of anti-Semitism.[62] To convince sceptics of his rejection of anti-Semitism, Strache – like other European populist-nationalist politicians – has expressed a commitment to defending Israel and Jews against Muslim threats.[63] Strache said during a visit to Israel in April 2016: 'I always say, if one defines the Judeo-Christian West, then Israel represents a kind of border. If Israel fails, Europe fails. And if Europe fails, Israel fails.'[64] Meanwhile, the Orbán government in Hungary and the Law and Justice Party government in Poland have adopted rhetoric and legislation targeting liberal NGOs and the courts in a manner comparable to Netanyahu-led governments in Israel. This reduces prospects of the EU Council collectively censuring Israel over such measures.

At the same time, the improving trajectory of Jeremy Corbyn and the Labour Party in the UK and Podemos in Spain illustrate significant hostility to Israel in rising left-wing parties. So far, however, this has caused much more discomfort for European Jews, whose relationship with Israel is central to their identity, than it has for Israel itself.[65] Even leaders from political parties with a history of hostility to Israel including support for BDS, such as Syriza in Greece, have found their ideological positions tempered by more pressing domestic challenges in the wake of the 2008 economic crisis. As a result, the Syriza-led government has continued the process of deepening relations with Israel which began under its predecessors.

Israel's rising power

Israel has become a stronger economic and security partner to Europe. Israel's population had grown to nearly nine million in 2017 and is set to reach 15m by 2048.[66] It has become a regional power, and in recent years has improved relations with India, China, Latin America and several African states.[67] While EU economies have struggled in the last decade, Israel's growth has continued. EU imports from Israel have never been higher, staying at around €13bn annually between 2011 and 2016. Meanwhile, most EU members enjoy a growing trade surplus with Israel. EU exports to Israel grew from €14bn in 2006 to more than €21bn in 2016, despite the subdued economic climate.[68] In January 2017 Israel issued €2.25bn in bonds on the London Stock Exchange and demand was four times the offering.[69] Indeed, an economic model recently devised by a British think tank identified Israel as one of four countries – alongside Canada, India and China – that the UK should engage with intensively post-Brexit on the basis of projected growth potential in bilateral trade.[70]

Israel's success, especially in the high-tech sector, for which Israel has been dubbed the 'Start-Up Nation',[71] makes Israel not only an increasingly valuable economic partner but also one admired by Europeans struggling for higher growth and employment. In a recent Brussels event celebrating EU–Israeli innovation cooperation, EU innovation commissioner Carlos Moedas said, 'Israel's successful and dynamic innovation ecosystem … is an inspiration … when designing our EU research and innovation policies.'[72] Since becoming the first non-EU country to join Europe's innovation and research framework in 1996, Israel has contributed €1.277bn, its entities have benefited from €1.721bn in grants, and Israeli and European researchers have undertaken thousands of collaborations.[73] The perception of Israel as a dynamic and innovative society has to some extent mitigated the very negative impact of Israel's occupation of the West Bank on Israel's soft power. So too has the success of Israel's cultural exports. For example, two dovish Israeli authors – David Grossman and Amos Oz – were among the six finalists of the 2017 Man Booker International Prize.

*   *   *

Frustration over aggressive right-wing Israeli policies on Palestine have held back the advance of EU–Israel relations, but have not as yet led to EU-wide pressure on Israel because that conflict remains deeply divisive for Europeans. Furthermore, there is now unparalleled potential for economic and strategic cooperation between Israel and Europe in the context of Middle East chaos, Europe's internal challenges and Israel's rising power. Yet while European and Israeli strategic and economic interests are more aligned than ever, public sympathy for Israel based on culture and values, a positive factor in the first 25 years of the relationship, is now a negative factor in Western Europe, and this looks set to worsen.

European politicians visiting Israel still generally feel themselves to be in familiar, Western-type cultural and political surroundings. These impressions matter as the foundation of a sense of shared identity. But declining belief in the possibility of a two-state solution, and dwindling confidence in Israeli democracy, threatens the stability of this shared identity. If Israel appears hostile to a Palestinian state and the Trump administration incapable of meaningful engagement, analogies between Israeli policies and apartheid and calls for sanctions will be harder to ignore, and sympathy for Israel during conflicts will be even less forthcoming. One trigger could be the application of Israeli law to the settlements, which is being advanced by elements within Israel's governing coalition.[74] The Israeli–Palestinian conflict – which is significant for several European states' domestic politics as well as their international relations – threatens diplomatic support for Israel, as demonstrated by the December 2016 UN Security Council vote. The long-term attitudinal trends in Western Europe especially – shaped by growing Muslim populations and younger generations more attuned to global human-rights issues and less to the Israeli and Jewish historical narrative – are working against Israel.

Israeli measures that put a Palestinian state further from reach would bolster the case of Europeans arguing for EU sanctions against settlements. Such measures, or an intensification of violence, would also boost the BDS movement, in turn shaping European firms' assessments of investments in Israel. More EU governments could also feel compelled to act unilaterally or as subgroups of the EU Council in support of the Palestinian cause, as Sweden did in recognising Palestine. Israel therefore cannot ignore European concerns over the Israeli–Palestinian issue. The current Israeli governing coalition is incapable of generating a credible renewed commitment to a two-state solution. If a future Israeli government were to take advantage of the unprecedented willingness of key Arab states to begin normalisation with Israel to advance the creation of a Palestinian state, however, Israel would be in a strong position to reap the benefits of a greatly improved relationship with Europe.

Notes

1   This article draws on numerous interviews conducted with officials and politicians in EU institutions, EU member states and Israel.

2   Muriel Asseburg, 'Tensions on the Rise: Israel's Right-wing Government and the EU', Israeli European Policy Network, June 2015, http://www. iepn.org/images/stories/papers/2015/tensions%20on%20the%20rise-muriel%20asseburg.pdf.

3   Yann Le Guernigou, 'Sarkozy Tells Obama Netanyahu Is A "Liar"', Reuters, 8 November 2011, https://www.reuters.com/article/us-mideast-netanyahu-sarkozy/

sarkozy-tells-obama-netanyahu-is-
a-liar-idUSTRE7A720120111108.

4 Sharon Pardo and Joel Peters, *Israel
and the European Union: A Documentary
History* (Lanham, MD: Lexington
Books, 2012), p. 324.

5 Mahmoud Abbas, 'The Long Overdue
Palestinian State', *New York Times*,
16 May 2011, http://www.nytimes.
com/2011/05/17/opinion/17abbas.
html?mcubz=3.

6 'Unreleased EU Report Slams Israeli
Settlements', *Jerusalem Post*, 27
February 2013, http://www.jpost.com/
Diplomacy-and-Politics/Unreleased-
EU-report-slams-Israeli-settlements.

7 Sharon Pardo, *Normative Power Europe
Meets Israel: Perceptions and Realities*
(Lanham, MD: Lexington Books,
2015), p. 61.

8 Hugh Lovatt and Mattia Toaldo,
'EU Differentiation and Israeli
Settlements', European Council
on Foreign Relations, 22 July
2015, http://www.ecfr.eu/page/-/
EuDifferentiation-final3.pdf.

9 Michael Herzog, 'Inside the Black
Box of Israeli–Palestinian Talks',
American Interest, 27 February 2017,
https://www.the-american-interest.
com/2017/02/27/inside-the-black-box-
of-israeli-palestinian-talks/.

10 Connie de Boer, 'The Polls: Attitudes
Toward the Arab–Israeli Conflict',
Public Opinion Quarterly, vol. 47, no. 1,
1983, p. 121.

11 'Ideological Gaps Over Israel on
Both Sides of Atlantic', Pew Research
Center, 29 January 2009, http://
www.pewglobal.org/2009/01/29/
ideology-and-views-toward-the-
middle-east-conflict. On the US, see
also Dana H. Allin and Steven Simon,

*Our Separate Ways: The Struggle for
the Future of the U.S.–Israel Alliance*
(New York: PublicAffairs, 2016); and
Jonathan Rynhold, *The Arab–Israeli
Conflict in American Political Culture*
(Cambridge: Cambridge University
Press, 2015), ch. 3.

12 Bruno Oliveira Martins, '"A Sense of
Urgency": The EU, EU Member States
and the Recognition of the Palestinian
State', *Mediterranean Politics*, vol. 20,
no. 2, 2015, pp. 281–7.

13 Richard Ottaway, *Hansard*, 13
October 2014, col. 49, https://
publications.parliament.uk/
pa/cm201415/cmhansrd/
cm141013/debtext/141013-0002.
htm#14101322000001.

14 European Agency for Fundamental
Rights, 'Antisemitism: Overview
of Data Available in the European
Union 2004–2014', October
2015, http://fra.europa.eu/
sites/default/files/fra_uploads/
fra-2015-antisemitism-update_en.pdf.

15 Peter Beaumont, 'Leaders Reject
Netanyahu Calls for Jewish Mass
Migration to Israel', *Guardian*,
16 February 2015, https://www.
theguardian.com/world/2015/feb/16/
leaders-criticise-netanyahu-calls-
jewish-mass-migration-israel.

16 Jeremy Diamond, 'Jewish Leaders
Rebuff Netanyahu's Call for Mass
Migration', CNN, 17 February 2017,
http://edition.cnn.com/2015/02/16/
politics/benjamin-netanyahu-jewish-
mass-immigration-rejected/index.
html.

17 European External Action Service,
'Statement by the Spokesperson on
the Passage of the New NGO Law
in the Israeli Knesset', 12 July 2016,

https://eeas.europa.eu/headquarters/ headquarters-homepage/7228/ statement-spokesperson-passage-new- ngo-law-israeli-knesset_en.

18 Letter available at https://static.guim. co.uk/ni/1431517700142/EEPG-letter. pdf.

19 Joel Peters, 'Israel and Europe: Flashpoints on the Horizon', Israeli European Policy Network, June 2015, http://www.iepn.org/images/ stories/papers/2015/israel%20and%20 europe%20flashpoints%20on%20 the%20horizon-joel%20peters.pdf.

20 Emily Tamkin, 'Israel's Naftali Bennett: With Trump, "The Era of the Palestinian State Is Over"', Foreign Policy, 14 November 2016, http://foreignpolicy.com/2016/11/14/ israels-naftali-bennett-with-trump-the- era-of-the-palestinian-state-is-over/.

21 Peter Beaumont, 'Netanyahu: Middle East Peace Talks Are a Rigged Move Against Israel', Guardian, 12 January 2017, https://www.theguardian.com/ world/2017/jan/12/netanyahu-middle- east-peace-conference-rigged-move- against-israel-paris-trump.

22 Sigmar Gabriel, 'Speech to 11th INSS Annual International Conference', INSS, 31 January 2018, http://www. inss.org.il/sigmar-gabriel-german- foreign-minister/.

23 European Commission, 'EU and Israel', http://ec.europa.eu/trade/ policy/countries-and-regions/ countries/israel/.

24 Author's private conversation with EU ambassador in Israel.

25 Raffaella A. Del Sarto, 'Borders, Power and Interdependence: A Borderlands Approach to Israel–Palestine and the European Union', in Rafaella A.

Del Sarto (ed.), Fragmented Borders, Interdependence and External Relations: The Israel–Palestine–European Union Triangle (Basingstoke: Palgrave, 2015), p. 14.

26 Raphael Ahren, 'In Hot Mic Comments, Netanyahu Lashes EU's "Crazy" Policy on Israel', Times of Israel, 19 July 2017, https://www.timesofisrael.com/ in-overheard-comments-netanyahu- lashes-eus-crazy-policy-on-israel/.

27 Tal Shalev, 'Israel Is Expected to Sign a Cooperation Agreement with Europol', Walla News, 18 June 2017, https://news.walla.co.il/item/3074083.

28 Author interview with diplomat from member-state delegation, 21 June 2017, Brussels.

29 Richard Wike, Bruce Stokes and Katie Simmons, 'Europeans Fear Wave of Refugees Will Mean More Terrorism, Fewer Jobs', Pew Research Center, 11 July 2016, http://www.pewglobal.org/ files/2016/07/Pew-Research-Center- EU-Refugees-and-National-Identity- Report-FINAL-July-11-2016.pdf.

30 Mission of Israel to the EU and NATO, 'Israel at Visegrad Group Summit', 19 July 2017, http://embassies.gov.il/ eu/NewsAndEvents/Pages/Israel--- Visegrad-Group-Summit.aspx#p.

31 Andrew Rettman, 'Two EU States Break Ranks on Jerusalem', EU Observer, 7 December 2017, https:// euobserver.com/foreign/140198.

32 'EU Diplomats Reportedly Angry after Netanyahu "Invites Self" to Summit', Times of Israel, 29 November 2017, https://www.timesofisrael.com/ eu-diplomats-reportedly-angry-after- netanyahu-invites-self-to-summit/.

33 Gaps are illustrated by draft texts sub-

mitted for a resolution on the Middle
East Peace Process in May 2017,
available at http://www.europarl.
europa.eu/sides/getDoc.do?pubRef=-//
EP//TEXT+MOTION+P8-RC-
2017-0345+0+DOC+XML+V0//
EN.

34 'Ideological Gaps Over Israel on
Both Sides of Atlantic', Pew Research
Center, 29 January 2009, http://
www.pewglobal.org/2009/01/29/
ideology-and-views-toward-the-
middle-east-conflict/.

35 Nizan Feldman, *In the Shadow of
Delegitimization: Israel's Sensitivity to
Economic Sanctions* (Tel Aviv: INSS,
2017).

36 'Remarks by High Representative/
Vice-President Federica Mogherini',
EEAS, 8 September 2017, https://
eeas.europa.eu/headquarters/
headquarters-homepage/31830/
remarks-high-representativevice-
president-federica-mogherini-joint-
press-conference-sven_en.

37 Author interview with diplomat from
member-state delegation in Brussels,
21 June 2017, Brussels.

38 Author interview with EEAS officials,
23 June 2017, Brussels.

39 'Israeli Officials Snub Swedish
Foreign Minister', AFP/The Local, 13
December 2016.

40 Daniel Brössler and Alexandra
Föderl-Schmid, 'Auf schmalem Grat',
Sueddeutsche Zeitung, 16 January
2018, http://www.sueddeutsche.de/
politik/nahost-konflikt-auf-schmalem-
grat-1.3827523.

41 EU High Representative, 'A Secure
Europe in a Better World: European
Security Strategy', December 2003,
https://www.consilium.europa.eu/

uedocs/cmsUpload/78367.pdf.

42 EU HR/VP, 'Shared Vision, Common
Action: A Stronger Europe: A Global
Strategy for the EU's Foreign and
Security Policy', June 2016, https://
europa.eu/ globalstrategy/sites/global-
strategy/files/eugs_review_web.pdf.

43 Behlül Ozkan, 'Turkey, Davutoglu and
the Idea of Pan-Islamism', *Survival*,
vol. 56, no. 4, August–September 2014,
pp. 119–40.

44 Roberto Roccu and Benedetta
Voltolini, 'Framing and Reframing
the EU's Engagement with the
Mediterranean: Examining the
Security–Stability Nexus before
and after the Arab Uprisings',
Mediterranean Politics, vol. 23, no. 1,
2018, pp. 1–22.

45 *Ibid.*; Vincent Durac,
'Counterterrorism and Democracy:
EU Policy in the Middle East and
North Africa after the Uprisings',
Mediterranean Politics, vol. 23, no. 1,
2018, pp. 103–21.

46 EU HR/VP, 'Shared Vision, Common
Action: A Stronger Europe'.

47 Author interview with Brando Benifei
MEP, 22 June 2017, Brussels.

48 Yasser El-Shiny and Anthony
Dworkin, 'Egypt on the Edge',
European Council on Foreign
Relations, 14 June 2017, http://www.
ecfr.eu/page/-/ECFR218_-_EGYPT_
ON_THE_EDGE.pdf.

49 Robert M. Danin, 'Israel Among the
Nations', *Foreign Affairs*, vol. 95, no. 4,
2016, pp. 28–36.

50 David D. Kirkpatrick, 'Arab Leaders,
Viewing Hamas as Worse than
Israel, Stay Silent', *New York Times*,
30 July 2014, https://www.nytimes.
com/2014/07/31/world/middleeast/

fighting-political-islam-arab-states-find-themselves-allied-with-israel.html?mcubz=0.

51 Author interview with Malcolm Rifkind, 2 February 2017, London.

52 Richard Spencer, 'Israel's Secret Raqqa Raid Led Britain to Ban Laptops on Planes', *Sunday Times*, 24 November 2017, https://www.thetimes.co.uk/article/israel-s-secret-raqqa-raid-led-britain-to-ban-laptops-on-planes-mzp3w05ks.

53 See, for example, Leon Symons, 'Sadiq Khan Sought Israel's Advice on Fighting Terror After Spate of UK Attacks', *Jewish News*, 13 June 2017, http://jewishnews.timesofisrael.com/exclusive-sadiq-khan-sought-counter-terrorism-advice-from-israel-after-spate-of-uk-attacks/; and Colonel Richard Kemp and Arsen Ostrovsky, 'What Europe Can Learn from Israel in its War Against Vehicle Attacks and Lone Wolf Terror', *International Business Times*, 22 August 2017, http://www.ibtimes.co.uk/what-europe-can-learn-israel-its-war-against-vehicle-attacks-lone-wolf-terror-1635945/.

54 John Irish, 'Despite EU Caution, France Pursues Tough Line on Iran Missile Program', Reuters, 15 November 2017, https://www.reuters.com/article/us-iran-nuclear-france-eu/despite-eu-caution-france-pursues-tough-line-on-iran-missile-program-idUSKBN1DF23M; and Mark Landler, David E. Sanger and Gardiner Harris, 'Rewrite Iran Deal? Europeans Offer a Different Solution: A New Chapter', *New York Times*, 26 February 2018, https://www.nytimes.com/2018/02/26/us/politics/trump-europe-iran-deal.html.

55 Zenonas Tziarras, 'Israel–Cyprus–Greece: A Comfortable "Quasi-Alliance"', *Mediterranean Politics*, vol. 21, no. 3, 2016, pp. 407–27.

56 Author interviews with EU and member-state officials, June 2017, Brussels.

57 Elai Rettig and Yotam Rosner, 'Europe's Challenges Open the Market for Israel's Arms Industry', INSS, 21 August 2017, http://www.haaretz.com/israel-news/1.780198.

58 'Optsat-3000 Earth Observation Satellite for Italy's Ministry of Defence Is Ready To Be Launched', *Telespazio*, 31 July 2017, http://www.telespazio.com/-/optsat-prelaunch.

59 Thomas Risse, *A Community of Europeans* (New York: Cornell University Press, 2010), p. 10.

60 Farid Hafez, 'Shifting Borders: Islamophobia as Common Ground for Building Pan-European Right-Wing Unity', *Patterns of Prejudice*, vol. 48, no. 5, 2014, pp. 479–99.

61 'How Austria's Far-Right Leader Strache Brought the Freedom Party Back from the Brink', AFP, 13 October 2017, https://www.thelocal.at/20171013/austria-far-right-leader-strache-election-deputy-chancellor-freedom-party.

62 Karin Stoegner, '"We Are the New Jews!" and "The Jewish Lobby" – Antisemitism and the Construction of a National Identity by the Austrian Freedom Party', *Nations and Nationalism*, vol. 22, no. 3, 2016, pp. 485–504.

63 José Pedro Zúquete, 'The European Extreme-Right and Islam: New Directions?', *Journal of Political Ideologies*, vol. 13, no. 3, 2008, pp. 321–44.

64 Luke Baker, 'Far-Right Austrian Leader Visits Israel's Holocaust Memorial', Reuters, 12 April 2016, https://www.reuters.com/article/us-israel-austria-strache/far-right-austrian-leader-visits-israels-holocaust-memorial-idUSKCN0X91NX.

65 Toby Greene and Yossi Shain, 'The Israelization of British Jewry: Balancing Between Home and Homeland', *British Journal of Politics and International Relations*, vol. 18, no. 4, 2016, pp. 848–65.

66 Lidar Garev-Lazi, 'Israel's Population to Reach 20 Million by 2065', *Jerusalem Post*, 21 May 2017, http://www.jpost.com/Israel-News/Report-Israels-population-to-reach-20-million-by-2065-492429.

67 Walter Russell Mead and Sam Keeley, 'The Eight Great Powers of 2017', *American Interest*, 24 January 2017, https://www.the-american-interest.com/2017/01/24/the-eight-great-powers-of-2017/.

68 European Commission DG Trade, 'Trade in Goods with Israel', 3 May 2017, http://trade.ec.europa.eu/doclib/docs/2006/september/tradoc_113402.pdf.

69 London Stock Exchange Group, 'Israel Issues Largest Ever Euro Bond Offering on London Stock Exchange', 18 January 2017, https://www.lseg.com/resources/media-centre/press-releases/israel-issues-largest-ever-euro-bond-offering-london-stock-exchange.

70 Henry Newman et al., *Global Britain: Priorities for Trade beyond the EU* (London: Open Europe, 2017), http://openeurope.org.uk/intelligence/economic-policy-and-trade/global-britain-priorities-for-trade-beyond-the-eu/.

71 Dan Senor and Saul Singer, *Start-Up Nation: The Story of Israel's Economic Miracle* (New York: Twelve, 2009).

72 Carlos Moedas, 'Speech: EU–Israel: 20 Years Research and Innovation Partnership', European Commission, 20 June 2017, https://ec.europa.eu/commission/commissioners/2014-2019/moedas/announcements/eu-israel-20-years-research-and-innovation-partnership_en.

73 Delegation of the European Union to Israel, 'EU Commissioner for Research, Science and Innovation Visits the Start-Up Nation', 17 May 2017, https://eeas.europa.eu/delegations/israel/26342/eu-commissioner-research-science-and-innovation-visits-start-nation_en.

74 Shlomi Eldar, 'Israeli Justice Minister's Stealthy Plan to Annex the West Bank', *Al-Monitor*, 26 February 2018, http://www.al-monitor.com/pulse/originals/2018/02/israel-west-bank-palestinians-ayelet-shaked-high-court-law.html#ixzz58KunWcxE.

Italy, Its Populists and the EU

Erik Jones

The current Italian government is the most sceptical of the European Union in the country's history. The deputy prime minister and minister of the interior, Matteo Salvini, seems to delight in confronting his European partners on immigration, the euro and the whole European way of doing business. The other deputy prime minister and minister of labour, Luigi Di Maio, is no less challenging; if he confuses or even insults Italy's European allies along the way, so be it. Labelling French President Emmanuel Macron 'public enemy number one' for his stand on immigration policy is a good illustration.[1]

While Prime Minister Giuseppe Conte may try to smooth ruffled feathers, few doubt that he is controlled by his deputies. Because of their role as party leaders, their behaviour is signally important. The coalition government is only as stable as the support Conte receives from Salvini's Lega Nord (Northern League) and Di Maio's Five Star Movement (M5S). Two weeks into this arrangement, close to 60% of the Italian public approved of what that government is doing. Small wonder, therefore, that so many outside Italy question whether the Italians have decided to turn their backs on Europe. The good news is that they have not; the bad news is that they have edged closer to doing so.

The response of Italy's European partners to this new government will make a difference. The challenge is to defuse popular frustration with the

Erik Jones is Professor of European Studies and Director of European and Eurasian Studies at the Paul H. Nitze School of Advanced International Studies (SAIS), Johns Hopkins University; Senior Research Fellow at Nuffield College, Oxford; and a Contributing Editor to *Survival*.

Survival | vol. 60 no. 4 | August–September | pp. 113–122   DOI 10.1080/00396338.2018.1495433

EU by focusing on the issues, listening to Italian voices, and thinking flexibly about how to construct possible solutions. This is going to be difficult because other European leaders have their own domestic considerations. European institutions are also about to start an intensive and controversial political process that will culminate in the elections to the European Parliament and the appointment of a new European Commission. Crafting a message to engage with Italy's new government – often in the face of provocation and always with the risk of being taken out of context and used by Italy's new governing elites as further evidence of European insensitivity or intransigence – will never be easy.

Yet the alternative strategy of trying to ignore or downplay Italian concerns would not only stoke popular frustration but could also raise the salience of eurosceptic impulses across the Italian population. Italian voters may not have supported M5S and Lega in the March 2018 parliamentary elections due to those parties' anti-European policies, but growing populist frustration with Europe could determine the outcome of upcoming elections to the European Parliament and subsequent elections.

Complex causes

According to data from Eurobarometer, Italian trust in the EU has fallen in recent years by more than the European average. That trust has also been slower to recover with the gradual improvement in economic circumstances.[2] The latest Eurobarometer shows just how much ground is left to recapture. If the gap between those who tend not to trust and those who tend to trust the EU is six percentage points across the EU as a whole, it is still 15 percentage points in Italy.[3] Italian frustration with European policies toward migration and banking resolution has been increasing. So has the willingness of Italians to say they would consider alternatives. Although still not a majority, greater numbers of Italians tell pollsters that they would vote for Italy's exit from either the euro or the EU itself.[4] The polling data comes from multiple sources, including national polling as well as Eurobarometer, and paints a consistent picture of discontent.

Notwithstanding these trends, the strong showing of M5S and Lega in the 4 March 2018 parliamentary elections – together with their decision to work together as a 'government of change' – was surprising. M5S was always expected to emerge from the elections as the largest political party. It nevertheless surpassed expectations by more than the margin of polling error – jumping from 27.6% of support in pre-election polls to over 32% actual support in both the Chamber of Deputies and the Senate and is emerging as the dominant political force in the south. Lega saw its support increase from 13.4% in the last round of public opinion polls to 17.5% in the actual contest.[5] This increase catapulted Lega to the leadership of the centre-right with a clear dominance in the north. The two parties represent very different versions of populism and have constituencies with legacies of outright mutual antagonism. Nevertheless, together they constituted a majority in parliament and managed to find enough common ground to form a coalition.

It is tempting to conclude that Italy has an M5S–Lega government today because of the growth in euroscepticism among voters. Support for both M5S and Lega has risen even as support for European integration has fallen. M5S and Lega politicians have adopted openly eurosceptic positions. M5S promised a referendum on continued membership in the eurozone; Lega promised to push back against European migration policies. The new government has focused its attention primarily on migration, which is not surprising given that M5S had walked back its euro-referendum commitment. Lega is even more openly critical of the euro and yet Salvini made it clear that he would tackle migration first, which is why he chose to be minister of the interior.

Italians have grown increasingly frustrated with the EU, and M5S and Lega have pushed strongly eurosceptic policy positions for the same reasons. Italy is suffering from a migration crisis, which may not seem critical in other countries but is certainly perceived as such by Italians.[6] Italians are also fed up with the prolonged and painful consequences of the global economic and financial crisis.[7] Moreover, politicians in both M5S and Lega recognise this frustration and are trying to tap into it – with considerable success on the migration front, but also with respect to economic and social issues.

More complications

The apparent correlation between worsening attitudes towards Europe and strengthening support for populist political parties does not mean, however, that Italians support M5S or Lega because those parties are eurosceptic. It also does not suggest that, when faced with a choice more significant than what response to give to a public-opinion pollster, Italians would decide to abandon the EU or even the euro. Italy today is not the United Kingdom in 2015 or even in 2013. On the contrary, there are indications that Italians would prefer it if Europe's migration problem faded away and a strong economic recovery raised income and employment so as to ease any discomfort they feel with the EU. Arguably, then, the connection between Italian discontent with the EU and popular support for the current government is coincidental and not directly causal. Euroscepticism and populism in Italy may have common roots. But Italians can embrace populism without necessarily rejecting Europe; conversely, they can feel uncomfortable with Europe without embracing populism.

Italians want to have less tension with Europe, but they also have long wanted to change their country's relationship with the EU. Hence, even the most pro-European parts of the Italian political spectrum are pushing for something different from the past. That something does not include leaving the EU, but it does include standing up to European partners when the situation calls for it. This compulsion is particularly evident when talk turns to the reform of European institutions and processes.

The substantially coincidental nature of the relationship between the Italian frustration with Europe and support for M5S and Lega is demonstrable, if subtle. It rests in part on the salience of the issue – that is, just how much Italians are willing to act on their frustration with Europe. Polling groups capture this factor by asking three types of question in addition to what respondents think about an issue. Those questions concern how important the issue is in general terms, how central it is to the upcoming election, and how much that issue is likely to make one want to vote for a particular party given the platform it puts forward. The Italian polling group SWG used this strategy to assess popular attitudes across a range of issues, from cutting taxes and throwing out the ruling elite, to fighting inequality, eliminating precarious employment, and changing relations with Europe. They did one round of polling in May 2017 and another in January 2018, just weeks before the March vote.

What the SWG pollsters found about the notion of changing Italy's EU relationship is revealing. In May 2017, 41% of Italian respondents thought the issue was an important one but only 22% thought it would be relevant in any upcoming elections and only 18% thought they would be attracted to vote for a party given their stand on relations with Europe. Eight months later, and less than two months before the elections, popular attention was more concentrated. By that time, however, only 35% of voters thought Europe was an important issue in general, only 17% thought it was relevant to the campaign, and only 17% thought it could influence their vote. Put simply, Europe was not a major issue for electoral consideration.[8]

The political parties responded quickly to this evolution in popular attitudes. Although both M5S and Lega came out with bold electoral proposals to change Italy's position within the EU and even to take Italy out of the euro, both parties quickly shelved these issues when it became obvious they were not gaining traction among the electorate. M5S walked back its promise to hold a referendum on eurozone membership and Lega made it clear that while it remained sceptical of the advantages of the single currency, the time was not ripe for a change in that arrangement. Both parties remained eurosceptic, but that was not the face they put forward to attract support at the polls.

This was not the first time that Italian political parties have tried to campaign on eurosceptic positions only to pull those off the table once they got into the heat of the contest. When Lega went to the polls with Silvio Berlusconi as leader of the Italian centre-right in 2006, for example, part of the initial campaign strategy was to claim that the changeover from the Italian lira to the euro gave shopkeepers the opportunity to gouge unwitting consumers. This was important for Berlusconi because the euro was wildly unpopular at the time owing both to that fear, and to the fact that Berlusconi's opponent, Romano Prodi, had paved the way for Italy's participation in the single currency as Italian prime minister and had helped establish the euro as European Commission president. But the claim did not resonate, so Berlusconi quietly dropped it in favour of other issues that he perceived to be more relevant.[9]

Berlusconi tried again to raise the issue of Europe in 2013, this time to greater effect, and he was not alone. The 2013 election was the first one joined by M5S, which put its eurosceptic views on display alongside the movement's central promise to overturn the country's ruling elites. Expert surveys during this period show that the Italian political system was beginning to focus on changing the country's relationship with the rest of the EU.[10] The issue was not decisive in the election, but it was influential across political elites who recognised that the growing influence of European authority in matters of domestic policy was becoming a major source of political vulnerability. The many concessions to both Brussels and other European partners made by Mario Monti as prime minister came back to haunt him in that respect. Thus, from 2013 onward, Italy's political class has sought to adjust the country's relationship with the EU to cultivate a greater sense of domestic accountability and control within the Italian electorate.

Necessity and self-confidence

The relationship Italian political leaders sought with the rest of Europe was grounded in a mixture of necessity and self-confidence.[11] The necessity emerged as a result of the difficult government-formation process that followed the February 2013 elections. Although the centre-left coalition was the largest group in parliament, M5S was the largest political party. Moreover, the surprisingly strong performance of Silvio Berlusconi's centre-right bloc deprived the centre-left of a workable majority. Worse, the president of the republic, Giorgio Napolitano, was in his last six months in office and so no longer possessed the power to dissolve parliament. Hence the challenge became to elect a new president who could impose some discipline on an unruly parliament.

Even that proved too much for Italy's politicians to manage, so Napolitano reluctantly accepted a second term in office. In exchange he demanded that the centre-left and centre-right form a grand coalition under Enrico Letta that could undertake an ambitious reform agenda. Napolitano threatened that, should they fail to fulfil that mandate, he would force Italy's politicians to go back and face the electorate. Neither the centre-left parties nor the centre-right ones were eager to take that risk.

Letta realised from the outset that gaining greater room for manoeuvre within the European context was critical to holding the grand coalition together. With his extensive contacts across the European People's Party, Letta proved to be an able negotiator. As the coalition became more stable, it gained confidence. Matteo Renzi made a bid for leadership of the Democratic Party in the autumn of 2013 and then used his new position to take over the premiership the following February. Immediately thereafter, Renzi led the Democratic Party to achieve a record 40% of the vote in the May 2014 elections to the European Parliament. Renzi described that victory as his own popular mandate and then used his popularity to try to assert his government's position more forcefully in the European context.

Renzi's more assertive posture won approval in Italy and respect abroad. Other European leaders did not always agree with the positions Renzi took in their deliberations, but they nevertheless accepted his right to participate in an active manner.[12] For their part, Renzi's ministers showed a strong commitment to extending his new assertiveness across the range of issues in which Italian and European policymaking intersect. They were even willing to engage in substantive and painful institutional reforms in order to bolster their creditworthiness with their European partners. The 'Jobs Act' is a good illustration. By reforming Italy's labour markets, the Renzi government not only removed an important supply-side constraint on domestic macro-economic performance, but also demonstrated its willingness to tackle powerful domestic interests.[13]

The European strategy followed by the Renzi government continued in the government headed by Paolo Gentiloni, albeit in a more low-key manner. Although Italy bumped against European rules regarding fiscal consolidation, banking resolution and migration policy, Gentiloni was able to find solutions that created enough flexibility to hold his coalition together and to advance his government's agenda. In this way, Gentiloni normalised the new relationship with Europe that the Letta and Renzi governments established. The reduction of tensions with Europe in the run-up to the March 2018 elections was a measure of Gentiloni's success.

Taste for conflict

The new Italian government wants to unravel that accomplishment. Both Salvini and Di Maio understand that they were previously unable to gain traction with the electorate by exploiting friction with Europe. Now they see a richer opportunity to employ that tactic. For Salvini, this means exploiting the migration issue. His goal is to underscore what he contends is the hypocrisy of Italy's European partners so that he can present himself as the only political figure willing to speak truth to power and to represent the country's true interests. Each time he faces criticism abroad it affords him a new opportunity to press the argument domestically. Indeed, he has shown a willingness to respond to even the slightest foreign comment.

There is no easy solution for European policymakers who want to bring Italy into the conversation and yet who cannot be seen to be folding in the face of Salvini's verbal onslaught. The temptation to lose patience with the new Italian government must be extreme. Nevertheless, it is worth considering that the underlying cleavage between those who support European integration and those who resent European interference in domestic politics is still lurking beneath the surface. Italians are frustrated with Europe for a number of other reasons as well. The more Italy's partners disregard or push back against the government, the more likely they are to combine these different Italian attitudes toward Europe into a single toxic mixture of disillusionment and resentment that politicians like Salvini will be able to nurture long into the future. Italy is not yet in a situation like the United Kingdom's. Perhaps it will never head down that path. But there are clearly politicians who would exploit such disenchantment. The challenge for Europe is to starve them of the oxygen of open conflict.

Notes

1   'Macron contro l'Italia: "Non ha crisi migratoria, proporrò sbarchi nei porti più vicini". Salvini: "Apri quelli francesi". E Di Maio: "Lui è il nemico numero 1 dell'Italia"', *Huffington Post* (Italian edition), 23 June 2018, https://www.huffingtonpost.it/2018/06/23/pilato-macron_a_23466276/.

2   See data for 'trust in the European Union' from the Eurobarometer interactive time-series database at http://ec.europa.eu/commfrontoffice/publicopinion/index.cfm/Chart/index.

3   See *Standard Eurobarometer 89 (Spring 2018): First Results* (Brussels: European Commission, 2018), p. 14.

4   See, for example, Dario Di Vico, 'Italia fuori dall'Ue? Solo un italiano su 4 dice di sì', *Corriere della Sera*, 3 June 2018, https://www.corriere.it/

politica/18_giugno_03/italia-fuori-ue-un-italiano-4-dice-si-eae5790c-6767-11e8-83d0-1e29d770f94c.shtml.

5   The polling data is reproduced from multiple sources on the website *Termometropolitico*, https://www.termometropolitico.it/sondaggi-politici-elettorali. The electoral data is taken from the *La Repubblica* website, https://elezioni.repubblica.it/2018/cameradeideputati.

6   The evidence here is the furious response generated in Italy by French President Emmanuel Macron's comments that anyone who says that Italy is facing a migration crisis like it did in the past, is lying. See 'Macron: Italia non ha crisi migratoria', *Ansa*, 23 June 2018, http://www.ansa.it/sito/notizie/mondo/europa/2018/06/23/macron-italia-non-ha-crisi-migratoria_d4ca06d4-9f99-43c7-94b0-24e08420e3c7.html.

7   When asked about the main concerns they face at the national level, 48% of Italians cite unemployment and 35% cite immigration; the next highest category is the 'general economic situation', cited by 25%. See *Standard Eurobarometer 89 (Spring 2018): First Results*, p. 11.

8   *Italia 4 Marzo: Progetto per la fornitura di dati preelettorali: Report #2* (Trieste: SWG, 16 February 2018), p. 13.

9   See Erik Jones, 'Italy and the Euro in the Global Economic Crisis', *International Spectator*, vol. 44, no. 4, December 2009, pp. 93–103.

10 See Aldo Di Virgilio et al., 'Party Competition in the 2013 Italian Elections: Evidence from an Expert Survey', *Government and Opposition*, vol. 50, no. 1, January 2015, pp. 65–89.

11 Much of this section is adapted from Erik Jones, 'Relations with Europe: Beyond the Vincolo Esterno', in Alessandro Chiaramonte and Alex Wilson (eds), *Italian Politics: The Great Reform that Never Was* (New York: Berghahn Books, 2017), pp. 51–69.

12 Interview with a member of the President of the European Commission Jean-Claude Juncker's cabinet, May 2015.

13 This point has been underscored in conversations with some of Renzi's former advisers.

Restraining Rome: Lessons in Grand Strategy from Emperor Hadrian

Christopher J. Fettweis

For many scholars of international relations, ancient wisdom seems to begin and end with Thucydides. His *History of the Peloponnesian War* is regularly read, dissected and plumbed for insights applicable to modern problems. Requiring aspiring strategists to study the contest between Athens and Sparta made sense during the Cold War, when it seemed to echo modern times. Once the USSR imploded, however, the quest to understand the geopolitics of the bipolar Greek city-state system lost a bit of its urgency. While few would suggest that scholars stop reading Thucydides, it may be time to expand the canon, to seek advice from other sources more relevant to the current era.[1] There is an obvious, under-appreciated, more appropriate analogue from the ancient Mediterranean. Today's strategists would be better served by studying the wisdom – and occasional lack thereof – of the Roman emperors, whose system and security environment more resembled our own.

It is probably safe to say that Donald Trump reminds precisely no one of the Roman Emperor Hadrian. The 45th president of the United States and 14th Augustus appear to be as different as can be: the latter was a military leader of some consequence, an experienced politician and renowned poet; the former made his name in real estate, avoided public service for 70 years and brags about never reading books. The only thing they seem to have in common, aside from the desire for walls to keep out perceived barbarians, is the determination to change the course charted by their predecessors.

Christopher J. Fettweis is Associate Professor of Political Science at Tulane University. His most recent book is *Psychology of a Superpower: Security and Dominance in U.S. Foreign Policy* (Columbia University Press, 2018).

Survival | vol. 60 no. 4 | August–September | pp. 123–150   DOI 10.1080/00396338.2018.1495438

The states led by these two men have more in common than a cursory reading might suggest, however. The United States of 2017 and Rome of 117 were both the strongest actors in their system, and faced neither peer competitors nor existential threats. Their leaders had to forge strategy in profoundly asymmetric environments where they were the dominant actors, which can be more challenging than it might seem. For a variety of reasons, concentrated power often serves as an impediment to strategic thought.[2] The decisions Hadrian made, many of which were profoundly unpopular at the time, contain a good deal of wisdom for those struggling to make strategy in an era containing some relevant similarities. At the very least, it might be helpful to understand how an earlier unipolar power identified and pursued its interests in a world of minimal existential threat.

The reign of Hadrian began at the peak of the empire's expansion in 117 and lasted for nearly 21 years. Throughout the era, Rome followed a clear strategic path, shaped by intuitive understandings of what are now recognised as the security dilemma and the offence–defence balance. Hadrian faced internal revolts by irregular forces and an ancient version of the so-called 'Lippmann gap', or an imbalance between national commitments and resources. The emperor made a series of strategic decisions that he knew would be unpopular – some on his very first day – but found ways to placate the troops and masses alike. Overall, Hadrian constructed a coherent grand strategy that helped the empire flourish and become stronger, safer and more prosperous, and could serve as a model for how to match means to ends in a unipolar system.

Rome and grand strategy

Analysis of Roman grand strategy began with Edward Luttwak's justly famous book, *The Grand Strategy of the Roman Empire*.[3] Luttwak described the evolution of Roman thinking about strategy across three broad eras, each largely determined by its prevailing attitude toward the frontier. In the early decades of the empire, Roman emperors relied upon permeable borders and client states in the periphery. Over time those borders hardened as the emperors searched for the optimal, rather than the most, territory to rule. In the third era, as Rome's fortunes began to change in the face of stronger enemies, border defence was essentially abandoned in favour of a general defence-in-depth approach.

Luttwak's work sparked controversy among historians, many of whom rejected the notion that Rome had a central grand strategy at all. Roman foreign policy seemed more reactive than proactive, particularly to specialists in the study of its frontiers.[4] As Kimberly Kagan has pointed out, however, this disagreement largely stems from a misunderstanding about the concept of grand strategy.[5] While the Romans had no Clausewitz and did not use modern terms, they certainly thought strategically and marshalled resources in pursuit of their interests. A different group of historians recognised the essential strategic nature of Roman action and engaged Luttwak in a more productive manner, correcting what they see as his misinterpretations of, or mistakes regarding, Roman policy.[6]

For all its minor flaws, *The Grand Strategy of the Roman Empire* remains enormously useful for laying out the general outlines of its subject. In the process of simplifying centuries of history into manageable eras, however, it sacrifices nuance and misses the substantial variation across imperial administrations. Few earlier historians saw commonality between the grand strategy of Hadrian and that of his predecessor Trajan, for example, but the two are lumped together in Luttwak's narrative. Rome's successes and blunders within eras are explicable only by a closer examination of the decisions made by its leaders, who hardly chose identical paths. Emperors had neither checks nor balances, and as a result had the freedom to mould foreign policy as they saw fit. Concentrating on the choices made by individual emperors, assessing what they did well and where they went wrong, has considerable potential to provide insight for strategists of today.

That said, the bulk of scholarly and popular attention paid to Hadrian has been skewed towards a few features of his rule that are tangential from a strategic standpoint: the famous, eponymous wall in northern England; his Hellenophilia, which dominated his poetry and outlook, and can be seen on his busts (he was the first emperor to sport a beard, which was considered the Greek style); and his tragic relationship with the young Bithynian boy Antinous. Others have examined his restless and curious nature, which led to a great deal of travel throughout his two decades in power.[7] Of his grand strategy, however, not much has been said. Surviving source material on Hadrian's reign is particularly thin. No contemporaneous analysis of his reign survives, in part because there was a semi-official but serious taboo on writing about an emperor while he was in office. The two main ancient sources are a chapter in the *Historia Augusta*, published today as the bulk of the *Lives of the Later Caesars*, which was written anonymously in the fourth century and is not widely respected by historians; and Cassius Dio's *History of Rome*, of which a 5,500-word summary of the Hadrian volume survives. Other, less direct sources exist, and archaeological evidence has helped historians fill some gaps. Accordingly, Hadrian's grand strategy, even more than that of other emperors, must be pieced together from his actions. Nevertheless, enough is known about them to make the inferences not merely supportable but strong.

Hadrian's grand strategy

When Publius Aelius Hadrianus became emperor in August 117, the Roman Empire had reached its greatest size. His predecessor, Trajan (98–117), had engaged in a series of campaigns that brought more territory under Roman control than ever before. Few emperors had showered as much glory upon the empire as did Trajan, and modern maps of the empire at its height invariably show the area under control in the last year of his reign. His successor, however, had other ideas.

Trajan was far more aggressive than most emperors of the *principate*, or period of imperial rule that began with Augustus. The empire was built during the Republican period, when the Senate ordered generals to conquer first neighbouring and then far-flung polities.[8] Early emperors generally led what we would call today a status quo power, a state more interested in stability than expansion.[9] They had quite consciously followed the deathbed advice of Augustus, who supposedly told his chosen successor Tiberius to *consilium coercendi intra terminus imperii*, or 'confine the empire within its present limits'.[10] The days of conquest were all but over, and Rome was to spend most of the next five centuries seeking to maintain its status. There were exceptions – Emperor Claudius completed the conquest of Britain within a few decades of Augustus's death, for one, and Nero ordered a punitive expedition into Armenia – but not until Trajan's time did Rome consistently march its legions outward, both to the north into Dacia (roughly modern-day Romania) and eastward into Persia, which was run by the Parthian dynasty. The victories were complete and, especially in the latter case, swift.

These were no ordinary wars of conquest. The invasion of Dacia was an enormous undertaking, involving the greatest concentration of Roman power since the civil wars that ended the republic. It necessitated tremendous feats of engineering, including the construction of canals along unnavigable sections of the Danube and roads through deep gorges. Other sections of the river were diverted entirely to facilitate the movement of Roman troops and supplies. Under Trajan's orders, the legions built a series of great bridges, one of which was larger than any seen in Europe for the next 1,000 years. All told, the pre-war build-up took nearly three years to complete.[11] Rome had invested a great deal of blood and treasure in this adventure, in other words, and by all accounts its society took a great deal of pride in its accomplishment. Some 123 days of celebrations followed. The famous column that still stands in Rome tells the story of the courageous emperor who finally shook Rome out of its centuries-long, inglorious slumber.

Conquest was always quite popular among the Roman elite and populace alike, and restraint generated discontent. Metaphors evoking the life of a person appear to have been common. 'From the time of Caesar Augustus down to our own age there has been a period of not much less than two hundred years,' wrote Florus during Trajan's reign.

> During that time, owing to the inactivity of the emperors, the Roman people grew old and impotent, except that under the rule of Trajan it again stirred its arms and, contrary to general expectation, again renewed its vigor with youth as if it were restored.[12]

Trajan was at least as important to Rome's pride and glory, then, as he was to its interests. Any reversals to this course would have met substantial opposition. In ancient Rome, that sometimes translated into palace coups and decapitated emperors.

Trajan died before he was able to complete his dream of following the path of Alexander the Great into India. As he was declining, he adhered to the long-established Roman pattern of adopting a son to succeed him. His choice was a controversial one, a successful general from Spain who, despite only being in his mid-thirties, had substantial political experience. It is doubtful that Trajan knew the plans young Hadrian had for the new territories.[13] Although Hadrian took over at a high point of both Roman territory and glory, he immediately set Rome on a new path.

Among his initial acts as emperor – orders that might have been issued on his very first day – was reversing the aggressive policies of his predecessor.[14] Rome abandoned all territory beyond the Tigris and Euphrates, returning Mesopotamia, Assyria and Greater Armenia to the Parthian king. Hadrian also ordered the evacuation of Roman soldiers from eastern Dacia, known at the time as 'Moesia Inferior'. He did not pull the legions out of southern Dacia, in large part because doing so would have meant abandoning Roman colonists who had been dispatched to settle in the region in the aftermath of Trajan's conquest. Hadrian did have his predecessor's enormous bridge dismantled, however, and put an end to all further talk of expansion in the region. Overall, although the Roman Empire reached its peak at the beginning of 117, by year's end it had shrunk by tens of thousands of square miles. Hadrian did not share his predecessor's admiration of Alexander and instead returned to the received wisdom of Augustus, on whom he was to pattern the rest of his reign.

Popular though they were, Trajan's conquests look more stable on twenty-first-century maps than they did in second-century practice. Many new provinces were in open revolt by summer 117. Hadrian inherited rebellious Moors and Samaritans, riots in Egypt, and restive populations in Libya and Palestine, which appeared to strike ancient sources as a particularly ominous development.[15] The new emperor decided that the costs of pacifying these provinces outweighed their benefits, especially with problems popping up elsewhere in the empire. He apparently made direct reference to Cato the Elder, who argued nearly three centuries before that troublesome peoples were not worth ruling.[16] Hadrian agreed, and pulled the legions back to their previous positions.

The politics of the empire supported the maintenance of Trajan's new status quo, which meant that Hadrian ran a great risk in conducting what must have seemed to be a retreat in the face of his enemies. Given the popularity of Trajan's conquests – then as now, nothing succeeds like success – it would have been far easier for the new emperor to succumb to the pressures of inertia and continue the policies of his predecessor. Hadrian's policies did not endear him to his fellow Romans, who were far more sympathetic to Trajan's aggression than to Hadrian's restraint. Elites were especially hawkish, often resembling the kind of armchair warriors ridiculed by Juvenal as men who study battles and dream of war from the safety of their marble villas.[17] Tacitus may well have been speaking indirectly of his own era when he lamented that

> I am not unaware that very many of the events I have described, and shall describe, may perhaps seem little things, trifles too slight for record; but no parallel can be drawn between these chronicles of mine and the work of the men who composed the ancient history of the Roman people. Gigantic wars, cities stormed, routed and captive kings, or, when they turned by choice to domestic affairs, the feuds of consul and tribune, land-laws and corn-laws, the duel of nobles and commons – such were the themes on which *they* dwelt, or digressed, at will. Mine is an inglorious labor in a narrow field; for this was an age of peace unbroken or half-heartedly challenged, of tragedy in the capital, of a *princeps* careless to extend the empire.[18]

Peace and stability can bore the historian eager to relate exciting stories of invasion and slaughter. Largely because of his refusal to indulge Rome's desire for excitement, according to the *Historia Augusta*, Hadrian was 'hated by all'.[19] The Roman people were less interested in peace and prosperity than glory and conquest.

Such negative reactions are understandable, if irrational. Retrenchment invariably faces substantial psychological barriers. Prospect theory helps explain why voluntary, unforced steps backward are uncommon in history.[20] The Roman people reacted badly to Hadrian's abandonment of their hard-won gains in part because it is difficult for human beings to accept loss, and to adjust to a new reality worse than that which they currently have, whether measured in money, living standards or status. Hadrian certainly anticipated a negative reaction to his strategic adjustments, and seems to have had a plan to deal with it.

Hadrian had options for dealing with his critics unavailable to US presidents. Within a few months of his ascension, the emperor had a group of four potential opponents tracked down and killed. Hadrian accused these senior senators of plotting against him, a claim of which ancient sources are sceptical.[21] Perhaps their main sin was that they were, in one historian's words, 'Trajan's men'.[22] Hadrian's relationship with the Roman elite never recovered from these extra-judicial killings, which were one of the reasons that the Senate refused to deify him after his death. Even the most powerful of Roman emperors could not kill all those who objected to their policies. Hadrian knew that he had some fence-mending to do with a variety of groups in Roman society if his reign was not to come to a premature end. The elites were fuming over the assassinations, and the masses were not ready to forgive his retreat.[23] He appears to have been well aware of the discontent, and responded as many before and after, with bread and circuses. This time it was quite literal: Hadrian ordered free distributions of grain for citizens of Rome, as well as regular salaries for those public officials, such as consuls and praetors, who up until then had no take-home pay. The emperor cancelled all unpaid public debts to the imperial treasury incurred in the previous 15 years. He also put on an enormous round of games, where untold numbers of gladiators, slaves and exotic animals gave their lives in an attempt to cheer up Romans otherwise dispirited by diminished glory.[24]

Hadrian also embarked upon a campaign to win over the troops, to assure that their loyalty – upon which, after all, his power rested – would not waiver in the face of restraint. He had led legions in the Dacian wars and distinguished himself in command, so he brought a veteran's credibility to the job. He also took pains to make clear to his soldiers that he considered himself one of them, spending a good deal of time in their camps during his travels and, if sources are to be believed, training with the men and eating what they ate. Bonuses and gifts did not hurt his efforts.[25] The emperor also seems to have understood that idle military hands often lead to problems, and compensated for the absence of campaigning by compelling the legions to increase their training regimens. He kept the men busy with massive construction projects, including a 350-mile palisade throughout modern-day Germany and a series of famous walls elsewhere.[26] Unlike the projects of his predecessor, Hadrian's engineering marvels were inherently defensive, not a prelude to invasion.

In the end, no amount of opposition was going to reverse the course set by the emperor. Roman troops pulled back to most of their pre-117 borders, and Hadrian set about what we would acknowledge today as a grand strategy of strategic restraint. Borders hardened and offensive actions curtailed, and as a result the empire entered a time of great peace, security and prosperity.

Hadrianic restraint in practice

The actions of the first few days foreshadowed the foreign policy of Hadrian's reign. Under his leadership, the Romans adopted an essentially defensive posture. Despite the fact that he possessed the finest military of the era, the emperor was reluctant to use it. Dio writes that Hadrian 'did not stir up any war, and he terminated those already in progress'.[27] The military instrument of Roman power took a back seat to diplomacy and economics. Hadrian relied on negotiation rather than ultimatum, and entered into a series of new treaties with the small powers across the border. 'To petty rulers and kings he made offers of friendship,' notes the *Historia Augusta*, and he returned a princess of Parthia, captured during Trajan's conquest, to her father.[28] Hadrian was quite willing to make deals to please rivals and potential enemies, often giving more than he got. He summoned leaders to his court or even met them near the border when on one of his frequent extended travels throughout the empire. Prior experience with Roman diplomacy, which was what we would today call coercive, probably made some of the invitees rather dubious. 'When some of the kings came to him,' however, 'he treated them in such a way that those who had refused to come regretted it.'[29] Hadrian understood that it is cheaper, if less glorious, to pursue national interests at the negotiating table than on the battlefield. His deals were often sweetened with gold from the imperial treasury or other monetary incentives.

Hadrian was not the first emperor to open Rome's purse in pursuit of its interests, even if he did so with increased alacrity. Domitian had paid off the Dacian king Decebalus in 88 as part of a peace agreement following an aborted campaign, and promised to keep the subsidies coming. This appears to have set a precedent, as there is evidence that Trajan had made some payments to the Roxolani, and many of Hadrian's successors were to do the same with other problematic peoples.[30] Using economic tools became a central part of later Roman strategy, especially in the rich east, where the empire's wealth helped fend off assault from barbarians like Attila and many similar nomadic invaders over the course of the millennium that followed the fall of the west.[31]

None of this is to imply that Hadrian's Rome let down its guard. Quite the opposite; Rome's legions increased the pace of their training, improving what we would today call readiness. 'So excellently, indeed, had his soldiery been trained,' writes Dio, that 'the barbarians stood in terror of the Romans.'[32] When external threats materialised – as when the Alani raided Asia Minor in 135 – the legions were prepared to deal with them swiftly. Hadrian was thus reluctant to use his sword but kept it sharp. The army was both a deterrent to invasion and the ultimate insurance policy for a defensive, restrained grand strategy. 'This best explains why he lived for the most part at peace with foreign nations,' says Dio, 'for as they saw his state of preparation and were themselves not only free from aggression but received money besides, they made no uprising.'[33]

Nor did Hadrian retrench because he was a pacifist. When crises arose, the emperor reacted with rather sensational violence. In 130, the empire faced a revolt by one of its most troublesome groups, the Jews. Due to grievances that were essentially religious in nature – relating to either a Roman ban on the practice of circumcision, or a perceived defilement of their holy city, or some combination of both – the Jewish people engaged in an irregular war that took nearly five years for Hadrian to crush. But crush it he did, and harshly. Dio suggests that nearly 1,000 Jewish villages were burned to the ground, and over a half-million Jewish men slain in the various battles that took place during the campaigns. More believably, he wrote that 'the number of those that perished by famine, disease and fire was past finding out,' and 'nearly the whole of Judaea was made desolate' as 'many wolves and hyenas rushed howling into their cities.'[34] As had happened before, the Romans made an example of the Jewish people, and Hadrian faced no further rebellion. Restraint did not imply weakness.

The walls

Restraint abroad allowed Hadrian to concentrate on needs inside the empire, and embark on a series of well-known infrastructure projects. His famous walls are the source of much speculation and some controversy among historians. Northern England is the home to the most famous but perhaps least important of these. Hadrian's Wall played a symbolic role in the development of English nationhood, but its fame is out of proportion to its limited practical significance for the empire. In fact, the northern wall marked a far-flung, relatively unimportant border. The walls between the Rhine and the Danube (the *limes Germanicus*) as well as the intermittent structures south of Carthage (the *fossatum Africae*) delineated the edge of vital imperial provinces, and were of greater strategic interest.

As generations of historians have pointed out, these walls cannot have served much defensive purpose. They were not large, crenelated castle-esque walls that would allow defenders to hold out against sustained assault while awaiting reinforcements, but rather unmanned, two- to three-metre-high barriers with outposts every mile or so, easily overcome by even mildly determined attackers. The *limes Germanicus* were not constructed in a way that suggests a defensive purpose, since even its guard towers do not appear to have much protection.[35] Germanic barbarians would have had little trouble getting past them. The *fossatum Africae* were built at a time when there was no threat from nomadic peoples to the south.[36] The Picts and other peoples of Scotland posed virtually no danger to Britannia. Hadrian's Wall was not protecting against invasion, in other words, because such a threat did not exist.

If Hadrian's various walls were not meant to defend the empire, then what purpose did they serve? Opinions are split on what the emperor had in mind when he ordered their construction. Brent Sterling has argued that the walls were essentially deterrents, with defensive importance only because they symbolised Roman power. To cross them, even if technically uncomplicated, was to engage the legions.[37] Other historians have suggested that the walls were constabulary rather than military, meant to control traffic and collect taxes on trade, as if they were essentially long tollbooths.[38] To Luttwak, the walls were built to encourage people on the other side to 'self-Romanize' by making it clear that life was better on the inside.[39]

None of these explanations is necessarily wrong; complex historical phenomena (and long walls were about as complex as it got in those days) have complex causes. But it is quite possible that the walls played another role in Hadrian's strategy. Historians have generally concentrated on the signals the walls sent outward in terms of potential deterrent or intimidation capabilities, rather than on the signals they sent inward. While Hadrian certainly wanted to keep the barbarians out, he also wanted to keep the Romans in. By delineating the frontiers of empire, the walls made it clear to those on both sides that expansion would not be taking place on Hadrian's watch. The walls were concrete and wooden manifestations of restraint, through which Hadrian hoped to encourage future emperors to adopt his grand strategy.[40] In the words of a modern historian, the walls were

> Hadrian's way of making plain that the policy of expansion really was at an end. The ideology of 'boundless empire,' immortalised in Virgil by the divine promise of an *imperium sine fine*, without an end in time or space, was thereby unmistakably buried. It was a clear signal to any surviving admirers of Trajan's expansionist policies that the empire was indeed precisely defined; thus far and no further.[41]

With construction of the walls, Hadrian promoted an offence–defence balance that favoured the latter. He was not only marking the limits of empire with the construction of *limes* but sending messages to the peoples beyond that they had little to fear from the superpower on the other side. By doing so, he decreased the threat that the unipolar power posed to its neighbours, and increased the chance for peaceful coexistence.

Glory and fear

Hadrian broke most dramatically with standard imperial practice regarding the psychological aspects of Roman foreign policy, which he seems to have interpreted in ways that not only differed from his predecessors and successors but that clashed with prevailing popular beliefs. Most importantly, he approached one of his era's cardinal virtues – glory – like no other emperor. Hadrian not only failed to associate glory with war, as so many did, but seemed relatively indifferent to the concept. While no Roman was immune to glory's appeal, Hadrian seems to have been uninterested in accolades won through conquest.[42] Today Hadrian would be considered a foreign-policy realist, focused more on Rome's interest than its mission, and unwilling to go abroad in search of barbarian monsters to destroy. Throughout his reign, Hadrian concentrated on Rome's tangible interests (security, prosperity) and minimised the importance of the intangibles (glory, honour, credibility), which was no mean feat in his time. That such an emphasis should lead to peace and stability should come as no surprise. As Thucydides wrote some seven centuries earlier, 'self-interest goes hand in hand with achievement of safety, whereas justice and honor are practiced with danger.'[43] Leaders interested in peace are well advised to focus on tangible goals, since interest and glory often inhabit opposite ends of the security spectrum. Hadrian chose the former, and his empire was better off as a result.

Perhaps Hadrian's greatest accomplishment was to keep the empire's threats in perspective. Roman emperors never shied away from challenge, and there is little reason to believe that Hadrian would have left a serious enemy alone in the hope that it would be pacified by Roman retrenchment. Indeed, the spectre of the external enemy was one of the main drivers of the empire's expansion from its earliest days. Rome's conquests were inspired by not only the desire for glory but also insecurity – that is, the sincere belief that untamed populations along its widening periphery represented threats to the core.[44] Cicero spoke for many of his countrymen when he explained that expansion was thrust upon Rome by the empire's various 'frightening neighbors'.[45] The fact that most of these neighbours were manifestly weaker did not matter; as its power grew, so too did Rome's insecurity. On this notion, known to historians as defensive imperialism, Joseph Schumpeter is probably unsurpassable:

> There was no corner of the known world where some interest was not alleged to be in danger or under actual attack … Rome was always being attacked by evil-minded neighbors, always fighting for a breathing space. The whole world was pervaded by a host of enemies, and it was manifestly Rome's duty to guard against their indubitably aggressive designs. They were enemies only waiting to fall on the Roman people.[46]

The most powerful, and in many ways safest, society in the ancient world was never convinced that its security was assured as long as potential enemies existed anywhere.

Hadrian simultaneously resisted the desire for glory-through-conquest displayed by so many of his contemporaries and the fear of the other that motivated earlier ventures in defensive imperialism. He understood that the empire's threats did not necessitate aggressive action. The Roman Empire under Hadrian maintained a substantial insurance policy in the form of well-trained legions, but the emperor saw little reason to set them in motion. Instead he felt that Roman interests were best served by sagacious diplomacy and economic action, both of which were cheaper and delivered more stable outcomes. As a result, according to Dio, 'Hadrian was hated by the people, in spite of his generally excellent reign.'[47] He refused to indulge their fears, nor did he sate their desires for conquest and glory. It took courage for an emperor to restrain Rome, but Hadrian understood its interests better than those he led.

Results of restraint

While restraint may have angered the Roman people, its material results were clear: the empire flourished. Hadrian's grand strategy yielded peace and prosperity, maximising security at a minimum cost. He abandoned quarrelsome areas that were not worth pacifying; he embarked on no new, expensive campaigns; he opened the Roman purse to buy peace, which was immeasurably less costly, in terms of blood and treasure, than conquest would have been; and he shared the imperial largesse with the people. Despite the hand-wringing and disquiet generated by Hadrian's policies, the decades that followed the abandonment of Trajan's conquests were in many ways Rome's greatest, when the empire faced no major, and very few minor, threats. Hadrian handed a far more stable, secure and prosperous empire to his successor than Trajan bequeathed to him.

Hadrian is supposed to have bragged on occasion that he 'achieved more by peace, than others have by war'.[48] Most observers who have examined his boast seem to agree. Some 16 centuries later, English historian Edward Gibbon famously praised the era. 'If a man were called upon to fix that period in the history of the world during which the condition of the human race was most happy and prosperous,' he wrote, 'he would, without hesitation, name that which elapsed from the death of Domitian to the accession of Commodus.'[49] That period, roughly 96–180, was the peak of Pax Romana and the time of the 'five good emperors', of which Hadrian was the middle one. During this time, and for centuries to come, the greatest threats to Rome were internal. Civil war followed Commodus's assassination in 192, and five decades of near-constant internecine fighting marked the middle of the third century, but the Western Roman Empire survived for nearly 340 years after Hadrian's retrenchment. Premonitions of catastrophe that must have accompanied the emperor's grand-strategic decisions were not borne out by events. Restraint worked.

Hadrian's lessons

Presidents of the United States exist in a very different world than did the emperors of Rome, and there is little need to rehash the familiar arguments about the perils of analogical reasoning.[50] Ancient Rome is more than just a foreign country.[51] No one would suggest that its experience holds the answers to all current US challenges, or that a close study of Hadrian's grand strategy would reveal precisely what the United States should do today. History can suggest how to think about grand strategy, however, if not what exactly to think about. Surely it is worth contemplating the experience of other unipolar powers, to try to understand how their leaders made strategy in asymmetric security environments.[52] Hadrian's experience can offer food for a few categories of thought, because he did some things very well. He assessed the dangers that Rome faced in a reasonable, rational manner; he dealt with overstretch in a way that relieved the burden on the imperial treasury, resisting calls for conquest from glory-seeking corners; and he mitigated the risks that accompany retrenchment. Perhaps most fundamentally, Hadrian chose to emphasise Rome's tangible interests over the intangible concerns that his critics focused on, and the empire benefited.

Security environment

The threats of the twenty-first century are not the same as those of the second, but the danger they pose to unipolar powers is comparable. Hadrian had rogue states as well as non-state actors to worry about, and much stronger ones, relatively speaking, than those bedevilling the United States. The Alani, who lurked just beyond Asia Minor, were one such group, as were the Brigantes and other tribes of lower Scotland, who were causing problems as Trajan's rule came to an end. The Jewish revolt of 130 was a more serious threat to systemic stability than any posed by the various Islamist groups that harass the modern West. It involved far more people, including tens of thousands of warriors, and was closely watched by other would-be revolutionaries across the empire.

Still, these were relatively minor actors who did not pose existential threats to the empire. The Jews were not going to sack Rome. In fact, Rome faced no such dangers in the second century. The Parthian Empire, centred in modern-day Iran and Iraq, was more a target than a threat. Roman troops marched into its capital, Ctesiphon, on five separate occasions. The various Germanic tribes who would come to cause so much havoc in future centuries were still rather small and unorganised.[53] The peoples of northern Europe had few permanent settlements and lacked both written language and currency. Towns established in the empire during this era, even those near the imperial boundaries, often were not accompanied by circumvallating walls because they faced no real threats. Hadrian recognised that Rome needed a grand strategy for a safe era, one focused on stability and prosperity rather than security, since the latter was essentially assured.

Like second-century Rome, the United States faces a low level of threat. Security is, it is worth recalling, relative: no state is ever fully safe, just as no individual is ever completely free from danger. As long as ideology, religion or psychopathology are available to inspire non-state actors, there will be threats from within; as long as other states maintain some level of military power, there will be threats from without. The United States will always face danger, which is good news for its politicians and news media, neither of which ever tire of highlighting the various bogeymen lurking in the shadows.

When US security is viewed comparatively, in relation to that of other states, one is hard-pressed to conclude that the United States faces much serious danger. The United States has always been blessed by vast oceans and weak neighbours, and today its power dwarfs not only all potential competitors but most realistic hostile coalitions. If there is any state in an anarchic system that should not fear for its security, it is a unipolar power. By any reasonable measure, the post-Cold War system is much safer for the US than the one that preceded it.[54] Over the past 25 years, the world has experienced a steady decline in all types of warfare, from major wars to small ethno-nationalist conflicts.[55] At the beginning of 2018, for the first time in eight decades, there were no known active nuclear-weapons development programmes whereby states were pursuing their first nuclear bomb – an under-appreciated phenomenon. Nuclear testing has effectively ground to a halt, at least outside of the Korean Peninsula, where Pyongyang is no more (or less, unfortunately) irrational in its behaviour than it was prior to its nuclearisation.[56] Terrorism remains a problem, but hardly an existential threat. The number of failed states is not increasing, and the threat posed by them remains minimal.[57] Since the end of the Cold War, no UN members have disappeared against their will; a few, such as Yugoslavia and Ukraine, have been dismembered, but for the most part conquest is dead. Overall, the era of the 'New Peace', to use Steven Pinker's memorable phrase, is one in which states are essentially safe.[58] The strongest is the safest.

Most members of the US security community do not interpret the steadily accumulating data as evidence of essential American safety. Trump-administration officials in particular inhabit the far end of the threat-perception spectrum. They see danger lurking everywhere, and trust no other states. 'The United States faces an extraordinarily dangerous world,' according to the December 2017 National Security Strategy, which then goes on to paint a rather terrifying picture of threats and evil that can only be met by a strong United States.[59] The president, like the people around him, interprets twenty-first-century danger much more like Trajan than Hadrian, and as a result risks putting his country on a counterproductive path.

The unipolar state is simultaneously the safest and most fearful of all modern great powers.[60] This is not a coincidence. As it turns out, perception and misperception are, in large part, functions of relative power.[61] Asymmetry has important, at times counter-intuitive effects on the formation of images. Threats are more likely to be identified, by core and peripheral states alike, when one power effectively dominates the rest. Misperception is always common in international politics, but in unipolar orders it is the rule. And given the asymmetry of power that such orders contain, such misperception often leads to tragedy. Restraint, in turn, is the antidote to the mistakes fuelled by fear.

Lippmann gaps

The first challenge Hadrian faced was imperial overextension. Rather than make the easy and popular choice to reinforce his predecessor's conquests, to 'double-down' in an attempt to stabilise the new provinces, he pulled the troops back. By doing so, he brought the empire's commitments and resources into balance, and set the foundation for a much more manageable reign. He addressed what two millennia later would be called a 'Lippmann gap' in a way that would be equally prudent today. 'In foreign relations,' wrote columnist Walter Lippmann in 1943, 'a policy has been formed only when commitments and power have been brought into balance.'[62] The art of policymaking, according to this way of thinking, is maintaining a balance, making sure that commitments do not extend beyond that which power can support. Samuel Huntington appears to have been the first to label a disparity between resources and commitments a Lippmann gap, incorporating the term into the lexicon of foreign affairs.[63]

To many observers, the United States operates today inside a Lippmann gap. Its myriad commitments in every corner of the world, from Afghanistan to Yemen, are underfunded and deteriorating. Its defence spending, although enormous, is insufficient to accomplish the expansive goals promoted by its internationalist foreign-policy community. Indications of under-spending seem to be everywhere. Military training and readiness are suffering, rendering the US Navy incapable of navigating in the open water without colliding with civilian vessels. US Secretary of Defense James Mattis told the House Armed Services Committee in June 2017 that he was 'shocked by what I've seen with our readiness to fight … It took us years to get into this situation. It will require years of stable budgets and increased funding to get out of it.'[64] Readers of the Heritage Foundation's *2018 Index of Military Strength* would think that the United States is in imminent danger of being overrun by twenty-first-century barbarians, rather than a unipolar power that spends more on its security than the next eight to ten countries combined.[65] Inside the security community there is a widespread, if hardly universal, impression that the commitments of the United States cannot be fulfilled with its current level of expenditure. The resources the United States devotes to its defence, though substantial relative to that of other states, are insufficient to achieve its goals.

Lippmann gaps can be addressed in other ways. Most obviously, states can bring this hypothetical equation into balance by reducing commitments, and by making foreign policy less costly so the current level of expenditure is sufficient to address security needs. Rarely do modern analysts consider seriously the possibility that US under-spending is not the problem, but rather that US commitments are unsustainably broad and in need of adjustment. Hadrian identified a proto-Lippmann gap and immediately contracted the empire's commitments and cut down its obligations. Such a move by the United States would require a revolution in its grand strategy, one for which Hadrian also provides a precedent.

Restraint and risk

Hadrian implemented a restrained grand strategy, one that relied more on the non-military components of national power to address national goals, without ever neglecting the legions. His actions made it clear that Rome would not pose an offensive threat to its neighbours while he was in charge.

Once that change was made, the basic behavioural norms of the system also changed. The strongest member of any system plays the largest role in determining its character; when Hadrian decided upon restraint, peace and security came not just to the empire, but to the entire region.

A similar option is open to the United States today. The strongest country of the twenty-first century's globalised system will also determine its character, for better or for worse. By keeping its threats in proper perspective, the United States could recognise that its security does not demand robust international military action. By restraining itself, the United States could demonstrate to the world that force should be a last resort, even for the strongest, most capable state in history, and thus do more to promote peace than all its misguided attempts at global policing. And it would waste far less blood and treasure in the process.

The most useful description of restraint remains that of Eric Nordlinger, who more than 20 years ago recommended US grand strategy be built on three pillars: 'minimally effortful national strategy in the security realm; moderately activist policies to advance our liberal ideas among and within states; and a fully activist economic diplomacy on behalf of free trade'.[66] Restraint is thus hardly isolationism. No serious analyst of foreign affairs thinks that states should wall themselves off from the rest of the world, à la Tokugawa Japan. A restrained United States would continue to trade, participate in international organisations and play a role in humanitarian-relief efforts. It would merely define threats, interests and obligations narrowly, and arrange security commitments and military spending accordingly.

Hadrian was able to adjust Roman grand strategy away from Trajanic excess because Rome was the strongest power in its neighbourhood, which gave it a substantial margin for error. Hadrian did not take safety for granted, however, and instituted policies that mitigated the risks inherent in restraint. He kept the legions prepared and their readiness high to assure that the peoples of the periphery did not mistake restraint for weakness. He made examples of transgressors when necessary, although it rarely was. Overall, Roman restraint was not challenged.

Retrenchment need not result in national catastrophe.[67] History is fairly clear on this point. Imperial Spain was the closest thing to a world-spanning empire in the sixteenth and seventeenth centuries. Its slow-motion collapse dealt a serious blow to Spanish glory, but not necessarily to its interests. By the beginning of the eighteenth century, Spain had become a much less significant player in European politics, but its people had been relieved of the burden of paying for an empire. The string of bankruptcies that had been a recurring feature of the monarchy ended, and its young men no longer risked death from Dutch bullets or Peruvian yellow fever. The Spanish were much better off in 1850, by which time Madrid's empire had drastically contracted, than they were two centuries earlier at its height. By almost any reasonable measure, decline was actually good for Spain's tangible, material interests.[68]

The British experience offers much the same lesson: the people of Great Britain are hardly worse off without their empire. Their pride may have suffered during the era of imperial decline, but their interests – their security and prosperity – were unaffected.[69] The cost of lost glory was most acutely paid by elites. Historian Bernard Porter points out that the working classes in England, the masses that constitute the 'silent majority', were mostly indifferent to the loss of the dominions.[70] As it turns out, England was able to adjust rather quickly to the prospect of being a normal state rather than an empire.

Still, as Hadrian understood, insurance is a wise accompaniment to restraint. Fortunately, the United States has plenty. The extraordinary capacity of the United States to respond to emergencies is one of the most important and overlooked lessons from twentieth-century history. Prior to both world wars, Washington maintained a small standing military; by their end, it had produced the best the world had to offer. Surging today might be a bit more difficult, since modern weapons systems are more complex and production chains more globalised. At the end of the 1930s, many under-used production lines stood ready to be transformed toward war production, and a large labour pool was available to fill them. But the capacity of the United States to respond to threats – and the ingenuity of the entrepreneur – should not be underestimated. The United States retains a considerable surge potential at the beginning of the twenty-first century, one that surely could be improved as a hedge against future crises. Richard Betts advocates relying on what he calls a 'mobilization strategy', which would insure against the rise of a peer competitor by 'developing plans and organizing resources now so that military capabilities can be expanded quickly later if necessary'.[71] By concentrating on the maintenance and improvement of its surge capacity, the United States could mitigate risk without spending itself into oblivion addressing threats that currently do not exist.

Internationalists seem curiously unwilling to place trust in the ability of the United States to respond rapidly to future threats, should they arise, acting instead as if restraint would permanently neuter the country and leave it vulnerable to any number of dangers. This need not be the case. We ought not treat retrenchment as if it would herald the end of the second American Century. As Roman experience suggests, it can be a necessary step toward a far greater era, one in which interests and expenditures are aligned to maximise security, prosperity and stability. In the era of the New Peace, when borders have essentially hardened, the United States can pull back without fear. There are no barbarians at the gates.

*   *   *

What would a Hadrianic grand strategy look like today? Addressing the Lippmann gap through contraction would invite a fundamental re-examination of foreign entanglements, including everything from alliances to aid to forward deployments. What good do they serve? Do their costs outweigh their benefits? Most importantly, how much are our policies in place because they serve our pride – the twenty-first-century version of what the Romans called *superbia* – rather than our interests? How much are intangible factors clouding our judgement?

The Romans might have had no concept of the physical laws of inertia, but Hadrian innately understood its political effects. Policies persist unless acted upon by a force. Hadrian must have realised that using political force to alter popular policies entails a cost, but he considered it one worth paying. It is not clear that our modern leaders would be sufficiently courageous to make similar decisions. Only by putting reason ahead of fear, and interest ahead of glory, can the United States hope to scale the heights that Rome reached following Emperor Hadrian's sagacious decisions to make a drastic break with the grand strategy of his predecessors.

Notes

1   David A. Welch is an exception. See his 'Why International Relations Theorists Should Stop Reading Thucydides', *Review of International Studies*, vol. 29, no. 3, July 2003, pp. 301–19.

2   Christopher J. Fettweis, *Psychology of a Superpower: Security and Dominance in U.S. Foreign Policy* (New York: Columbia University Press, 2018).

3   Edward N. Luttwak, *The Grand Strategy of the Roman Empire: From the First Century A.D. to the Third* (Baltimore, MD: Johns Hopkins University Press, 1976).

4   This specific charge is made by J.C. Mann, 'Power, Force and the Frontiers of the Empire', *Journal of Roman Studies*, vol. 69, 1979, pp. 175–83. See also Fergus Millar, 'Emperors, Frontiers and Foreign Relations, 31 B.C. to A.D. 378', *Britannia*, vol. 13, 1982, pp. 1–23; Benjamin Isaac, *The Limits of Empire: The Roman Army in the East* (Oxford: Clarendon Press, 1990), ch. 9; and C.R. Whittaker, *Rome and Its Frontiers: The Dynamics of Empire* (New York: Routledge, 2004), esp. pp. 28–49.

5   Kimberly Kagan, 'Redefining Roman Grand Strategy', *Journal of Military History*, vol. 70, no. 2, April 2006, pp. 333–62, esp. pp. 334–5. One of the best definitions of grand strategy describes it as a guide for national action that encompasses all aspects of national power (military, political, economic, cultural, etc.) both in times of war and peace. Paul Kennedy, 'Grand Strategy in War and Peace: Toward a Broader Definition', in Paul Kennedy (ed.), *Grand Strategies in War and Peace* (New Haven, CT: Yale University Press, 1991), p. 4.

6   In addition to Kagan, see Everett L. Wheeler, 'Methodological Limits and the Mirage of Roman Strategy', *Journal of Military History*, vol. 57, no. 1, January 1993, pp. 7–41 [part 1] and vol. 57, no. 2, April 1993, pp. 215–40 [part 2]; and Arther Ferrill, *Roman Imperial Grand Strategy* (Lanham, MD: University Press of America, 1991).

7   See Elizabeth Speller, *Following Hadrian: A Second-Century Journey through the Roman Empire* (New York: Oxford University Press, 2003).

8   Arthur Eckstein argues that the Republic was not exceptionally imperial or warlike, but was rather shaped by the rules of its time. Arthur M. Eckstein, *Mediterranean Anarchy, Interstate War, and the Rise of Rome* (Berkeley, CA: University of California Press, 2006).

9   For discussions of revisionist and status quo states, see Arnold Wolfers, *Discord and Collaboration: Essays on International Politics* (Baltimore, MD: Johns Hopkins University Press, 1962), pp. 125–6; and Randall L. Schweller, 'Bandwagoning for Profit: Bringing the Revisionist State Back In', *International Security*, vol. 19, no. 1, Summer 1994, pp. 72–107.

10 Tacitus, *Annals*, 1:11.

11 Anthony Everett, *Hadrian and the Triumph of Rome* (New York: Random House, 2009), pp. 107–8. He notes that the nine legions Trajan assembled for the invasion may have been 'the largest army a Roman general had ever commanded'.

12 Florus, *Epitome of Roman History*,
    1:8. Anthropomorphic metaphors
    in Roman sources are discussed by
    Greg Woolf in *Rome: An Empire's Story*
    (New York: Oxford University Press,
    2012), p. 201.

13 Hadrian apparently tried to convince
    people that Trajan secretly endorsed
    a course change, a claim widely
    doubted by his contemporaries. 'These
    measures, unpopular enough in them-
    selves, were still more displeasing to
    the public because of his pretense that
    all acts which he thought would be
    offensive had been secretly enjoined
    upon him by Trajan.' *Historia Augusta*,
    Vol. I, 9:2. Indeed, history contains
    few examples of a dying leader
    imploring a successor to reverse his
    life's work.

14 For speculation about this occurring
    on Hadrian's first day in the purple,
    see Anthony R. Birley, *Hadrian:
    The Restless Emperor* (New York:
    Routledge, 1997), p. 78.

15 *Historia Augusta*, Vol. I, 5:37–42.

16 Cato was speaking specifically about
    the Macedonians, who, 'because they
    could not be held as subjects, should
    be declared free and independent'.
    Historia Augusta, Vol. I, 5:42.

17 Juvenal, *Satire IV*, 111–12. See also
    Everett, *Hadrian and the Triumph of
    Rome*, p. 55.

18 Tacitus, *Annals*, Book IV, 32:1. See also
    Birley, *Hadrian*, p. 116.

19 *Historia Augusta*, Vol. I, 11:7 and 25:7;
    see also 27:1.

20 Daniel Kahneman and Amos Tversky,
    'Prospect Theory: An Analysis of
    Decision under Risk', *Econometrica*,
    vol. 47, no. 2, March 1979, pp. 263–91.
    See also Robert Jervis, 'Political

Implications of Loss Aversion',
Political Psychology, vol. 13, no. 2, June
1992, pp. 17–204.

21 Dio, *The History of Rome*, Vol. VIII, 2:5.

22 Speller, *Following Hadrian*, p. 30. Some
    historians have suggested that the
    four men were leading figures in a fac-
    tion dedicated to Trajan's expansionist
    policies, making their killing an act
    of foreign policy. See Michel Christol
    and Daniel Nony, *Rome et son Empire*
    (Paris: Hachette, 2003), p. 158. This is
    possible, but has no support from the
    ancient sources.

23 Everett describes the popular attitude
    toward Trajan's conquests as 'delight'.
    Hadrian and the Triumph of Rome, p.
    117.

24 For an analysis of the various breads
    and circuses, see Everett, *Hadrian and
    the Triumph of Rome*, pp. 188–90.

25 *Historia Augusta*, Vol. I, 10:1–8.

26 Everett, *Hadrian and the Triumph of
    Rome*, p. 211.

27 Dio, *The History of Rome*, Vol. VIII, 5:1.
    'There were no campaigns of impor-
    tance during his reign', concurs the
    Historia Augusta (Vol. I, 21:8), 'and the
    wars that he did wage were brought
    to a close almost without arousing
    comment.'

28 *Historia Augusta*, Vol. I, 13:8.

29 *Historia Augusta*, Vol. I, 13:9.

30 See Susan P. Mattern, *Rome and
    the Enemy: Imperial Strategy in the
    Principate* (Berkeley, CA: University
    of California Press, 1999), pp. 121 and
    159.

31 See Edward N. Luttwak, *The Grand
    Strategy of the Byzantine Empire*
    (Cambridge, MA: Harvard University
    Press, 2009), *passim*.

32 Dio, *The History of Rome*, Vol. VIII, 9:6.

33   Dio, *The History of Rome*, Vol. VIII, 9:5.

34   Dio, *The History of Rome*, Vol. VIII, 14:1–2.

35   Isaac, *The Limits of Empire*, p. 415.

36   This is the conclusion reached by Isaac in *The Limits of Empire*, pp. 414–15.

37   Brent L. Sterling, *Do Good Fences Make Good Neighbors? What History Teaches Us about Strategic Barriers and International Security* (Washington DC: Georgetown University Press, 2009), pp. 76–7.

38   David J. Breeze and Brian Dobson, *Hadrian's Wall* (London: Allen Lane, 1976); and Isaac, *The Limits of Empire*, p. 414. See also Adrian Goldsworthy, *Hadrian's Wall* (London: Head of Zeus, 2018).

39   Luttwak, *The Grand Strategy of the Roman Empire*, pp. 88–9.

40   Sterling also speculates about the possibility that the walls were built to make restraint permanent. *Do Good Fences Make Good Neighbors?*, p. 77.

41   Birley, *Hadrian*, p. 116.

42   For the influence of glory on foreign-policy decisions, see Christopher J. Fettweis, *The Pathologies of Power: Fear, Honor, Glory, and Hubris in U.S. Foreign Policy* (New York: Cambridge University Press, 2013), ch. 3.

43   The Athenians remind the Melians of this during their famous dialogue. Thucydides, *History of the Peloponnesian War*, Book V, 107.

44   For good reviews, see Robert M. Errington, *The Dawn of Empire: Rome's Rise to Power* (London: Hamish Hamilton Ltd., 1971); Erich S. Gruen, *The Hellenistic World and the Coming of Rome* (Berkeley, CA: University of California Press, 1986); and P.A. Brunt, *Roman Imperial Themes* (Oxford: Clarendon Press, 1990), esp. p. 102.

45   Quoted by William V. Harris in *War and Imperialism in Republican Rome, 327–70 B.C.* (Oxford: Clarendon Press, 1985), p. 164.

46   Joseph A. Schumpeter, *Imperialism and Social Classes* (Oxford: Basil Blackwell, 1951), p. 65.

47   Dio, *The History of Rome*, Vol. VIII, 23:2.

48   The only source we have for this oft-quoted boast (in Hadrian circles, at least) – *plus se otio adeptum quam armis ceteros* – is a booklet about the manners of the Caesars sometimes attributed to the unknown Sextus Aurelius Victor called *Epitome De Caesaribus*, 14:10, written at the end of the fourth century.

49   Edward Gibbon, *The History of the Decline and Fall of the Roman Empire* (New York: Penguin, 2000), p. 83.

50   The arguments are sufficiently hashed out by Ernest May, *'Lessons' of the Past: The Uses and Misuses of History in American Foreign Policy* (New York: Oxford University Press, 1973); Richard E. Neustadt and Ernest R. May, *Thinking in Time: The Uses of History for Policymakers* (New York: Free Press, 1986); and Yuen Foong Khong, *Analogies at War: Korea, Munich, Dien Bien Phu and the Vietnam Decisions of 1965* (Princeton, NJ: Princeton University Press, 1992).

51   The reference here is to David Lowenthal, *The Past is a Foreign Country* (New York: Cambridge University Press, 1999).

52   It will be easier to convince the modern reader that the ancient Mediterranean was more unipolar than the international system of 2017.

Many observers, especially in the age of Trump-induced pessimism, doubt that the United States asserts the influence it once did in the international system. See Simon Reich and Richard Ned Lebow, *Good-Bye Hegemony! Power and Influence in the Global System* (Princeton, NJ: Princeton University Press, 2014). While this may be true, it also conflates influence with power. In terms of raw, measurable national capability, there is little doubt that one state towers over all others. 'The question [of polarity] is an empirical one,' wrote Kenneth Waltz, 'and common sense can answer it.' Kenneth N. Waltz, *Theory of International Politics* (Reading, MA: Addison-Wesley Pub. Co., 1979), p. 131. Despite scepticism in some quarters, common sense – and the overwhelming preponderance of the evidence – suggests that the world remains unambiguously unipolar. The classification and defence of unipolarity is discussed at length by Fettweis in *Psychology of a Superpower*, ch. 1.

53   For a great discussion of the evolution of these groups and their implications for the empire, see Peter Heather, *The Fall of the Roman Empire: A New History of Rome and the Barbarians* (New York: Oxford University Press, 2006).

54   See the essays in Christopher A. Preble and John Mueller (eds), *A Dangerous World? Threat Perception and U.S. National Security* (Washington DC: Cato Institute, 2014).

55   For the data, see the Human Security Report Project, *Human Security Report 2013: The Decline in Global Violence* (Vancouver: Human Security Press, 2013); Monty G. Marshall and Benjamin R. Cole, *Global Report 2014: Conflict, Governance, and State Fragility* (Vienna, VA: Center for Systemic Peace, 2014); and David A. Backer, Ravi Bhavnani and Paul K. Huth (eds), *Peace and Conflict 2016* (New York: Routledge, 2016). The most comprehensive analysis is Steven Pinker, *The Better Angels of Our Nature: Why Violence Has Declined* (New York: Viking, 2011), but see also Robert Jervis, 'Theories of War in an Era of Leading Power Peace', *American Political Science Review*, vol. 96, no. 1, March 2002, pp. 1–14; John Mueller, *The Remnants of War* (Ithaca, NY: Cornell University Press, 2004); Christopher J. Fettweis, *Dangerous Times? The International Politics of Great Power Peace* (Washington DC: Georgetown University Press, 2010); Richard Ned Lebow, *Why Nations Fight: Past and Future Motives for War* (New York: Cambridge University Press, 2010); and Joshua Goldstein, *Winning the War on War* (New York: Dutton, 2011).

56   On North Korea's essential rationality, see Dennis Roy, 'North Korea and the "Madman Theory"', *Security Dialogue*, vol. 25, no. 3, September 1994, pp. 307–16; Leon V. Sigal, *Disarming Strangers: Nuclear Diplomacy with North Korea* (Princeton, NJ: Princeton University Press, 1998); David C. Kang, 'International Relations Theory and the Second Korean War', *International Studies Quarterly*, vol. 47, no. 3, September 2003, pp. 301–24; and Victor D. Cha, 'Five Myths about North Korea', *Washington Post*, 10 December 2010.

57   Michael J. Mazarr in 'The Rise and Fall of the Failed-State Paradigm: Requiem

for a Decade of Distraction', *Foreign Affairs*, vol. 93, no. 1, January/February 2014, pp. 113–21.

58 Pinker, *The Better Angels of Our Nature*, pp. 295–377.

59 The White House, *National Security Strategy of the United States of America* (Washington DC: Government Printing Office, December 2017), p. 1.

60 For an elaboration of this point, see Fettweis, *Pathologies of Power*, esp. ch. 1, 'Fear'.

61 See Fettweis, *Psychology of a Superpower, passim*.

62 Walter Lippmann, *U.S. Foreign Policy: Shield of the Republic* (Boston, MA: Little, Brown and Company, 1943), p. 7.

63 Samuel P. Huntington, 'Coping with the Lippmann Gap', *Foreign Affairs*, vol. 66, no. 3, 1987/88, pp. 453–77.

64 Sandra Erwin, 'Mattis is "Shocked" by U.S. Military Readiness Crisis', National Interest Online, 13 June 2017, available at http://nationalinterest.org/blog/the-buzz/mattis-shocked-by-us-military-readiness-crisis-21132.

65 Heritage Foundation, *2018 Index of U.S. Military Strength*, October 2017, available at http://www.heritage.org/military-strength.

66 Eric A. Nordlinger, *Isolationism Reconfigured: American Foreign Policy for a New Century* (Princeton, NJ: Princeton University Press, 1995),

p. 4. See also Eugene Gholz, Daryl G. Press and Harvey M. Sapolsky, 'Come Home America: The Strategy of Restraint in the Face of Temptation', *International Security*, vol. 21, no. 4, Spring 1997, pp. 5–48; Christopher A. Preble, *The Power Problem: How American Military Dominance Makes Us Less Safe, Less Prosperous and Less Free* (Ithaca, NY: Cornell University Press, 2009); and Barry Posen, *Restraint: A New Foundation for U.S. Grand Strategy* (Ithaca, NY: Cornell University Press, 2014).

67 Paul K. MacDonald and Joseph A. Parent, 'Graceful Decline: The Surprising Success of Great Power Retrenchment', *International Security*, vol. 35, no. 4, Spring 2011, pp. 7–44.

68 William S. Maltby, *The Rise and Decline of the Spanish Empire* (New York: Palgrave Macmillan, 2008), pp. 191–2.

69 George L. Bernstein, *The Myth of Decline: The Rise of Britain Since 1945* (London: Pimlico, 2004).

70 Bernard Porter, *The Lion's Share: A Short History of British Imperialism 1850–1995* (New York: Longman, 1996), pp. 290–2 and 346–7. See also Bernstein, *The Myth of Decline*, pp. 9–10.

71 Richard K. Betts, 'A Disciplined Defense: How to Regain Strategic Solvency', *Foreign Affairs*, vol. 86, no. 6, November/December 2007, pp. 67–80.

Nation Building: Why Some Countries Come Together While Others Fall Apart

Andreas Wimmer

Why do some countries fall apart, often along their ethnic fault lines, while others have held together over decades and centuries, despite governing an equally diverse population? Why is it, in other words, that nation building succeeds in some places while it fails in others? What happens when political integration fails is dramatically demonstrated by the current tragedy in Syria. Outside of the Western-media spotlight, South Sudan and the Central African Republic have gone through similar experiences in recent years. In some rich and democratic countries in Western Europe, such as Spain, Belgium and the United Kingdom, long-standing secessionist movements have regained momentum. They may very well succeed, within a couple of years or a generation, to break these states apart. Why, on the other hand, is there no secessionist movement among the Cantonese speakers of southern China or among the Tamils of India? Why has no serious politician ever questioned national unity in such diverse countries as Switzerland and Burkina Faso? Because in such countries, I will argue, three long-term, slow-moving political processes encouraged ties of political alliance and support to stretch across ethnic divides: the early development of civil-society organisations, the rise of a state capable of providing public goods evenly across a territory, and the emergence of a shared medium of communication.

Andreas Wimmer is Lieber Professor of Sociology and Political Philosophy at Columbia University. His most recent book is *Nation Building: Why Some Countries Come Together While Others Fall Apart* (Princeton University Press, 2018).

Survival | vol. 60 no. 4 | August–September | pp. 151–164   DOI 10.1080/00396338.2018.1495442

What is nation building – and what is it not?

Most American policymakers believe that democracy is the best tool to achieve political cohesion in the global South – so much so that many have equated nation building with democratisation.[1] Democratic elections draw diverse ethnic constituencies towards the political centre, or so the argument goes, by encouraging politicians to build broad coalitions beyond the pool of voters that share their own ethnic background. To be sure, almost all states that have failed at nation building and are governed by minority elites are autocratic, like Syria under Alawi rule. Conversely, democratic countries are on average more likely to include minority representatives in their ruling coalitions.

However, this is not so because societies *become* more inclusionary over time after transitioning to democracy. In many recently democratised countries, ethnic majorities sweep to power only to take revenge on hitherto dominant ethnic elites and their followers. Iraq after the fall of Saddam Hussein showed this clearly: much of al-Qaeda's and the Islamic State's domestic support came from the former Ba'ath elites and from disaffected Sunni tribes that resented having lost the power they had held under Saddam Hussein. Furthermore, some democracies have excluded even sizeable minorities for generations. The United States maintained slavery during the first 70 years of its democratic existence and denied African Americans any meaningful form of political representation for another full century after slavery ended. Democracy and inclusion go hand in hand because countries that are *already* governed by a more inclusive coalition will democratise earlier than exclusionary regimes that fight democracy tooth and nail. In a nutshell: democracy doesn't build nations, but nations that are already built democratise more easily.

There are two main aspects of nation building: the extension of political alliances across the terrain of a country (the political-integration aspect); and the emergence of a sense of loyalty to and identification with the institutions of the state, independent of who currently governs (the political-identity aspect). To foster both, political ties between citizens and the state need to reach across ethnic divides. Such ties of alliance connect national governments directly with individual citizens or indirectly through political organisations – voluntary associations, parties, professional groups and so on. Ideally, all citizens are linked into these networks of alliances centred on the state, and thus see themselves represented at the centre of power. Even if their favourite party or political patron is not currently occupying one of the seats of government, there will be other ties to powerful politicians of their own ethnic background whom individuals can perceive as 'one of their own'. In such inclusive regimes, intellectuals and political elites, as well as the average individual, will define the national community in broad terms to include all citizens equally and irrespective of their racial or ethnic background.

Nation building has important and positive consequences. Cross-cutting alliances de-politicise ethnic divisions such that politics is not perceived as a zero-sum game in which ethnic groups struggle over who controls the state. Rather, more substantial policy issues concerning what the state should actually do can come to the foreground. Furthermore, inclusive coalitions foster a sense of ownership of the state and promote the idea of a collective purpose beyond one's family, village, clan or profession. Thus, citizens of inclusionary countries will identify with and feel loyal to the nation, rather than their ethnic group, social class or region.[2] Even the best crafted of propaganda mechanisms – flag rituals, the collective singing of anthems, tombs of unknown soldiers – cannot produce such a shared identity. It emerges only when one sees one's own people in the seats of government. Citizens who identify with the nation, in turn, are less resistant to paying taxes and supporting a welfare state, and are governed by more effective states.[3] Even more importantly, inclusive coalitions that comprise minorities and majorities alike reduce the risk of civil war[4] and promote economic growth.[5]

What are the conditions under which such coalitions emerge? There are ways of analysing the alliances between individuals and the state: organisational, political-economic and communicative. For each of these aspects, a crucial factor can be identified that enables alliances to reach across regional and ethnic divides, generating a more inclusive coalition. Comparisons between Switzerland and Belgium, Botswana and Somalia, and Russia and China illuminate how these factors shape the historical process.

Networks of voluntary organisations: Switzerland and Belgium

The organisational perspective focuses on the institutional form that political alliances between the state and its citizens assume. They can appear in an ad hoc form, as when a citizen exchanges her vote against a politician's promise to implement a specific policy, or in the form of personalised patronage relationships in which the political loyalty of a client is exchanged against the patron's support in the event of a future emergency. They can be fully institutionalised, as in countries with strong, independent parties; or they can appear as networks of ties between state institutions and voluntary organisations such as local political clubs, professional associations and the like.

It is easiest to establish ties across ethnic divides if a dense network of such voluntary organisations already exists. These organisations bundle individual interests, such that politicians or state agencies can connect with them more efficiently. In patronage systems, by contrast, each individual alliance needs to be taken care of separately. Furthermore, voluntary organisations can build horizontal alliances with one another. Local nursing associations in California, for example, can form a statewide coalition. In patronage systems, by contrast, ties proliferate vertically between patrons and clients who in turn become the patrons of other clients further down the pyramid of power and influence. Alliance networks built on voluntary organisations therefore proliferate across the territory and across ethnic divides, while this is less frequently the case with patronage systems, which often remain mono-ethnic. It is easy, to stick with the example, to found a nationwide umbrella organisation of all nursing associations, which might then be tied to state institutions or to a political party that controls the state.

How far such voluntary organisations have developed matters especially in the early years of a country's modern existence, that is, after an absolutist monarchy has been overthrown or a former colony has become independent. If a dense web of such organisations has already emerged, the new power-holders can tap into these networks to mobilise supporters and to recruit political leaders. The political exclusion of ethnic minorities or even majorities becomes less likely under these circumstances: voluntary organisations have often already developed branches in different parts of the country inhabited by different ethnic communities. The support base of the new leaders and the leadership itself will therefore be multi-ethnic as well.

This can be shown empirically by comparing Switzerland and Belgium. In Switzerland, civil-society organisations – shooting clubs, reading circles, choral societies and so on – developed throughout the territory during the late eighteenth century and first half of the nineteenth century. They spread evenly because all major regions developed economically and because the small city-states of which Switzerland was composed lacked both the capacity and the motivation to suppress their growth. In Belgium, by contrast, Napoleon, as well as the Dutch king who succeeded him, suppressed these associations. More importantly, Belgian associations remained confined to the more economically developed and more educated French-speaking regions and segments of the population.

When Belgium became independent of the kingdom of the Netherlands in 1831, the new rulers of the country were linked into these French-speaking associational networks. Without giving it much thought, they declared French the official language of the administration, army and judiciary. Individuals who spoke Flemish only were not part of these associational networks and were therefore not represented in central government, despite forming a slight demographic majority. In Belgium, therefore, the Flemish were ruled as an internal colony until the end of the century. Early nation building failed and language issues became heavily politicised later in the century. The country is now close to breaking apart along the linguistic divide.

In Switzerland, the transition to the nation-state occurred after a brief civil war in 1848. The liberal elites who won the war and dominated the country for generations relied on the existing cross-regional, multi-ethnic networks of civil-society organisations to recruit followers and leaders. The power structure that emerged therefore had a multi-ethnic character as well: each language group was represented in the highest level of government as well as the federal administration, roughly according to the size of its population. French, German and Italian became official languages of the state. Language diversity was a political non-issue during most of the subsequent political history of the country, and remains so to this day.

State provision of public goods: Botswana and Somalia

The political-economy aspect of the ties between the state and its citizens concerns the resources that they exchange. Citizens are more likely to politically support a government that provides public goods in exchange for the taxes, dues and fees collected from them. The relationship between government and citizen is then no longer based on extraction under the threat of force – as was typically the case for the more coercive regimes that preceded the nation-state, such as an absolutist kingdom, an imperial governor or a colonial administration. The more a government is capable of providing public goods across all regions of a country, the more attractive it will be as an exchange partner, and the more citizens will attempt to establish an alliance with it. The composition of government will reflect such encompassing alliance structures and thus the ethnic diversity of the population. Citizens that receive public goods in return for their political loyalty and their taxes are also more likely to embrace the nationalist rhetoric generated and propagated by governing elites and their intellectual aides.

Somalia and Botswana illustrate this second mechanism. When Botswana became an independent country in 1966, its government efficiently created and managed export opportunities for cattle breeders; massively expanded transportation infrastructure, schools and health facilities; and created emergency programmes to address droughts that periodically devastated the cattle economy. These initiatives profited all regions equally, and there is little evidence that bureaucrats favoured their own ethnic groups when allocating these resources to specific villages or districts. Correspondingly, the ruling party gained support across regions and ethnic constituencies, which in turn translated into a parliament and cabinet that showed no signs of ethno-political inequality. This inclusionary power configuration then produced, over time, a strong identification with the state and the Tswana majority, into which more and more minority individuals assimilated over time.

In Somalia, conditions for nation building through public-goods provision were less favourable. After the formerly British and Italian colonies were unified into an independent state, there was little capacity to provide public goods to the population overall. The rapidly expanding bureaucracy was nourished by foreign aid rather than domestic taxes. When it came to distributing government projects, bureaucrats favoured those who could afford the highest bribe or members of their own clan and lineage. Mohamed Siad Barre's military coup in 1969 changed this dynamic only temporarily. Given the lack of institutional capacity, his regime tried to provide public goods through short-term, military-style campaigns, such as the one to bring relief to drought victims. No durable political alliances centred on the national government could be built in this way. Barre therefore had to base his rule increasingly on loyal followers from his own clan. Those left out resented this ethnic tilting of the power structure. Decades of civil war fuelled by changing alliances among clans and warlords have broken the country into pieces.

Shared medium of communication: China and Russia

Establishing ties across regions and across ethnic divides is easier if individuals can converse with each other in a shared language. This decreases 'transaction costs', meaning the effort needed to understand each other's intentions, to solve disagreements and negotiate compromise, and thus to build durable relationships of trust. Linguistic divides therefore slow down the spread of political networks across the territory of a country. Compare China and Russia from the early nineteenth century to the end of the twentieth century. China's population speaks many different tongues, which should make nation building more difficult. However, letters, newspapers and books have been written in a uniform script, allowing individuals from different corners of the vast country to understand one another effortlessly. The Chinese writing system is logogrammatic and, in contrast to European languages, disconnects sign from sound. Until the middle of the twentieth century, Chinese was pronounced differently depending on the actual language spoken by a person. The script therefore is equally accessible to speakers of all the various Chinese languages.

Throughout the imperial period, scriptural homogeneity enabled the national government to recruit a bureaucratic elite through a system of written examinations administered in all regions of the country, none of which was disadvantaged because its spoken language differed from that of the centre. This ensured that the elite was as polyglot as the population at large. The same held true for the political factions that formed among its members, as men who could not understand one another when speaking could correspond in writing to exchange ideas and form an alliance.

The anti-imperial, republican associations that emerged in the late nine-teenth century also had a polyglot membership. After these forces rose to power under the Kuomintang and overthrew the imperial dynasty in 1911, the power structure remained multi-regional and showed few signs of a lin-guistic tilt. The same can be said of the Communist Party that took power in 1949. Given the inclusive nature of the ruling coalition, no linguistic nation-alism ever emerged among the non-Mandarin-speaking groups of the Han majority. The Han were imagined as a multilingual but ethnically homoge-neous nation. The dogs of linguistic nationalism have never barked among China's Han majority.

They have barked throughout the modern history of Russia, however, and the empire twice fell apart along ethno-linguistic lines: after the Bolshevik revolution in October 1917 and again in the thaw of Mikhail Gorbachev's reforms around 1989. One of the reasons is that it is difficult to form political alliances across a population that speaks a great many languages of entirely different linguistic stock, from Finnish to German, from Russian to Turkish, from Korean to Romanian. In stark contrast to China, moreover, these lan-guages were also written in different scripts, including in Latin, Arabic, Cyrillic and Mongolian. When the age of mass politics set in during the late nineteenth century, alliance networks tended to cluster along linguistic lines because reaching a literate public through propaganda and news-papers demanded a shared script and language. The popular parties that emerged during the last decade of the nineteenth and the first decades of the twentieth centuries therefore either catered exclusively to specific linguistic communities (Armenians, Georgians, Finns, Poles) or at best represented a patchwork of linguistically confined alliance networks. National conscious-ness became cast in dozens of separate, linguistically defined moulds rather than in an overarching identity comparable to that of the Han Chinese.

The Soviet nationalities policy after the 1917 revolution cemented this state of affairs by alphabetising and educating minorities in their own language. Their elites were allowed to rule the new, linguistically defined provinces and districts under Moscow's tight supervision. This ensured that clientelist networks formed within separate ethnic compartments. Minorities continued to be heavily under-represented in the party leadership, the highest ranks of the bureaucracy and the army. It is not surprising, then, that the USSR was not able to forge an integrated 'Soviet people' even after it shifted to a more assimilationist policy under Khrushchev. The political field continued to resemble a patchwork of siloed ethnic groups, and the country finally fell apart along these linguistic fault lines.

State formation and nation building

Why are some countries better at providing public goods to their citizens, and why are some populations more linguistically fragmented than others? Both state capacity and linguistic homogeneity appear to be historical legacies of centralised states already established before colonisation and before the transition to the modern nation-state. Where highly centralised polities had developed, bureaucratic administrations learned how to organisationally integrate and politically control the various regions of the state. The governments of newly formed nation-states could rely on this know-how and bureaucratic infrastructure to provide public goods equitably across regions. Over the very long run, such highly centralised states also encouraged peripheral elites and their followers to adopt the language (or in the Chinese case, the script) of the central elites. This promoted their own careers and allowed them to lay claim to the prestigious 'high' culture of the political centre. In pre-colonial Botswana, a series of centralised and tightly integrated kingdoms had emerged, ruled by Tswana-speaking noblemen. Once subsumed and subdued by the post-colonial government, these kingdoms greatly facilitated the provision of public goods by the central state, affording it legitimacy as well as an institutional infrastructure on which to build an administration. They also promoted, throughout the pre-colonial, colonial and post-colonial periods, the assimilation of non-Tswana populations into the dominant Tswana language.

In Somalia's history, no centralised polity governing the interior of the country and its nomad majority ever emerged. This was a notable impediment to post-colonial public-goods provision. China's extraordinarily high levels of political centralisation over millennia provided the background for the emergence and empire-wide adoption of the unified script, as well as the assimilation of a wide variety of political elites into the neo-Confucian canons of the empire. Centralised indigenous states, on which colonial rule often rested, therefore provided an important background condition for successful nation building because they left the dual legacy of a bureaucratic-political infrastructure and a uniform language or script.

Beyond case studies: a global analysis

These case studies don't permit the assessment of the differing relative influences of the three mechanisms they illustrate. Somalis, for example, all speak the same language, while Switzerland is linguistically more diverse, yet their two histories of nation building diverge. Compared to Switzerland, China lacked much civil-society development up to 1911, yet a trans-ethnic alliance structure emerged in both.

Furthermore, other factors could be crucial for nation building. Firstly, colonial experience could make a difference. Countries like Somalia and Botswana suffered from the divide-and-rule policies of colonial powers, which could have made post-colonial nation building more difficult in those countries than in Switzerland and Russia, which were never colonised. Secondly, nation building may be a function of economic development. Switzerland had a successful export industry and became an international centre for banking and insurance, while Botswana had diamonds. Somalia and China, by contrast, remained poor agricultural economies for generations. Thirdly, the structure of ethnic cleavages may matter. Where linguistic and religious divides reinforce each other, as in Romanov Russia, nation building might be more difficult than in Switzerland, where speakers of the same language are separated by religion. Finally, nation building may work best where countries have fought wars with other countries, gluing their citizens together by mobilising them for total war and instilling in them a strong sense of national solidarity. Similarly, centuries of boundary adjustments and ethnic cleansings in Europe may have led to more homogeneous populations that are easier to integrate into a national polity. Yet there is not much support for these other possible explanations of nation building. Statistically, countries are not more likely to fail at nation building if they were subjected to colonial rule for a very long time or if that rule assumed a specific form (such as settler colonialism or indirect rule); if their economies are underdeveloped; if they have no history of inter-state wars or ethnonationalist conflicts; or if religious and linguistic cleavages overlap.

The three mechanisms specified above – organisational, political-economic and communicative – turn out to be the best predictors of nation building. To measure how successful nation building has been, one can calculate a country's population share of the ethnic communities represented at the highest level of government. Data is available from 1946 to 2005 and for 155 countries.[6] The data shows that political exclusion is less pronounced where voluntary associations have spread among a population, where the state is providing public goods, and where the linguistic landscape is more uniform. Literacy rates, strongly influenced by public school systems, measure public-goods provision. The global mean is 65%. Statistical analysis shows that if 80% of the adult population can read and write in a country, the share of the excluded population will be roughly 30% lower than in a country in which only half of the population is literate. The probability that two randomly chosen citizens speak the same language measures linguistic diversity. The global mean is 38%. If the probability is 52%, the share of the excluded population will be about 30% lower than in a country where the likelihood is only 25%. The share of the excluded population is also reduced by roughly the same amount if a society with 12 voluntary associations per 500 individuals – the global mean is four per 500 – is compared with a society that has a negligible number of voluntary organisations.

Finally, the analysis also shows that where highly centralised states had emerged before the colonial interlude and before the transition to the nation-state, contemporary governments provided more public goods and the population spoke fewer tongues. This forms another crucial element of the tectonic view on nation building advocated here. To demonstrate, there are two useful sources on the history of state formation. The first is available for 74 countries of Asia and Africa whose pre-colonial political structures were documented by social anthropologists. The second, collected by economists, covers 141 countries and measures how far an indigenous state controlled the territory of a present-day country during the second half of the nineteenth century. To illustrate, increasing the share of the population that lived in states (as opposed to stateless societies) before colonisation by 40% increases post-war literacy rates by roughly 9%, and the chances that two randomly chosen individuals in the early 1960s spoke the same language by 17%. The effects are similar if the second data source, which measures levels of state development in the late nineteenth century with an index that runs from 0 to 50, is used. If this index is increased by 12 points, 4% more adults were likely to read and write and there was a 10% higher chance that two citizens spoke the same language in the early 1960s.

*　　*　　*

Obviously, the past cannot be engineered retrospectively to create a historical state that would favour contemporary nation building. Nor can a state's capacity to provide public goods be enhanced in a couple of years. A shared language of communication cannot be taught to a population within a short time span. Voluntary organisations around which political alliances coalesce will not take root in a society over the short run. The time it takes to develop these three crucial political factors is measured in generations, not years. Fixing failed states or building nations therefore cannot be done within the time span of an American presidency or two.

Over at least two decades or so, global institutions such as the World Bank have attempted to build the institutional capacity to provide public goods in developing countries. This steady emphasis on governance and capacity building represents a welcome corrective to the more erratic foreign policies that elected governments of Western countries often pursue. A consistent and long-term commitment to strengthening government institutions and making them more efficient at public-goods delivery represents the best international policy to help nation building around the world.

Public goods should be provided by national and local governments, rather than private agencies, foreign NGOs or intervening armies. Public goods provided by outside forces do little to enhance the legitimacy of the national government. According to the *Survey of the Afghan People,* conducted by the Asia Foundation annually from 2006 to 2015, public-goods projects conducted by foreigners are far less effective in creating satisfaction with the national government or in motivating citizens to turn to government institutions to solve their local disputes, rather than to traditional authorities or warlords. It is especially disheartening to find that Afghans think more positively about the Taliban after foreigners have sponsored public-goods projects in their district.

A coherent strategy for nation building must also promote the communicative integration of a country by supporting its unified school system. Countries around the world have come a long way in schooling their populations and teaching them to speak a common language. Continued support for national school systems in the face of budgetary pressures is therefore a meaningful long-term strategy not only to achieve sustained growth and gender equity, but also to foster nation building.

In addition, indigenous civil-society organisations merit international support. Such support can lead to political backlash, as shown by the recent crackdowns on foreign-funded NGOs in many Eastern European countries. But in the long run, such organisations will provide a political infrastructure that helps establish ties across ethnic divides and foster political integration.

Finally, and admittedly more problematically, outside support for groups that fight for a more inclusionary regime and that are themselves built on a multi-ethnic coalition may enhance prospects for nation building in the long run. As history shows, highly exclusionary, minority-dominated regimes like the one ruling contemporary Syria can often be overcome only through armed struggle. Peaceful transitions such as South Africa's are rare. Violence in the present, then, is sometimes the price to be paid for the sustainable peace that political integration and nation building offer. Nothing guarantees, however, that new rulers after a violent regime change will not simply turn the tables, excluding the hitherto dominant groups from political representation in national government. One good example among many is how Iraqi Shia political elites marginalised Sunni politicians after the American invasion.

Insistence on arrangements for power-sharing, despite all its well-documented flaws,[7] might therefore still be the best option available for outside powers with some leverage in the local political arena. Few observers today would harbour the illusion that effectuating such arrangements is easy. The difficulties of implementing them against the will of major political forces are well illustrated by the case of Iraq, and perhaps even more dramatically by that of Bosnia, which would have fallen apart long ago if left to its own fate. Policymakers should therefore reject the idea that it is feasible to 'teach other people to govern themselves', as a prominent intellectual put it at the height of the nation-building enthusiasm of the George W. Bush era.[8] To build nations from the outside is next to impossible if local conditions are not conducive to putting minorities as well as majorities on an equitable political footing.

Notes

1 James Dobbins, 'America's Role in Nation-Building: From Germany to Iraq', *Survival*, vol. 45, no. 4, Winter 2003–04, pp. 87–110; Francis Fukuyama, 'Nation-Building 101', *Atlantic*, January–February 2004.

2 Andreas Wimmer, 'Power and Pride: National Identity and Ethno-Political Inequality Around the World', *World Politics*, vol. 69, no. 4, October 2017, pp. 1–35.

3 Pelle Ahlerup and Gustav Hansson, 'Nationalism and Government Effectiveness', *Journal of Comparative Economics*, vol. 39, no. 3, September 2011, pp. 431–51; Salwei Qari, Kai A. Konrad and Benny Geys, 'Patriotism, Taxation and International Mobility', *Public Choice*, vol. 151, no. 3, June 2012, pp. 695–717; Kai A. Konrad and Salmai Qari, 'The Last Refuge of a Scoundrel? Patriotism and Tax Compliance', *Economica*, vol. 79, no. 315, July 2012, pp. 516–33.

4 Andreas Wimmer, Lars-Erik Cedarman and Brian Min, 'Ethnic Politics and Armed Conflict: A Configurational Analysis of a New Global Data Set', *American Sociological Review*, vol. 74, no. 2, April 2009, pp. 316–37.

5 Alberto Alesina, Stelios Michalopoulos and Elias Papaioannou, 'Ethnic Inequality', *Journal of Political Economy*, vol. 124, no. 2, April 2016, pp. 428–88.

6 Wimmer et al., 'Ethnic Politics and Armed Conflict'.

7 Philip G. Roeder, 'Power Dividing as an Alternative to Ethnic Power Sharing', in Philip G. Roeder and Donald Rothchild, *Sustainable Peace: Power and Democracy After Civil War* (Ithaca, NY: Cornell University Press, 2005), pp. 51–82.

8 Fukuyama, 'Nation-Building 101'.

The Security Implications of Synthetic Biology

Gigi Gronvall

Consumers have grown accustomed to personalised products. There are T-shirts made to order, books printed on demand, music-streaming services that cater to individual tastes, personalised news feeds and lists of suggested apps. This trend towards personalisation has even been extended to biology: genetic information and biological techniques can now be used by individuals to meet their personal needs. Biological information, such as the number of steps one takes in a day, one's heart rate or one's genetic code, has become trackable, and can be compiled for individualised purposes. Biological laboratory techniques, once the sole purview of scientific professionals, are likewise becoming increasingly accessible to amateurs, yielding information such as what a person eats or where they live.

The trend towards the personalisation of biology would not be possible without synthetic biology, a growing technical field that aims to make biology easier to engineer. Synthetic biology is widely seen as an exciting new branch of the life sciences, but can be difficult to define.[1] One group of researchers has described synthetic biology as 'a) the design and fabrication of biological components and systems that do not already exist in the natural world and b) the re-design and fabrication of existing biological systems'.[2] Others define synthetic biology in terms of what the field aims to do: make biology easier to engineer.[3] While bioengineering has been around

Gigi Gronvall is a Senior Scholar at the Johns Hopkins Center for Health Security and an Associate Professor at the Johns Hopkins Bloomberg School of Public Health, Department of Environmental Health and Engineering. She is also the author of *Synthetic Biology: Safety, Security, and Promise* (Health Security Press, 2016).

Survival | vol. 60 no. 4 | August–September | pp. 165–180   DOI 10.1080/00396338.2018.1495443

for a while, synthetic biology is more powerful: it has been described as 'genetic engineering on steroids' by one of its founding practitioners.[4] Synthetic-biology tools, such as CRISPR (clustered regularly interspaced short palindromic repeats) for gene editing, gene synthesis and gene drives,[5] are being used in a wide range of life sciences.

Scientists working in synthetic biology envision a time when biological traits, functions and products may be programmed like a computer. While there is a great deal of research yet to be done to allow for this, the convergence of high-speed computing power, intense research interest and some early commercial successes during the last decade has spurred the growth of the field. Publications about synthetic biology have increased from 170 per year in 2000–05 to more than 1,200 per year in 2015.[6] More than 700 research organisations in over 40 countries are undertaking work in the field.[7]

One major outcome of this growth is that biology is becoming industrialised. While biological processes have long been used in industrial settings – for example, to produce some medicines and vaccines, as well as certain consumer products such as beer and wine – they are increasingly being exploited for manufacturing, replacing the use of petrochemicals and resource-intensive harvesting from nature. Synthetic biology is now used to alter the internal machinery of microbes so that they produce a variety of desired molecules, from biofuels to flavour compounds to pharmaceuticals.[8] This has expanded the biological footprint of a range of industries including fuel, agriculture, medicines and mining, and of products such as construction materials, perfumes, fibres and adhesives. The economic implications of synthetic biology are vast and growing: the global market was valued at $3.9 billion in 2016, and is anticipated to grow at an annual rate of 24.4% to reach over $11bn by 2021.[9] McKinsey and Company has reported that the total economic impact of synthetic biology, including applications in energy, agriculture and chemicals, could reach $700bn to $1.6 trillion annually by 2025.[10]

While clearly useful on an industrial scale, synthetic biology can also be useful to individuals. It can yield information that would never merit a traditional research grant from the National Institutes of Health (NIH) or the Wellcome Trust. In contrast to the research funded by agencies like these, which is intended to foster benefits at a societal level, personalisation allows for the acquisition of information and products that are immediately useful to particular individuals. Scientific advances and the democratisation of synthetic biology should bring about an exciting future, but will also lead to changes in national and international security, the governance of biological research, and safety.

Do-it-yourself biology

Synthetic biology has already produced one of the most promising developments in cancer treatments for years, known as chimeric antigen receptor T-cell therapy, or CAR-T therapies.[11] In this treatment, a patient's own T cells are altered in a laboratory so that they will attack cancer cells. The Food and Drug Administration (FDA) has approved two CAR-T therapies, one to treat children with acute lymphoblastic leukaemia and the other to treat adults with advanced lymphomas. The complete remission rate in a trial of 100 adults with refractory or relapsed large B-cell lymphoma was 51%.[12]

The trend towards the personalisation of biology is not limited to FDA-approved therapies, but is also in the hands of individuals curious about their own bodies. There is intense public interest in harvesting and making sense of personal biological information from health-monitoring devices.[13] Services like 23andMe and Ancestry.com provide clients with detailed genetic information, including clues – and sometimes surprises – about their ancestry.[14] Their users can find out whether they potentially have a higher likelihood of developing breast cancer (as established by the presence of BRCA genes) or Parkinson's disease.

PatientsLikeMe is another example of a service generating personalised health information. On this for-profit site, people who suffer from one or more of 2,800 listed conditions share their medical data and reactions to investigational drugs. The company claims that patients who use their service will learn more about their medications and conditions, make connections with others who share their illnesses, and ultimately 'change the future of personalised health'.[15] The data provided to this site has led to original published research, and to the development of an easier way to enrol patients in clinical studies.[16]

Non-traditional research environments, including home- or community-based laboratories, are becoming more common, an approach that has been called DIY Bio (do-it-yourself biology), bio-hacking or citizen science. Community laboratories where bio enthusiasts can gather and work together, alongside many more DIY communities that lack laboratory space, have been established in New York, Boston, Seattle, San Francisco and Baltimore – as well as in Budapest, Manchester, Munich, Paris and Prague.[17] According to DIYBio.org, a charitable organisation formed with the mission of 'establishing a vibrant, productive and safe community of DIY biologists', there were 44 DIY Bio groups across the US and Canada, 31 in Europe, and 17 in Asia, South America and Oceania as of early June 2018.[18] These laboratories, which typically charge membership fees to purchase equipment, are dedicated to making science accessible and frequently offer educational programmes.

The Baltimore Underground Science Space (BUGSS), for example, recently held a class for people aged ten and up to learn about bioluminescence in bacteria, during which a gadget was built that puffs air into bacterial cultures to make the bacteria glow.[19] Another class invited people to investigate their own microbiome – the bacteria living inside their gut.[20] Participants were directed to take a stool sample at home and to quickly inactivate it so that no living microbes were brought into the laboratory. At the lab, the participants attempted to use polymerase chain reaction (PCR) to amplify the DNA of the microbes so as to identify them. Participants could also compare samples taken before and after embarking on a diet, or of two different people.

In the hands of amateurs, straightforward 'DNA-barcoding' techniques can be used to determine whether purchased sushi is actually made from the species advertised.[21] Other techniques can be used to detect the presence of melamine, a poison, in baby formula.[22] The ease of use offered by such technologies has inspired new biological services as well. For instance, apartment-complex owners have required stool samples from tenants' pets to genetically identify them, for the purpose of identifying and deterring those who do not pick up after them.[23]

The pipeline for non-traditional biological exploration is expanding, thanks to iGEM, the International Genetically Engineered Machine competition. iGEM began more than a decade ago as a class offered at the

Massachusetts Institute of Technology (MIT) in Cambridge, MA, that was modelled on robotics competitions intended to draw students into engineering fields.[24] In iGEM competitions, teams comprising undergraduates from around the world are given a kit of standard biological parts called BioBricks. Over a summer, and with the help of instructors, the teams use the parts and others they create to engineer biological systems and operate them within living cells. The competition has grown from involving fewer than two dozen undergraduates in its early years to drawing more than 6,000 undergraduates, high-school students, DIY Bio practitioners and 'overgrads' per year from more than 40 countries, with 30,000 alumni having already participated. Many of the projects aim to tackle real-world problems and to develop solutions that can be used in low-resource settings, such as a bacteria-produced blood substitute that may be stored for long periods.[25]

As people acquire more biological information about their environment, they will increasingly have the opportunity to make more personalised and biologically informed choices to improve their health, pursue new hobbies and even care for new types of pets. While these are positive outcomes, there is also the potential for negative outcomes, given the possibility that synthetic biology could be misused to cause deliberate harm. There will also be many new opportunities for quackery and dangerous self-experimentation that could spread via social media and thus become a contagious phenomenon. Biological safety practices will be challenged, and there could be some unwelcome surprises.

The misuse of synthetic biology

Disease has long been used as a weapon. Carcasses have been thrown into wells and over castle walls in warfare, for example.[26] Yet the golden age of microbiology, which began at the turn of the nineteenth century, marked a turning point. Louis Pasteur's discovery that infectious *Bacillus anthracis* could be attenuated into a vaccine for anthrax, along with other breakthroughs, demonstrated that specific biological pathogens could be isolated, grown and manipulated. It was not long before microbes were specifically developed with the intent to use them as weapons.[27] National biological-weapons programmes founded during the twentieth century developed an array of weaponised pathogens, and the United States' and Soviet Union's pursuit of aerosol applications during the Cold War left no doubt that such weapons could kill or incapacitate millions of people. However, with a few exceptions (such as the activities of Japan's Unit 731 during the Second World War), biological weapons have rarely been used in wars between nation-states.

The US unilaterally abandoned the development of biological weapons in 1969, and worked towards an international convention to prohibit their use. The Biological Weapons Convention (BWC) entered into force in 1975 and now has 180 states parties, each of which

> undertakes never in any circumstances to develop, produce, stockpile or otherwise acquire or retain: (1) Microbial or other biological agents, or toxins whatever their origin or method of production, of types and in quantities that have no justification for prophylactic, protective or other peaceful purposes; (2) Weapons, equipment or means of delivery designed to use such agents or toxins for hostile purposes or in armed conflict.[28]

However, the terms of the BWC have at times been violated. The Soviet Union, and then Russia, employed thousands of scientists to put smallpox on intercontinental ballistic missiles (ICBMs), to grow anthrax by the tonne, and to experiment with genetic engineering. Iraq had a biological-weapons programme, discovered after the First Gulf War, as did South Africa.

Indeed, there are probably still national biological-weapons programmes in existence today. Most worryingly, a statement made on 12 March 2012 by then Russian minister of defence Anatoliy Serdyukov indicated that a governmental plan was being prepared for 'the development of weapons based on new physical principles: radiation, geophysical wave, genetic, psychophysical, etc.'.[29] A genetic weapon would likely constitute a violation of the BWC. In May 2018, a report of Ukrainian allegations that Russia was 'returning to the Soviet-era development of a deadly Ebola–smallpox virus mix' was submitted to the NATO Parliamentary Assembly. Iryna Friz, the head of the Ukrainian delegation, stated that this effort was 'confirmed by the analysis of more than 5,000 tenders in public procurement and scientific activity of several Russian institutions managed by the Russian defence ministry'.[30]

Importantly, however, no nation has claimed to already possess biological weapons, and there have been no documented examples of their use. Bioterrorism has also been relatively infrequent, though the capability to use biology to do harm has been within reach. The anthrax letter attacks of 2001, the failed attempt by Japanese cult Aum Shinrikyo to develop an anthrax weapon in the 1990s, and the deliberate contamination of salad bars with salmonella by the Rajneeshee movement in Oregon in 1984 are conspicuous exceptions that prove the norm of rarity.

While it is unclear why there have been so few incidents of biological-weapons use, for most of recorded history, the technical capacity for harm has lagged far behind malicious intent. It is possible that synthetic biology, the democratisation of biology and the expanding power of biological tools may increase the likelihood of biological-weapons use. One highly relevant technical development is that it is no longer necessary to acquire a pathogen from nature or a laboratory to be used as a weapon. Using synthetic-biology techniques, many pathogens – particularly viruses – can be made 'from scratch', including smallpox virus, which was declared eradicated from the natural world in 1980.[31] For this reason, there was some controversy when scientists from the University of Alberta in Edmonton, Canada, synthetically recreated horsepox virus for the purposes of developing a smallpox vaccine.[32] Horsepox is very similar to smallpox, and may have been used by Edward Jenner to develop his original smallpox vaccine.[33] The horsepox synthesis is an example of 'dual-use' research – that is, legitimate science that could be misused for malign purposes. Observers were concerned that the methods used by the Canadian scientists could be duplicated using smallpox, and that the horsepox work lowered technical barriers to misuse.[34] Others thought that even after publication, misuse of the horsepox study would still present a great deal of technical difficulty.[35]

When discussing the potential for biology to be misused for harm, opinions on the risks usually turn on how 'hard' or 'easy' a technique is, and for whom. This may be difficult to ascertain without a detailed analysis, as headlines may be deceiving. For example, a CRISPR kit may be purchased online and can be used by amateurs, as described in the 2017 *Scientific American* article 'Mail Order CRISPR Kits Allow Absolutely Anyone to Hack DNA'.[36] This description makes it sound as though a powerful and potentially dangerous technology has been placed in the hands of amateurs. In fact, the kit contains the materials required to carry out only one procedure – adding one gene to a single spot in E. coli – and so is unlikely to cause harm.

A great deal of public science communication is filled with hyperbole, hype and gee-whiz-ardry, and thus cannot be a reliable guide either for how accessible a technology might be for misuse, or what benefits may accrue from the technology in the future. While amateurs and citizen scientists may do amazing things in the laboratory with tools such as CRISPR, there are still gaps between the use of such technologies by amateurs and by well-resourced groups with institutional ties and expertise. More detailed science reporting that sets out the scientific context of new research is required both for the purposes of setting expectations for positive benefits as well as for ameliorating concerns about security or safety risks.

Sometimes, synthetic-biology projects prove to be too challenging. In 2013, a fundraising campaign on the crowdfunding site Kickstarter promised to produce glowing plants and to distribute the seeds to 8,000 supporters. The effort was controversial, and observers debated the environmental risks as well as the legality of the exercise. In the end, creating glowing plants proved to be too difficult in technical terms to achieve. The scientists involved decided to make scented moss instead, which was more straightforward.[37]

Donald S. Fredrickson, who headed the NIH during the recombinant-DNA debates in the 1970s, wrote that 'one of the most important lessons to be learned about controversy over use of high technologies … is the absolute requirement for expert opinion'.[38] For dual-use phenomena, scientific expertise is required to separate facts from fiction. To help determine which advances are truly concerning from a security standpoint, a National Academies of Sciences, Engineering, and Medicine committee produced the 'Imperiale Framework', named after its chairman, which may be used to evaluate emerging biotechnologies for novel risks.[39]

The misuse of biotechnologies also includes the potential for unsafe practices. The personalisation of biology has already led to scientifically dubious self-experimentation. Aaron Traywick, CEO of Ascendance Biomedical, achieved infamy during a so-called body-hacking conference known as BDYHAX 2018 – a 'celebration of human enhancement, transhumanism, and biohacking' – when he injected himself with an anti-herpes treatment his company had developed in front of a live audience, with many more watching in real time on Facebook.[40] In an *Atlantic* article published after he was found dead at age 28 in a flotation-therapy tank, it was claimed that Traywick 'wanted to cure cancer, herpes, HIV, and even aging, and he wanted to do it without having to deal with the rules and safety precautions of regulators and industry standards'.[41]

Self-experimentation using gene therapy has also taken place. Elizabeth Parrish, CEO of a small biotech company based in Seattle, self-experimented with a gene therapy intended to increase muscle mass and to protect telomeres (structures at the end of chromosomes that protect them from damage), in an attempt to reverse ageing in a way that has been demonstrated in mice.[42] Brian Hanley, CEO of a small biotech company called Butterfly Sciences, tested a therapy on himself that was intended to increase the muscle mass of HIV patients.[43] And Josiah Zayner, who started an online supply site for DIY Bio projects called The ODIN, sells kits that could, in theory, be used to increase muscle mass using CRISPR.[44] Regulatory agencies face a significant challenge in keeping up with this kind of development, and in mitigating the potential harm, which will likely be amplified by social media.[45]

Making personal biology safer

Synthetic biology and other advanced biological techniques are not used only for fun or novelty. They are also marshalled for profit on an international scale. This makes the oversight and control of their negative outcomes more complex. In addition to the many DIY Bio enthusiasts around the world, and the more than 40 nations represented at each iGEM competition, many multinational companies have investments in synthetic biology. DuPont, Pfizer, Bausch & Lomb, Coca-Cola and other Fortune 500 companies make or use products derived from engineered organisms, including food, clothing, beauty products and medicines.[46] There have also been large national investments in synthetic biology, particularly by China, the United

Kingdom and the United States. Many other nations have technology road maps intended to encourage research and their own bioeconomies.[47]

Individual countries have attempted to control various aspects of the field in a top-down manner. Germany, for example, has threatened that anyone caught doing genetic engineering outside of a licensed facility could face a €50,000 fine or three years in prison.[48] Yet some are concerned that oversight that is too heavy-handed will only push DIY Bio activity underground, making it harder to detect misuse and to implement safety programmes.[49] Such top-down control measures could also unnecessarily stifle innovation. What, then, should be done by nations to limit the potential misuse of synthetic biology?

Firstly, there is a need to support efforts to make practitioners aware of the potential safety and security risks of their work. The FBI, for example, has developed a successful outreach programme for university-based and amateur biologists alike to raise their awareness of the potential misuse of their work, and to give them points of contact to report suspicious behaviour.[50] These awareness-raising mechanisms may help to forestall an incident and give law enforcement a chance to intervene in the case of a security concern.

The DIY Bio community would also benefit from biosafety awareness. There used to be an 'ask a biosafety expert' feature on the DIY Bio website, funded by the Alfred P. Sloan Foundation and supported by the Woodrow Wilson International Center for Scholars.[51] Unfortunately, this programme has now closed due to a lack of funding.[52] The Open Philanthropy Project is launching a new initiative to evaluate the safety and security of numerous DIY Bio laboratories, and to create a biosafety and biosecurity pilot programme in three DIY Bio labs. This programme will allow for the hiring of three biosafety officers for the laboratories, who will develop a list of best practices for DIY labs and co-author a biosafety manual which could be used by any DIY practitioner.[53]

As a second principle, nations should embrace 'partial solutions' to address biosafety and biosecurity risks in crafting their oversight of synthetic biology. The use of synthetic-biology tools by non-professionals can be beneficial, and a blanket ban or heavy oversight would be difficult to enforce.

However, partial solutions that address specific security or safety concerns have the potential to be more effective in reducing risks. For example, more than 80% of gene-synthesis orders are screened by the companies carrying out the syntheses to ensure that dangerous sequences are not being procured by those who are not supposed to have them.[54] While sophisticated nefarious actors could still overcome these barriers, such efforts would reduce some risks and should be supported.[55] It should not be easy to order smallpox DNA from the internet, for example. For other potential applications, including for gene drives or germline editing, specific and limited oversight may help to reduce the potential for negative outcomes.

Finally, scientific standards of practice need to be shaped in ways that reduce risks. Regulations and standards always lag behind technology development, so the practice of science will necessarily be shaped by the scientists and practitioners at the technical leading edge. For example, when Jennifer Doudna, one of the biologists credited with developing CRISPR, became concerned about the potential for unintended uses and effects of the technology, she and others called a meeting to consider the ethical and safety ramifications of human-germline editing, which involves modifications to the DNA of sperm or egg cells that are not just applied to one person, but also to their progeny.[56] Doudna's efforts led to a National Academies of Science, Engineering, and Medicine initiative to inform decision-making for genome editing, including the clinical, ethical, legal and social implications of their use. Gatherings of concerned experts and rigorous peer review of potentially worrisome new technologies are important in setting guidelines and expectations for the field, and can work across national boundaries.

*　　*　　*

Synthetic biology is a fast-moving, complicated field. Many of its tools have been democratised and put to use by corporations, community laboratories and individuals. A wide variety of applications are being developed, fuelling a trend towards personalisation as well as industrialisation. While this is likely to produce benefits for medicine, manufacturing, agriculture and national economies, there are also risks that need to be continually monitored and mitigated. Biosecurity and biosafety concerns, including limiting the risks of dangerous self-experimentation, need to be specifically addressed by practitioners as well as governments, to minimise the risks inherent in these powerful technologies, and to safeguard their enormous promise.

Notes

[1] Synthetic Biology Project, 'What Is Synthetic Biology?', http://www.synbioproject.org/topics/synbio101/definition/.

[2] *Ibid.*

[3] See *Ibid.*; Synberc, 'What Is Synbio?', https://www.synberc.org/what-is-synbio; and Stephanie Joyce, Anne-Marie Mazza and Steven Kendall (rapporteurs), 'Positioning Synthetic Biology to Meet the Challenges of the 21st Century: Summary Report of a Six Academies Symposium Series', 2013, p. 7, http://www.nap.edu/catalog.php?record_id=13316.

[4] Paul Voosen, 'Synthetic Biology Comes Down to Earth', *Chronicle of Higher Education*, 4 March 2013, http://chronicle.com/article/Synthetic-Biology-Comes-Down/137587/. See also Steven A. Benner, Zunyi Yang and Fei Chen, 'Synthetic Biology, Tinkering Biology, and Artificial Biology: What Are We Learning?', *Comptes Rendus Chimie*, vol. 14, no. 4, 2011, pp. 372–87.

[5] Gene drives represent a special case of gene editing which can increase the prevalence of a gene in a sexually reproducing population, so that instead of half of an individual's progeny inheriting the gene, inheritance can reach close to 100%.

[6] Philip Shapira, Seokbeom Kwon and Jan Youtie, 'Tracking the Emergence of Synthetic Biology', *Scientometrics*, vol. 112, no. 3, September 2017, pp. 1,439–69.

[7] Yensi Flores Bueso and Mark Tangney, 'Synthetic Biology in the Driving Seat of the Bioeconomy', *Trends in Biotechnology*, vol. 35, no. 5, May 2017, pp. 373–8.

[8] See Xenia Priebe and Andrew J. Daugulis, 'Thermodynamic Affinity-Based Considerations for the Rational Selection of Biphasic Systems for Microbial Flavor and Fragrance Production', *Journal of Chemical Technology & Biotechnology*, vol. 93, no. 3, March 2018, pp. 656–66; Pamela B. Besada-Lombana, Tami L. McTaggart and Nancy A. Da Silva, 'Molecular Tools for Pathway Engineering in *Saccharomyces cerevisiae*', *Current Opinion in Biotechnology*, vol. 53, December 2018, pp. 39–49; and Eko Roy Marella et al., 'Engineering Microbial Fatty Acid Metabolism for Biofuels and Biochemicals', *Current Opinion in Biotechnology*, vol. 50, April 2018, pp. 39–46.

[9] John Bergin, 'Synthetic Biology: Global Markets', BCC Research, January 2017, https://www.bccresearch.com/market-research/biotechnology/synthetic-biology-markets-report-bio066d.html.

[10] James Manyika et al., 'Disruptive Technologies: Advances that Will

Transform Life, Business, and the Global Economy', McKinsey Global Institute, May 2013, p. 86, https://www.mckinsey.com/business-functions/digital-mckinsey/our-insights/disruptive-technologies.

11 National Cancer Institute, 'CAR T Cells: Engineering Patients' Immune Cells to Treat Their Cancers', https://www.cancer.gov/about-cancer/treatment/research/car-t-cells.

12 Food and Drug Administration, 'FDA Approves CAR-T Cell Therapy to Treat Adults with Certain Types of Large B-Cell Lymphoma', 18 October 2017, https://www.fda.gov/NewsEvents/Newsroom/PressAnnouncements/ucm581216.htm.

13 Bruce Japsen, 'Wearable Fitness Devices Attract More than the Young and Healthy', *Forbes*, 11 July 2016, https://www.forbes.com/sites/brucejapsen/2016/07/11/wearable-fitness-devices-attract-more-than-young-healthy/#33667d057df3.

14 Natalie Rahhal, '"Genetics Have a Dark Side": Trend of Gifting DNA Tests Might be More of a Curse than a Joy this Christmas, Ethicist Warns', *Daily Mail*, 17 December 2017, http://www.dailymail.co.uk/health/article-5192243/Trend-gifting-DNA-tests-cause-family-rifts.html.

15 See Jeana H. Frost and Michael P. Massagli, 'Social Uses of Personal Health Information Within PatientsLikeMe, an Online Patient Community: What Can Happen When Patients Have Access to One Another's Data', *Journal of Medical Internet Research*, vol. 10, no. 3, July–September 2008, p. e15; and Paul Wicks et al., 'Sharing Health Data for Better Outcomes on PatientsLikeMe', *Journal of Medical Internet Research*, vol. 12, no. 2, April–June 2010, p. 19.

16 Rahhal, '"Genetics Have a Dark Side"'.

17 DIY Bio, 'Local Groups', http://diybio.org/local/.

18 Data available at the DIY Bio website, https://diybio.org/.

19 See Baltimore Underground Science Space (BUGSS), 'Does It Glow or No?', course offered in June 2017, http://www.bugssonline.org/past-classes/.

20 See Baltimore Underground Science Space (BUGSS), 'GO WITH YOUR GUTS! (And the Billions of Bacteria in Them): A Personal Microbiome Course', course offered in April 2018, http://www.bugssonline.org/past-classes/.

21 See Ido Amit et al., 'Voices of Biotech', *Nature Biotechnology*, 10 March 2016, vol. 34, no. 3, pp. 270–5; John Scwartz, 'Sushi Study Finds Deception', *New York Times*, 22 August 2008, http://www.nytimes.com/2008/08/22/world/americas/22iht-fish.1.15539112.html?_r=0; and Demian A. Willette et al., 'Using DNA Barcoding to Track Seafood Mislabeling in Los Angeles Restaurants', *Conservation Biology*, vol. 31, no. 5, October 2017, pp. 1,076–85.

22 Thomas Landrain et al., 'Do-It-Yourself Biology: Challenges and Promises for an Open Science and Technology Movement', *Systems and Synthetic Biology*, vol. 7, no. 3, September 2013, pp. 115–26.

23 See Matt Peckham, 'Texas Apartment to Track Dog Poop Offenders Using DNA', *Time*, 24 January 2013, http://newsfeed.time.com/2013/01/24/

texas-apartment-to-track-dog-poop-
offenders-using-dna/; and Paul Walsh,
'Minneapolis Apartment Building
Collecting Pets' DNA to Catch Poop-
A-Trators', *Star Tribune*, 7 December
2017, http://www.startribune.com/
minneapolis-apartment-building-
collecting-pets-dna-to-catch-poop-a-
trators/462297273/.

24 For an example of a robotics competition, see NASA, 'The Robotics
Alliance Project', https://robotics.nasa.
gov/events/competitions.php.

25 See Catherine Goodman, 'Engineering
Ingenuity at iGEM', *Nature Chemical
Biology*, vol. 4, no. 13, 2008; and
Richard Gallagher, 'An iGEM of an
Idea', *Scientist*, vol. 21, no. 12, 2007.

26 W.S. Carus, 'The History of Biological
Weapons Use: What We Know and
What We Don't', *Health Security*,
vol. 13, no. 4, July–August 2015, pp.
219–55.

27 *Ibid.*

28 UN Office for Disarmament Affairs,
'Convention on the Prohibition
of the Development, Production
and Stockpiling of Bacteriological
(Biological) and Toxin Weapons and
on Their Destruction', available at
http://disarmament.un.org/treaties/t/
bwc.

29 Quoted in Raymond A. Zilinskas and
Philippe Mauger, *Biosecurity in Putin's
Russia* (Boulder, CO: Lynne Rienner
Publishers, 2018).

30 'Russia Renewing Development
of Ebola–Smallpox Virus Mix,
Ukraine Suggests', Unian, 27 May
2018, https://www.unian.info/
politics/10131959-russia-renewing-
development-of-ebola-smallpox-virus-
mix-ukraine-suggests.html.

31 World Health Organization, *Global
Eradication of Smallpox: Final Report
of the Global Commission for the
Certification of Smallpox Eradication*
(Geneva: World Health Organization,
December 1979), available at http://
whqlibdoc.who.int/publications/
a41438.pdf.

32 Ryan S. Noyce, Seth Lederman and
David H. Evans, 'Construction of an
Infectious Horsepox Virus Vaccine
from Chemically Synthesized DNA
Fragments', *PLoS ONE*, vol. 13, no. 1,
January 2018.

33 Livia Schrick et al., 'An Early
American Smallpox Vaccine Based
on Horsepox', *New England Journal of
Medicine*, vol. 377, no. 15, pp. 1,491–2.

34 See Tom Inglesby, 'Important
Questions Global Health and
Science Leaders Should Be Asking
in the Wake of Horsepox Synthesis',
Bifurcated Needle, 7 July 2017,
http://www.bifurcatedneedle.com/
new-blog/2017/7/7/
important-questions-global-health-
and-science-leaders-should-be-asking-
in-the-wake-of-horsepox-synthesis;
and Gregory D. Koblentz, 'The *De
Novo* Synthesis of Horsepox Virus:
Implications for Biosecurity and
Recommendations for Preventing the
Reemergence of Smallpox', *Health
Security*, vol. 15, no. 6, December 2017.

35 See Diane DiEuliis, Kavita Berger and
Gigi Gronvall, 'Biosecurity Implications
for the Synthesis of Horsepox, an
Orthopoxvirus', *Health Security*, vol. 15,
no. 6, November–December 2017, pp.
629–37; and Diane DiEuliis and Gigi
Gronvall, 'A Holistic Assessment of the
Risks and Benefits of the Synthesis of
Horsepox Virus', *mSphere*, vol. 3, no. 2,

March–April 2018.

36   Annie Sneed, 'Mail-Order CRISPR Kits Allow Absolutely Anyone to Hack DNA', *Scientific American*, 2 November 2017, https://www.scientificamerican.com/article/mail-order-crispr-kits-allow-absolutely-anyone-to-hack-dna/.

37   Ariel Schwartz, 'One of the Most Controversial Kickstarter Campaigns in History Is Dead – Here's the Product that Actually Got Made', *Business Insider*, 27 August 2017, http://www.businessinsider.com/glowing-plant-kickstarter-campaign-orbella-moss-2017-8.

38   Donald S. Fredrickson, *The Recombinant DNA Controversy – A Memoir: Science, Politics, and the Public Interest, 1974–1981* (Washington DC: ASM Press, 2001).

39   Committee on Strategies for Identifying and Addressing Potential Biodefense Vulnerabilities Posed by Synthetic Biology, 'Biodefense in the Age of Synthetic Biology', 19 June 2018, https://www.eventbrite.com/e/report-briefing-biodefense-in-the-age-of-synthetic-biology-tickets-46625113971.

40   'BDYHAX2018: The Body Hacking Convention', https://bodyhackingcon.com/.

41   Kristen V. Brown, 'What Does an Infamous Biohacker's Death Mean for the Future of DIY Science?', *Atlantic*, 5 May 2018, https://www.theatlantic.com/science/archive/2018/05/aaron-traywick-death-ascendance-biomedical/559745/. See also Alex Philippidis, 'Dead at Age 28, Ascendance Biomedical CEO Remembered for Pushing Boundaries', GEN News Highlights, 2 May 2018, https://www.genengnews.com/gen-news-highlights/dead-at-age-28-ascendance-biomedical-ceo-remembered-for-pushing-boundaries/81255775.

42   See Antonio Regalado, 'A Tale of Do-It-Yourself Gene Therapy', *MIT Technology Review*, 14 October 2015, https://www.technologyreview.com/s/542371/a-tale-of-do-it-yourself-gene-therapy/; and Bruno Bernardes de Jesus et al., 'Telomerase Gene Therapy in Adult and Old Mice Delays Aging and Increases Longevity Without Increasing Cancer', *EMBO Molecular Medicine*, vol. 4, no. 8, 2012, pp. 691–704, http://www.ncbi.nlm.nih.gov/pmc/articles/PMC3494070/.

43   Antonio Regalado, 'One Man's Quest to Hack His Own Genes', *MIT Technology Review*, 10 January 2017, https://www.technologyreview.com/s/603217/one-mans-quest-to-hack-his-own-genes/.

44   Tom Ireland, 'I Want to Help Humans Genetically Modify Themselves', *Guardian*, 24 December 2017, https://www.theguardian.com/science/2017/dec/24/josiah-zayner-diy-gene-editing-therapy-crispr-interview.

45   Kristen V. Brown, 'The FDA Is Not Cool with Selling DIY Gene Therapies', Gizmodo, 22 November 2017, https://gizmodo.com/the-feds-are-officially-cracking-down-on-basement-bioha-1820682025.

46   US Office of Technical Intelligence, 'Technical Assessment: Synthetic Biology', January 2015, http://defenseinnovationmarketplace.mil/resources/OTI-SyntheticBiologyTechnicalAssessment.pdf.

47 'Synthetic Biology in China, UK and US', *Synthetic and Systems Biotechnology*, vol. 1, no. 4, December 2016, p. 215, http://www.ncbi.nlm.nih.gov/pmc/articles/PMC5625731/; OECD, 'Emerging Policy Issues in Synthetic Biology', 4 June 2014, http://www.oecd-ilibrary.org/science-and-technology/emerging-policy-issues-in-synthetic-biology_9789264208421-en.

48 Kristen V. Brown, 'Germany Is Threatening Biohackers with Prison', Gizmodo, 9 February 2017, https://gizmodo.com/germany-is-threatening-biohackers-with-prison-1792143993.

49 See, for example, Robert Carlson, 'Causes and Consequences of Bioeconomic Proliferation: Implications for U.S. Physical and Economic Security', Biodefense Net Assessment, Department of Homeland Security Science and Technology Directorate, 2012, http://www.synthesis.cc/2012/09/causes-and-consequences-of-bioeconomic-proliferation.html.

50 See Laura Kwinn (ed.), 'FBI Connects Science and Security Communities', *Science, Safety, and Security Quarterly*, no. 2, May 2012, pp. 1, 5, http://www.phe.gov/s3/Documents/s3newsletter-may2012.pdf; and Edward W. Lempinen, 'FBI, AAAS Collaborate on Ambitious Outreach to Biotech Researchers and DIY Biologists', 1 April 2011, http://www.aaas.org/news/fbi-aaas-collaborate-ambitious-outreach-biotech-researchers-and-diy-biologists.

51 DIY Bio, 'Ask a Biosafety Professional Your Question', http://ask.diybio.org/.

52 DIY Bio, 'Ask a Biosafety Expert – Closed', https://diybio.org/ask-biosafety-notice/.

53 Open Philanthropy Project, 'Genspace – A DIY Bio Project', September 2017, https://www.openphilanthropy.org/focus/global-catastrophic-risks/biosecurity/genspace-diy-bio-labs-project.

54 See International Gene Synthesis Consortium (IGSC), 'Harmonized Screening Protocol v2.0: Gene Sequence & Customer Screening to Promote Biosecurity', 19 November 2017, available at https://genesynthesisconsortium.org/.

55 Diane DiEuliis, Sarah R. Carter and Gigi Kwik Gronvall, 'Options for Synthetic DNA Order Screening, Revisited', *mSphere*, July–August 2017, vol. 2, no. 4, 2017, https://www.ncbi.nlm.nih.gov/pubmed/28861521.

56 See David Baltimore et al., 'Biotechnology: A Prudent Path Forward for Genomic Engineering and Germline Gene Modification', *Science*, 3 April 2015, vol. 348, no. 6,230, pp. 36–8; and National Academies of Sciences, Engineering, and Medicine, 'Human Gene Editing Initiative'.

Review Essay

The Ghost of Jefferson Davis

Russell Crandall

This Vast Southern Empire: Slaveholders at the Helm of American Foreign Policy
Matthew Karp. Cambridge, MA: Harvard University Press, 2016.
£21.95/$29.95. 360 pp.

Recent debates about the legitimacy of monuments commemorating the Confederate States of America (also known as the Confederacy) in the American South – debates that have in some cases triggered violence, as in Charlottesville, VA, in August 2017 – have generated interest in the late-nineteenth and early-twentieth-century societies that erected them. It is all too easy to assume that such monuments were only ever of interest to a Southern racist fringe. Yet depictions of the Confederacy as a noble, if misguided, political experiment have been received with sympathy by a much wider range of people than some might believe. Nineteenth-century British prime minister William Gladstone, for one, lauded the Southern aristocracy's 'splendid virtues' despite the sins of slavery, describing Southern planters as 'worthy to sit with Sir Percival at the "table round" of King Arthur' (p. 255).

Princeton scholar Matthew Karp reminds us in his dazzling, essential history, *This Vast Southern Empire*, that the Southern slaveholding class had only been dead a short while before its legacy was resurrected, 'cast

Russell Crandall is a professor of American foreign policy at Davidson College in North Carolina, and a contributing editor to *Survival*.

Survival | vol. 60 no. 4 | August–September 2018 | pp. 181–186   DOI 10.1080/00396338.2018.1495444

in bronze and hauled atop pedestals of marble' (p. 252), not just in likely places such as Virginia, but in New England as well – the self-identified cradle of the abolitionist movement. By the late 1880s, narratives focusing on 'national white reconciliation', the 'lost cause' and a 'battle between brothers' had begun to eclipse previous understandings of the US Civil War as a 'revolutionary clash of nations' (p. 252). Politicians on both sides of the Atlantic began to 'decorate slavery's tomb with garlands of myth, romance, and false antiquity' (p. 255).

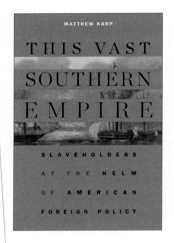

MATTHEW KARP

THIS VAST
SOUTHERN
EMPIRE

SLAVEHOLDERS
AT THE HELM
OF AMERICAN
FOREIGN POLICY

Slavery and imperialism

In summer 1890 – the same year a large statue by the famed French sculptor Antonin Mercié of Confederate General Robert E. Lee was unveiled in Richmond, VA – the commencement address at Harvard University was delivered for the first time by a black man, William Edward Burghardt Du Bois. The topic of his address was 'Jefferson Davis as Representative of Civilization' (p. 251). Davis, who had died only months earlier on 6 December 1889, had been the president of the Confederate States of America and the last remaining Southern senator to have joined the rebellion after Abraham Lincoln was elected president in November 1860.

In what was likely intended as a stab at the moral vanity of New England's learned society, Du Bois's address suggested that it was not the Founding Fathers – men like George Washington, Thomas Jefferson and James Madison – nor even wartime Lincoln, but Davis, 'the ghost of a treasonous Confederate commander', who was the United States' 'chief representative of civilization' in 1890 (p. 252). The type of civilisation embodied by Davis, according to Du Bois, was founded on 'the idea of the strong man – individualism coupled with the rule of might'. 'Whenever this idea has … escaped from the individual realm,' he continued, 'it has found an even more secure foothold in the policy and philosophy of the State.' Du Bois argued that this idea could be seen in the 'cool logic of the Club' then driving the imperial aspirations of American, British, Dutch, French, German and Japanese leaders. The racial justifications underpinning their predations on vulnerable societies would, believes Karp, have resonated with American slaveholders prior to the Civil War. He cites, among others, George Frederick Holmes, who in 1856 observed that 'conquest, extension, appropriation, assimilation, and even the extermination of inferior races has been and must be the curse pursued in the development of civilization' (p. 255). Three decades later, in 1889, Harvard graduate and future US president Theodore Roosevelt wrote in *The Winning of the West* that 'it is of incalculable importance that America, Australia, and Siberia should pass out of the hands of their red, black, and yellow aboriginal owners, and become the heritage of the dominant world races' (p. 253).

Karp believes that Du Bois's address was 'strikingly original' not merely because it discussed a burgeoning imperialism, but because it argued that this imperialism was rooted in a belief in the rightness of slavery. According to Karp, US foreign policy in the run-up to the Civil War had slavery at its core. During the 1840s and 1850s, Southern politicians and their 'largely compliant northern allies' held a disproportionate yet hermetic grip on national power, and especially over the country's foreign policy, or what Karp calls the 'outward state' (p. 5). Pro-slavery figures such as Andrew Jackson, the seventh president of the United States, used the tremendous diplomatic and military powers at their disposal to advance the institution of slavery, especially in the western hemisphere. Their purpose was not just to safeguard their own chattel or to maintain their grip on society, although these were important goals. Rather, as Karp sees it, American elites regarded the advance of slavery as a 'vital element of global progress' (p. 256). It is easy to forget that it cost upwards of 750,000 lives and untold economic and social destruction to defeat this project in the United States. Karp believes that its legacy – so evident in the late nineteenth and early twentieth centuries, and arguably still with us today – demonstrates the 'vast breadth and fierce confidence of the proslavery political vision' (p. 256).

Karp accurately points out that history remembers the nominally unauthorised ('filibuster') incursions into Latin America, during which 'swashbuckling imperialists' commanded militias to invade Cuba, Mexico and Nicaragua (p. 7) – missions that typically ended in disaster. Yet Karp sees beyond the historical appeal of 'wild-eyed soldiers of fortune' like William Walker, who made several attempts in the 1850s to establish slave-holding colonies under his personal control in Latin America, to Southern slaveholding elites not just in Charleston, Richmond and New Orleans, but also at West Point, the State Department and the White House. Men like South Carolina native John C. Calhoun, who served as the seventh vice president of the United States, were 'weighty statesmen' who 'acquired Texas, protected slavery in Cuba, and oversaw the conquest of Mexico' (p. 7). By the 1850s, these savvy politicians 'ruled over the most dynamic slave society the world had ever known' – the United States of America (p. 2).

Slavery's champion

Karp does not forget that 'American soil was not the only slave soil' (p. 7). For hundreds of years, African slaves had 'formed the backbone' of colonial societies throughout the New World (p. 1). By the 1850s, the slave-based economies of Brazil and Cuba, for example, were pumping out 'unprece-dented quantities' of staples such as sugar, cotton and coffee. Slaveholding elites in the United States, where more than six million people – the largest slave population in the Americas – 'toiled in bondage' at the outset of the Civil War in 1861, felt a deep solidarity with their counterparts in other countries (p. 1).

Yet slavery, despite its prevalence, was 'patently on the decline' by the mid-eighteenth century (p. 3). 'Great revolutions' in the United States, France and Haiti had ushered in political and philosophical notions fiercely antagonistic to slavery (p. 1). And there were complete or partial anti-slavery successes in states such as Vermont and Pennsylvania, and countries including Chile and Peru. Southern aristocrats increasingly felt the need to take action. Although they frequently decried the reach of the federal government when it came to domestic affairs, 'whenever a question arose of extending or protecting slavery,' as Henry Adams pithily observed in 1882, 'the slave-holders became friends of centralized power, and used that dangerous weapon with a kind of frenzy' (p. 5).

The annexation of Texas in 1845 serves as a case in point. In the early 1840s, the independent Republic of Texas had the fourth-highest rate of enslavement in the Americas. Yet abolitionist sentiment in both Great Britain and Mexico was increasingly seen as a threat to slaveholders' way of life on both sides of the US–Texas border (pp. 84–5). Thus, on 1 March 1845, US president John Tyler, a Virginian aristocrat, signed an offer of annexation that was quickly ratified by Texas. Tyler and other annexationists, such as John Calhoun and Abel Upshur (Tyler's secretary of state), publicly claimed that Texas 'would be a boon to the national economy and a market for northern manufactures, a key addition to block British encirclement from the Gulf of Mexico all the way up to Canada, and … a safety valve for the ultimate diffusion of American slavery'. Yet Karp contends that such arguments still 'rested atop the essential foundation of slavery'. After all, the principal contribution that Texas could make to the national economy would be to enlarge the production of cotton; the main threat posed by Great Britain to the United States was its potential ability to undermine Southern slavery; and the argument that the movement of slaves into Texas would ultimately reduce the slave population in the South was a fiction 'intended for credulous northern audiences only. Slaveholders themselves knew better' (p. 85). For example, Karp cites a speech given after annexation by Willian Lowndes, a Southern congressman and orator who would later help lead the secessionist movement, in which he argued that the annexation of Texas would help to demonstrate the 'immense superiority of a system of associated slave labor over free individual labor in every species of tropical cultivation' (p. 101).

Not surprisingly, the annexation of Texas produced revulsion among the political and cultural adversaries of slavery and its advocates. Writing at the time, British scholar T.B. Macaulay observed that 'the United States' Government has openly declared itself the patron, the champion, and the upholder of slavery' (p. 100). New England writer Ralph Waldo Emerson declared that 'the annexation of Texas looks like one of those events which retard or retrograde the civilization of the ages' (p. 100).

In his 1890 remarks at Harvard, W.E.B. Du Bois did not deny that Southern aristocrats displayed some admirable qualities; in fact, he acknowledged their 'stalwart manhood and heroic character', and the ambition of their crusade (p. 255). His purpose was to highlight the vigour of their project so as to dispute the notion, already taking hold by the 1890s, that slavery was little more than a regrettable sideshow in the otherwise noble sweep of American history. As Karp puts it, 'if one read all antebellum history backward from the perspective of Appomattox, it became easy to see the South as weak, defensive, and archaic. Only these illusions could permit later observers, from Westminster to Hollywood, to view the proud slaveholding civilization of Jefferson Davis with such demeaning nostalgia' (pp. 255–6).

Karp's appraisal certainly seems prescient now that Donald Trump appears to be presiding over a mission stoked by Steve Bannon and Breitbart News to revive white nationalism in the United States. Is it possible that the administration has made a conscious choice to identify more with Jefferson Davis than with Du Bois? It is probably risky to assume that the commander-in-chief knows who these two men were, though one can be sure that Bannon does. Anyone wishing to resist the revival of Davis's 'treasonous ghost' could do worse than reading Karp's masterful history.

Book Reviews

Politics and International Relations
Gilles Andréani

From Fascism to Populism in History
Federico Finchelstein. Oakland, CA: University of California
Press, 2017. £24.00/$29.95. 328 pp.

The apparent rise of populist leaders from Asia to Europe and the United States
has prompted an abundance of books and essays on populism, some of which
have already been reviewed in these pages. Yet, taken together, they have not
fully clarified what populism is. The concept is intrinsically difficult to capture,
caught as it is between generalities and the specifics of its diverse manifestations.

With *From Fascism to Populism in History*, Federico Finchelstein has made an
interesting contribution to this ongoing debate. A professor of history at the
New School for Social Research in New York, he has published extensively on
Latin American populism, and on contemporary Argentine history. He thus
brings to the debate a dual perspective: that of a historian familiar with the story
of the immediate post-war wave of populism in Latin America, and of someone
with a global – rather than a European – perspective on populism.

The book's main thesis is that post-war populism emerged from fascism,
but substantially differed from it by drawing its legitimacy from electoral processes. Whereas there are few examples of populism eventually giving rise to
fascist regimes, in the post-war period quite a few fascist or dictatorial regimes
evolved into populist ones, especially in Latin America, where Peronism offers
the most telling example of such a transformation. This historical perspective
suggests that populism should not be seen as 'fascism light', but rather as a
'repudiation, and a democratic reformulation' of fascism (p. 247). Situated
somewhere between liberal democracy and fascism, twentieth-century popu-

Survival | vol. 60 no. 4 | August–September | pp. 187–192   DOI 10.1080/00396338.2018.1495446

lism 'drew on the residues of the former to challenge the latter' (p. 247). As a result, it transformed the dictatorial tradition of fascism into 'an antiliberal and intolerant form of democracy' (p. 248).

Finchelstein substantiates his thesis by drawing extensively on Latin American examples such as Getúlio Vargas in Brazil, Jorge Eliécer Gaitán in Colombia and, more recently, Carlos Menem in Argentina. All these leaders claimed to embody a third way between capitalism and socialism, and often leaned to the left. Finchelstein does not confine himself to the western hemisphere, however, and discusses contemporary leaders in other regions as well, such as Recep Tayyip Erdogan in Turkey, Jacob Zuma in South Africa and Suthep Thaugsuban in Thailand. He thus manages to look beyond the narrow Euro-American circle in which populism studies are too often confined.

The book does have a few shortcomings. The text can be repetitive at times, and the introduction is somewhat unfocused. Moreover, Finchelstein occasionally adopts some highly debatable propositions without qualifying them, as where he blindly accepts Zeev Sternhell's distorted view of the French writer Maurice Barrès as a proto-fascist (p. 51).

Be that as it may, *From Fascism to Populism in History* serves the important purpose of reminding us that populism was in evidence throughout the twentieth century, especially in Latin America, and thus is a global phenomenon of long standing. Moreover, Finchelstein usefully highlights three truths about populism. Firstly, he notes that populism can come from the left as well as from the right – indeed, most populists have claimed to repudiate the left– right divide, and some have genuinely adopted policies which favoured the working class. Secondly, he observes that leaders cannot thrive without followers. Populist leaders may be devious, but simply dismissing their supporters as misguided, as Barack Obama did with reference to Donald Trump's supporters, is not going to solve the problem. Thirdly, Finchelstein argues that populism is not mainly a perversion of democracy that inverts its main features, but rather is deeply rooted in dictatorship and fascism. All this makes populism an ambiguous phenomenon. On the one hand, it displays affinities with the worst political ideas of the past century. On the other, it has helped some dictatorial regimes to evolve into a kind of democracy based on genuine electoral processes and popular support, as seen in the case of Juan Péron's Argentina. In this sense, populism may be an unpleasant but necessary step in the transition from dictatorship to democracy. The current wave of populism in post-communist Europe could be seen in this light.

**The Opinion of Mankind: Sociability and the Theory of the
State from Hobbes to Smith**
Paul Sagar. Princeton, NJ: Princeton University Press, 2018.
£35.00/$45.00. 248 pp.

Ever since the end of the sixteenth century, sovereignty has stood out as the central question of political philosophy. The internecine quarrels of Christianity and the secularisation of societies in the 1500s undermined the proposition that all power proceeded from God, leaving open the key question of the legitimate source of political authority – that is, of sovereignty. It took the better part of two centuries to answer this question, through a series of attempts beginning with Thomas Hobbes and continuing to the French and American revolutions, and to the works of John Locke and Jean-Jacques Rousseau. The proposed answers were diverse and often at odds with one another, but nonetheless had two essential features in common: the notion that political authority should derive from a contract rather than from the unilateral imposition of a ruler's will; and that it needed the consent of the governed to be regarded as legitimate.

In addition to this 'main road' of modern political thought, however, there have been secondary paths which have offered answers no less valuable and relevant to our understanding of modern democracies. So argues Paul Sagar, a lecturer in political theory at King's College London, in *The Opinion of Mankind*. He contends that, beyond and against the Hobbesian tradition of the state, David Hume and Adam Smith made an original contribution that is insufficiently acknowledged today. He attempts to present and justify this contribution in his erudite and easy-to-read book. Sagar first shows how, within the larger context of the political thought of the Enlightenment – including the works of Lord Shaftesbury and Bernard Mandeville – Hume developed a view of human nature that, by including a capacity for empathy and a propensity to live in society, was at odds with Hobbes's dire conception of humanity. The need for justice, rather than a mere instinct for self-preservation, prompted men to create state institutions that could regulate the pursuit of individual self-interest. That process, based on utility rather than coercion or formal consent, formed the basis of government.

Sagar moves on to show how Hume's view of the family and society, as well as of history, parts ways with the idea of a contract-based political system as proposed by Hobbes and Locke. Hume's key contribution to political thought, however, is identified by Sagar as his ability to circumvent the issue of sovereignty while developing his own theory of political obligation. For Hume, the rightful source of authority depended on its utility: 'interest is the immediate sanction of Government' (p. 125). At the same time, obedience itself, to an established but admittedly unjust government, also had its utility. In the end, the balance between the two rested on 'opinion', which for Hume was a complex concept which went beyond public opinion to encompass a more general normative and sociological assent to being governed.

This understanding of opinion, which provided Sagar with the title of his book, accounts for Hume's famous observation that 'nothing appears more surprising than the easiness with which the many are governed by the few', when the latter 'have nothing more to support them than opinion'.

At this point, Sagar argues in a chapter entitled 'The State Without Sovereignty' that not only did Hume circumvent the issue of sovereignty, he also 'embraced secular political theory whilst abandoning any external justificatory grounding for our moral and political practices, settling instead for internal vindication by the lights of the opinion of mankind' (p. 137).

Sagar then turns to a lengthy discussion of Rousseau, thus exploring the main road of modern political thought before returning to the secondary paths he seeks to emphasise. In this long chapter, he overstates the commonalities between Rousseau and Hobbes, and misses the opportunity to evoke the quarrel between Hume and Rousseau, which might have been worth mentioning in this context.

Finally, Sagar turns to Smith, whose promise to provide a general discourse on the principles of law and government went unfulfilled, and whose political thought remains unfinished. For Smith, there was no conceivable property or economy without government, given the need to defend the poor against the rich – an obviously utilitarian conception of government. Power could be based on ability, age, wealth or birth, but was ultimately rooted in 'the natural modesty of mankind, who are not generally inclined to dispute the authority of those above them' (p. 205). Like Hume, Smith developed a pragmatic, utilitarian view of the state, which depended in the end on the state's ability to justify its utility in a world increasingly governed by opinion, as wealth and commerce continued to develop.

At the end of this excellent book, Sagar argues that neither Hume nor Smith can provide ready-made solutions to the political dilemmas of our age. They still can inspire us, however, with their aspiration to base politics in facts, in the actual aspirations of populations, and in the practical functioning of societies, rather than in abstractions. As such, they complement more than they contradict the main road of modern politics.

The Ordinary Virtues: Moral Order in a Divided World
Michael Ignatieff. Cambridge, MA: Harvard University Press,
2017. £20.95/$27.95. 263 pp.

Michael Ignatieff does not belong to any recognisable intellectual category. A prolific writer, he is at the same time a moralist, a historian of ideas, a political advocate – he was briefly a politician – and a perceptive witness to our time. His writings combine the talents of a journalist, an academic and an activist. A Canadian citizen of Russian origin who has lived in Europe and the United States, he is a man of many cultures who displays a sense of belonging to the wider world while retaining a deep affinity with local events and people.

With *The Ordinary Virtues*, Ignatieff takes his readers once again on a journey into divided lands. He had previously done so in 1993, with *Blood and Belonging: Journeys Into the New Nationalism*, which explored nationalist impulses in Serbia and Croatia, Germany, Ukraine, Quebec, Kurdistan and Northern Ireland. Three years later, he published *The Warrior's Honour: Ethnic War and the Modern Conscience*, in which, based on the horrors of conflicts in Bosnia, Central Africa and the Middle East, he advocated a more proactive stance on the part of the United Nations and the West.

The Ordinary Virtues is of a different order. Ignatieff's journeys in this book, unlike those he embarked upon 20 years ago, are not about wars or nationalism. This time, he ventures into places where people are coping not so much with hostile forces as with the tensions arising from memories, divisions or challenges which, on the face of it, seem insuperable. Among other questions, Ignatieff asks how families affected by the mass murders at Srebrenica can coexist with those who deny or dismiss the crime in a nominally unified Bosnia; how the inhabitants of Fukushima cope with the consequences of the 2011 nuclear disaster; how a global city like Los Angeles manages its ethnic and social tensions; and how South African society is handling the delusions of the post-transition period.

Ignatieff does a magnificent job of simply describing these situations, without insisting on moral clarity or outside intervention. He bears witness with accuracy and sensitivity to the simple courage and fortitude displayed by the individuals concerned. Two episodes stand out in this respect. Firstly, his chapter on Bosnia displays a level of commitment that is absent in some of the other chapters. He soberly concludes with the thought that reconciliation may be taking place there after all: 'not with the enemy, with "the other", with "them", but with the fact that the past is past and done with' (p. 115). Elsewhere, he renders the resilience and civic spirit displayed by the inhabitants of Fukushima both during and after the catastrophe in a sober and utterly impressive way.

Thus, Ignatieff's book is about ordinary people drawing on their moral resources to cope with uncommon situations, and the possibility of different groups of people living together amid tensions that are seemingly too great to overcome. Their ability to do so, and the resilience and tolerance this requires, are not, says Ignatieff, a function of the progress of any global norm, or of the convergence of moral attitudes worldwide. Rather, these virtues are mostly local, displayed by neighbours, next of kin, friends and passers-by. The presence of unrepentant or indifferent Serbs around Srebrenica, among other examples, reminds us that globalisation is doing little to advance what should be its most distinctive feature, the propensity to welcome and, if need be, help people of different races, religions or ethnicities.

Ultimately, *The Ordinary Virtues* is suffused both with hope and with a distinct melancholy. Previous works by Ignatieff had a similar quality: in *The Warrior's Honour*, for example, Ignatieff quotes a Serbian soldier who is trying to explain the difference between Serbs and Croats. 'Look, here's how it is,' he says. 'Those Croats, they think they're better than us. They want to be the gentlemen. Think they're fancy Europeans. I'll tell you something. We're all just Balkan shit.'

The difference between the two books is that, back in the 1990s, along with disillusionment there was still room for advocacy (in favour of outside intervention) and politics (siding with the weaker side, namely the Bosniaks). Entrusting the world of 2018 to ordinary virtues may be prudent and morally sound, but doing so nonetheless testifies to the narrow straits in which globalisation has left politics, which is just another word for the common good. This implicit message is one of the book's virtues, but also its limit.

Russia and Eurasia
Angela Stent

The Long Hangover: Putin's New Russia and the Ghosts of the Past
Shaun Walker. Oxford: Oxford University Press, 2018. £20.00.
278 pp.

The collapse of the Soviet Union was both unexpected and traumatic, and its aftershocks continue to reverberate in today's Russia. In this lively and engrossing book, Shaun Walker chronicles Vladimir Putin's mission to fill the void left after 1991, and to forge a new sense of nationhood and pride. His vehicle has been to create a cult of the Second World War – the Great Patriotic War – in which the Soviet victory is the glue that holds the new Russia together.

Putin has forged a new Russian national identity by selectively combining elements from the country's tsarist and Soviet past, highlighting features that can provide continuity, such as restoring the tune of the old Soviet national anthem in 2001, while providing new lyrics. Increasingly, the focus has been the victory over Nazi Germany, the one moment in Russia's recent history around which the population can unite. It is an 'official narrative, of a unified Soviet people marching forward to a glorious victory, a black-and-white tale of the triumph of good over evil' (p. 22).

To question any aspect of what happened during the war is tantamount to treason. What began under Mikhail Gorbachev and continued under Boris Yeltsin was a painful process of confronting Russia's difficult past. This process has all but ended. In 2009, the Kremlin established the Commission to Prevent the Falsification of History to the Detriment of Russia's Interests to counter Baltic and Central European narratives about Soviet occupation and wartime collaboration.

Moreover, in the sanitised Russian version of the war, 'fascism' is defined as Adolf Hitler's attack on the Soviet Union, and the other aspects of Hitler's system and the Holocaust are treated as incidental issues. 'It was not unusual, in eastern Ukraine,' Walker notes, 'for someone to express furious hatred for "fascists" and then in the same breath rant about the Jews or the gays as the root of all evil in the modern world' (p. 207).

The sanitisation of history extends to Joseph Stalin and to the Gulag. Walker travelled to Kolyma, the epicentre of the Gulag system, to talk to survivors and historians. Discussion of the camps was all but forbidden after Stalin's death and the freeing of prisoners, and only in the late 1980s did the non-governmental organisation Memorial begin systematically to uncover the atrocities of the

Gulag. Today, Memorial is under constant pressure from the Kremlin. During his visit, Walker also attended a history class at a school in Magadan, during which the teacher divided the blackboard into two halves. On one side she wrote the 'military and industrial achievements' of the Stalin era. On the other, 'unfortunate side-effects'. She reminded Walker that there was a threat from Germany, and that Stalin did not have time to decide who was guilty and who was not.

Putin has succeeded in creating a historical narrative that has restored the Russian people's national pride. 'Russia's glorious past has become a national obsession,' concludes Walker, 'but a prosperous future still seems a long way off' (p. 253).

China and Russia: The New Rapprochement
Alexander Lukin. Cambridge: Polity Press, 2018. £16.99.
220 pp.

Alexander Lukin has produced an informative book on the evolution of Sino-Russian ties that is part chronicle and part polemic. He begins by criticising Western scholars for not understanding how Russia and China see each other, but is equally critical of some of his Russian colleagues who, in his view, misunderstand the true nature of the relationship. He promises to acquaint the English-speaking world with the full reality of Sino-Russian ties.

Arguing that the Sino-Russian rapprochement is the natural outgrowth of developments in the late twentieth and early twenty-first centuries, he focuses on the West's attempts to impose its will on the rest of the world after the Soviet collapse. The US, Europe and allied countries viewed themselves as 'one center of power cemented together by the common totalitarian ideology of "democratism", that is, the desire to impose their model on the rest of the world' (p. 5). Lukin blames this 'dictatorial hegemony' for driving both Russia and China closer toward each other.

The USSR had begun the process of moving beyond the Sino-Soviet split under Gorbachev, but the rapprochement accelerated after post-Soviet Russia's attempts to integrate with the West were rebuffed by Washington and Brussels in the 1990s, says Lukin. Indeed, he argues that 'the West's model has reached cultural and civilizational limits' (p. 6). Brazil, Russia, India and China (the original BRICs) reject this model and the unipolar world that the West tried to create, and are moving toward the establishment of new centres of power in the 'multipolar world' that Russian officials and scholars incessantly evoke.

The Ukraine crisis accelerated the process of Sino-Russian rapprochement. Western sanctions and attempts to isolate Russia caused Moscow to intensify its ties to Beijing. Lukin points out that China, which emphasises the importance of territorial integrity given its own issues with separatists, does not agree with all of Russia's actions in Ukraine. Nevertheless, it has not publicly criticised Russia for its policies.

Lukin offers an instructive analysis of the internal politics of policymaking in both countries and how their attitudes toward each other have evolved. The Chinese were appalled by the Soviet collapse and wary of Russia in the 1990s, but view Putin's Russia as a bulwark of stability in an uncertain world. The Russians' fears of a rising China and possible Chinese designs on their territory have receded as the relationship has strengthened.

Lukin's detailed chronology of bilateral ties underscores that China and Russia have created a productive strategic partnership, but that neither side desires a full-blown alliance that would limit their respective freedom of manoeuvre. Neither country seeks a sphere of influence, he contends. They would like to create a new international order that serves their interests better than the current one. Their partnership is here to stay, he argues, and Donald Trump's initial hopes of forging an anti-Chinese partnership with Russia demonstrate that the US president profoundly misread the enduring nature of this relationship.

Putinomics: Power and Money in Resurgent Russia
Chris Miller. Chapel Hill, NC: University of North Carolina Press, 2018. $28.00. 217 pp.

In his balanced and persuasive account of the rise of 'Putinomics', Chris Miller explains how Putin has successfully crafted an economic system whose major accomplishment has been the preservation of state power and authority, and its projection abroad. He challenges the conventional Western wisdom that often depicts the Russian economy as that of a petro-state characterised by widespread corruption and an inability to modernise.

Russia under Putin, argues Miller, has sought to achieve its major goals of maintaining power, expanding Russian influence abroad and developing the domestic economy by implementing a three-pronged strategy: strengthening central authority, preventing popular unrest by guaranteeing low unemployment and adequate pensions, and relying on private business to improve efficiency – provided the latter does not compromise the first two efforts. However, while sensible macroeconomic policy has helped to stimulate growth, on 'issues such as market competition, regulation and the rule of law, the pillars of Putinomics are conducive to political control but not to economic growth' (p. xv).

The success of Putinomics is largely the product of the government's consistently conservative fiscal and monetary policy, primarily associated with Alexei Kudrin, finance minister from 2000–11 and newly appointed head of the Accounts Chamber. Russia paid back its foreign debt early. Kudrin and his allies revised the system of taxation so that the oil sector was taxed on production and export, arguing that a revenue tax was harder to cheat. Most importantly, Putin backed Kudrin when he insisted, against considerable opposition, on creating various savings funds for budget surpluses as oil prices rose in the early 2000s, instead of allowing them to be spent on pet projects. As a result, Russia entered the 2008 and 2014 economic crises with billions of dollars in reserve as a cushion.

When Putin came to power, in the wake of the 1998 financial crash, he was determined to tame the Yeltsin-era oligarchs and to ensure that private businesses did not act against the interests of the state. Two of the most powerful businessmen – Vladimir Gusinsky and Boris Berezovsky – were exiled, and one – Mikhail Khodorkovsky – was jailed for ten years and his Yukos company absorbed into the state-controlled Rosneft. The others agreed to eschew politics and work with the Kremlin. What is perhaps surprising, Miller says, is that so many oligarchs have stayed in Russia.

Russia, argues Miller, quoting economist Philip Hanson, 'has a "dual economy", with different rules and different outcomes' (p. 83). In the spheres dominated by state-owned firms and crony capitalists, corruption is rife and productivity gains limited. In other sectors, particularly those more isolated from Kremlin politics and Putin cronies, business is more efficient, transparent, modern and productive.

So far, Putinomics has given Russia stability and, in recent years, modest growth. But Miller questions the future adequacy of this model based on informal rules, arguing that, unless Russia commits itself to more thorough modernisation of the state and the economy, it will become a twenty-first-century laggard.

Rival Power: Russia in Southeast Europe
Dimitar Bechev. New Haven, CT: Yale University Press, 2017.
$27.50. 300 pp.

In this comprehensive and readable book, Dimitar Bechev explains how and why Russia has returned to the Balkans. Rejecting explanations that focus on Russia's traditional religious, historical or civilisational ties to the region, he states that the 'book's core message is that pragmatism and calculations of interest inform Russia's moves as well as the response of local players' (p. 4). Russia, he says, has no grand plan for the Balkans, nor does it have an alternative model to offer. For southeastern Europe, closer ties to Russia are a useful means of balancing relations with the European Union and the United States, and they bring the added benefit of Russian money, oil and gas.

Russia's involvement in the Yugoslav wars of the 1990s enabled it to gain a foothold in the area after the Soviet collapse, but its role in supporting NATO's military campaigns in Bosnia and Kosovo represents a painful period in its post-Soviet recovery, particularly the war for Kosovo, which led to a rift between Yeltsin and the West.

Today, Russia has returned to the western Balkans in ways which have caused their EU partners some concerns. Serbia occupies a special place. It has signed a strategic-partnership declaration with Moscow and is an observer at the Russian-led Collective Security Treaty Organisation. Russia refused to recognise Kosovo's independence and has backed Serbia on the Kosovo issue. Most Serbs believe that they should not have to choose between good relations with the EU and Russia.

Montenegro and Russia also enjoyed close ties, and Russian business is very active there. But it became a battleground in the tug of war between Russia and the West when it announced its intention to join NATO. In October 2016, the Montenegrin government accused Russia of taking part in a conspiracy to stage a coup spearheaded by a retired Serbian general. Montenegro subsequently joined NATO.

Russia has become more active in Bosnia-Herzegovina, whose fragile statehood makes it especially vulnerable to outside influences. Russia's support for the Republika Srpska (RS) has aligned it with the RS leadership's effort to shore up the autonomy of the Serb-dominated part of Bosnia, and Russia has also intervened in the RS's domestic politics, leading some EU members to call for accelerating Bosnia's EU accession.

Elsewhere in southeastern Europe, the majority of Bulgarian politicians hold favourable views of Russia, while their Romanian counterparts tend to see Russia as a threat. Russia's ties with Bulgaria today are much warmer than its ties with Romania. And the on-again, off-again Russo-Turkish relationship today is flourishing, as President Recep Tayyip Erdogan becomes increasingly alienated from the West.

Russia's military activities in the Black Sea and its energy dominance of parts of southeastern Europe make it an effective competitor with the West, as do its soft-power activities, writes Bechev. Russia, he argues, has behaved opportunistically in the Balkans: 'Its goal is to undercut and upset the existing institutions and rules set by the West' (p. 246).

The Ukrainian Night: An Intimate History of Revolution
Marci Shore. New Haven, CT: Yale University Press, 2017.
$26.00. 290 pp.

As the war in southeastern Ukraine continues to simmer, the heady days of the 2014 Maidan Revolution seem distant. Marci Shore, in this compelling, kaleidoscopic account of the 'revolution of dignity', reminds us what Ukrainians were fighting for. She has travelled both to Kiev and to the war-torn Donbas region, and has interviewed protagonists from several sides of the conflict, presenting their different stories and creating a human picture of the complexities of identity and loyalty in today's Ukraine.

Shore reminds her readers that, a decade before 'Euromaidan', Ukrainians had taken to the streets during the Orange Revolution, protesting falsified presidential-election results. The protests brought to power Victor Yushchenko in 2005, who promised to lead Ukraine to Europe. But Yushchenko, she argues, spent more time on memory politics and the rehabilitation of nationalist icons than on reforms, and the 'reign of oligarchy and corruption continued' (p. 27).

In 2010, Victor Yanukovych was elected and vacillated between Moscow and Brussels, ultimately refusing to sign an Association Agreement with the EU. In November 2013, thousands of Ukrainians heeded the call of Afghan Ukrainian journalist Mustafa Nayyem, who summoned his disillusioned fellow-citizens to the Maidan on his Facebook page. The protesters were multi-ethnic and their politics ranged from extreme left to extreme right. 'Yanukovych,' writes Shore, 'claimed to the Western media that the Maidan was filled with fascists and anti-semites – while telling his own riot police that the Maidan was filled with gays and Jews' (p. 69).

Shore's interview subjects give harrowing accounts of the brutal response of the Ukrainian special forces to the protesters, culminating, during the third week of February 2014, in the massacre of at least 100 protesters and Yanukovych's subsequent flight to Russia. Then came the Russian annexation of Crimea and the launch of a separatist war in the Donbas region. Shore criticises Europe for its response: 'The passive condoning of Putin's annexation of the Black Sea peninsula was reminiscent of Neville Chamberlain's appeasement at Munich' (p. 150).

Shore talked to those in Luhansk who both oppose and support the separatists. She describes Donbas as a special region where time has stood still. It has had a particularly difficult time coping with the aftermath of the Soviet collapse, and many of its inhabitants still regard themselves as Soviet, as opposed to Russian or Ukrainian. Kiev largely neglected the region after 1991, and this alienation from the centre created fertile soil for recruitment to the separatist cause. Some joined the separatists for money, some because they genuinely believed – as the Russians told them – that there had been a 'fascist coup' in Kiev, and others were politically indifferent but could not imagine life anywhere else. Donbas is a place where the Ukrainian state has failed.

Shore has great sympathy for the people who went to the Maidan and brought about Yanukovych's ouster, and for those who are fighting the separatists in Donbas. But the reader is left wondering how Ukrainians will judge the events of 2014 in a decade's time.

Asia-Pacific
Lanxin Xiang

The World According to Xi: Everything You Need to Know About the New China
Kerry Brown. London: I.B. Tauris, 2018. £8.99. 147 pp.

This is a very pretentious book, as its subtitle suggests. Yet Kerry Brown ultimately fails to deliver 'everything you need to know about the new China' under Xi Jinping. He starts by debunking 'Xi's story' as told by the propaganda machine of the Chinese Communist Party. Asserting that it is important to understand Xi's background (p. 5), Brown duly discusses the more than six years Xi spent being 're-educated' in rural China under Mao Zedong. According to official accounts, Xi succeeded in gaining the respect of the peasants during his time in the countryside, a claim Brown dismisses as 'contemporary hagiography' (p. 11). As someone who underwent a similar experience during the same period, I find this assessment unfair. It would have been impossible for Xi to join the party and become a team leader in the people's commune without having demonstrated exemplary performance given that his father had been purged by Mao. As the author himself notes, Xi applied for party membership ten times before being accepted (p. 15).

Brown claims that Xi's approach to dealing with internal party issues is completely different than Mao's: 'unlike Mao', he writes, 'Xi is a Party man through and through', unwilling or incapable of defying the party as Mao did during the Cultural Revolution (p. 41). This is clearly off the mark, since Xi's anti-corruption campaign has equally dismantled the party, state and military machines through ruthless purges and large-scale reshuffling. This is not the only instance in which the author's analysis of 'Xi Thought' is more imaginative than accurate.

As with Brown's previous, quickly prepared books on China, factual mistakes abound in *The World According to Xi*. For example, in discussing the anti-corruption campaign, Ling Jihua, one of the so-called 'tigers' to be jailed, is described as a 'full member of the politburo' (p. 69). Yet Ling, who served as president Hu Jintao's chief of staff for years, never entered the politburo. Similarly, Xi's marriage to the popular singer Peng Liyuan is said to have boosted Xi's career by demonstrating that 'he was a member of the elite' (pp. 16–17). In fact, the opposite is true. Peng, originally from a small town in Shandong, could not have contributed any more to Xi's career path than being the son of a leading politburo member had already done. Furthermore, the party document that officially unleashed the Cultural Revolution in 1966 is not the '16 of

July Notification' (p. 13) but the '16 of May Notification'. Many other examples could be cited.

China's Crisis of Success
William H. Overholt. Cambridge: Cambridge University Press,
2018. £19.99. 275 pp.

William Overholt, who may have been the first to identify the 'rise of China' in his 1993 book of that name, goes straight to the heart of the puzzles presented by contemporary China. He asks why the country has been so successful, why it is now facing a political–economic crisis, and what the future might hold, adding that his answers will 'vary considerably from what most readers are likely to read elsewhere' (p. viii).

Overholt has maintained a cool head since he predicted that perestroika and glasnost would end in disaster for the Soviet Union, and enthusiastically embraced the early rise of China. Since 2012, he has begun to cast doubts on China's continued success, believing that the country's earlier success derived mainly from studying and emulating the successful 'Asian Model'. Since then, the Chinese leadership – and Xi Jinping in particular – seems to have abandoned this approach, replacing it with an indigenous 'China model'. The Asian Model begins as an economy-first development strategy, but eventually leads to political reforms. The China model will not.

Overholt is not at all dogmatic on the question of whether China should democratise, finding little reason to believe that democracy could deliver economic development any better than China's existing regime. Yet he acknowledges that 'there is no successful precedent among Asian miracles for a strategy that accedes to the complexity revolution economically but tries to repress it politically' (p. 256).

The author analyses most of the pressing issues China now faces: the exhaustion of past drivers of growth, obsolete priorities and a serious financial squeeze (p. 51); as well as inequality, corruption, environmental crisis and more (p. 101). He concludes that much depends on whether Xi's administration 'is centralizing the right things and decentralizing the right things, and whether it can actually implement the needed reforms' (p. 221). He is critical of China's international policies, especially in the area of maritime disputes and Beijing's poorly implemented 'soft-power' offensive. 'There is no Beijing Consensus that is widely applicable', he writes, adding that 'illusions about a nonexistent Beijing Consensus and a practicable Washington Consensus form the basis of a remarkable amount of high-level policy thinking; if these are wrong, we need to know it. They are wrong' (p. xvi). This is an eye-opening book that debunks many established notions held by disciplinary academics, as well as by policy-makers both in China and the West.

Explaining the East Asian Peace: A Research Story
Stein Tønnesson. Copenhagen: Nordic Institute of Asian
Studies, 2017. £19.99. 263 pp.

International-peace researchers, especially in the Nordic countries, are particularly active in explaining peace phenomena from unique and innovative angles. Their analysis usually starts with a determination of whether 'peace' actually exists; if so, an inquiry is conducted into its root causes (or 'how deep' it is, to use their jargon). Finally, researchers offer their opinion on whether this peace condition is sustainable.

The first step is to look at the relevant statistics. According to Stein Tønnesson in *Explaining the East Asian Peace*, armed conflict in East Asia has dropped significantly. From 1946 to 1979, battle deaths in the region represented 80% of the global total, meaning that East Asia was the world's bloodiest region. The 1980s, however, witnessed a sharp drop, from 80% to 6.2%. Between 1990 and 2015, East Asia's share of world battle deaths dropped further still, to 1.7%, and in 2015 it was a mere 1.3% (p. 10).

What was the turning point? The author believes it arrived after the end of the Sino-Vietnamese border war in 1979 with the rapprochement between Hanoi and Beijing (p. 15). Shifting national priorities in the region, starting with post-war Japan's pacifist constitution, gradually saw territorial issues give way to economic development. According to the author, prioritising development 'can motivate governments to resolve conflicts, shelve disputes, show restraint or avoid open conflict in a crisis' (p. 77).

As for the question of whether this peace condition is viable in the long run, the author has some doubts, not least because he believes inter-state relations in Asia have deteriorated since the 2008 financial crisis. He cites five troubling trends: the shifting relative economic power of the US and China, which he predicts will accelerate their strategic rivalry; increasing Sino-Russian solidarity against US hegemony, which he believes signals a 'partial return to the dominant pattern of great power alignments in the 1950s–60s' (p. 200), as well as the annexation of Crimea, which he fears might inspire China to act similarly toward Taiwan (p. 201); a widespread regional arms race in terms of conventional weapons systems, which may be used for limited warfare; rising nationalistic sentiments across the region combined with differing interpretations of history and territorial disputes, especially in the maritime domain; and last but not least, slowing economic growth across the region.

The author concludes that, since the 2008 crisis, 'national leaders in East Asia have not done much to make regional peace more viable', instead becoming 'more vigilant in defending their narrow interests' (p. 205). The author believes that Xi Jinping's idea of building a 'new type of power relations' is worth considering, but the gap between the United States' and China's perceptions of each other remains vast. 'It is easy for a superpower, sitting on its own continent with huge oceans on either side to berate others for thinking of spheres of influence', he writes, adding that 'China will continue to feel vulnerable and therefore seek reductions in what it perceives as US military containment' (p. 218). This is a thought-provoking work.

The Secret War for China: Espionage, Revolution and the Rise of Mao
Panagiotis Dimitrakis. London: I.B. Tauris, 2017. £79.00. 272 pp.

Panagiotis Dimitrakis has made a useful contribution to our understanding of the use of espionage during China's civil war. In *The Secret War for China* he explores the complicated battlefield of the clandestine world during the Republican period. The scope of this work is impressive, encompassing the activities of both Communist and Nationalist spymasters, the astonishing war between Mao Zedong and Chiang Kai-shek on the secret front, the extraordinary rivalry between British intelligence and Comintern agents in China, Chiang's plots against his wartime allies (Britain and the US in particular), and Mao's targeting of pro-Moscow elements within his own party.

The spymasters in question include Zhou Enlai, Li Kenong, Chen Geng and Pan Hannian on the Communist side, and Dai Li, Xu Enzeng and Chen Lifu on the Kuomintang (KMT) side. Both sides engaged in assassination, sabotage, the recruitment of defectors and codebreaking during the war. The Communist intelligence network seems to have performed better in an extraordinarily harsh environment, while the government had far more resources and manpower in counter-intelligence.

The author does well in describing the failures of radio and telegraphic intelligence gathering, more often on the government side. From early on, the Communist leadership paid careful attention to this issue and succeeded in penetrating the KMT's top civilian intelligence agency, an episode that produced the Communist Party's legendary 'three musketeers', Li Kenong (the party's future spy chief), Qian Zhuangfei (misspelt by the author as 'Qian Zhunzhang', p. 27) and Hu Di. Their interception of top-secret messages via telegram saved the entire party leadership during the 1930s when a high-ranking Communist defector disclosed the whereabouts of the party's underground headquarters in Shanghai, led by Zhou Enlai (pp. 28–31).

Unlike the unified Communist system, the KMT spy network was divided into civilian and military agencies, producing a bitter rivalry between them that often hindered their work. General Dai Li's military-intelligence organisation proved to be far more resourceful and gained the confidence of Chiang Kai-shek. British intelligence in China considered Dai a formidable threat to British interests, styling him the 'Himmler of Asia'. Tensions ran so high that, in June 1940, the British decided to detain him during a secret trip to Hong Kong (p. 106).

On the Communist side, Mao emerged as the party's top leader from 1935. He was one of very few politburo members who had never been to Moscow, and was not among Joseph Stalin's favourites. As he consolidated power in the 1930s, he skilfully used the party's intelligence network to get rid of many pro-Stalin officials.

Given that the author relies almost entirely on English-language sources, this book is valuable mainly for what it tells us about international espionage. The Chinese story is murkier, with multiple misspellings of key players' names. For example, the names of KMT generals Liao Yunzhou and Zhang Kexia, both Communist moles who tipped the military balance during the crucial Huai-hai Campaign of 1948, are misspelt as 'Liao Yunsheng' and 'Zhang Gongxia'. More seriously, the author seems unaware of the critical contributions made by undercover agents such as Shen Anna (1915–2010), the stenographer for Chiang, and General Guo Rugui (1907–97), who served as director of operations within Chiang's high command during the civil war.

Origins of the North Korean Garrison State: The People's Army and the Korean War
Youngjun Kim. Abingdon: Routledge, 2018. £105.00. 248 pp.

There are very few books about North Korea's Korean People's Army (KPA), mainly because primary sources are hard to come by. This volume *does* make use of North Korean documents, as well as the personal testimonies of veterans, to illustrate how the Korean War and the KPA shaped North Korea into a closed, militarised and xenophobic garrison state.

The KPA once had several cultural factions, as many of its members had been trained by the Russians and the Chinese. Kim Il-sung's group, which had strong links with China, was the largest. It had worked with the Chinese Communist Party for more than a decade, and the guerrilla tactics it used during its 'people's war' originated in China. Indeed, more than half of the KPA's soldiers had returned to the homeland from China after the Second World War. These soldiers were seasoned fighters, having participated in guerrilla warfare against the Japanese in occupied Manchuria. In sharp contrast, the South Korean army at the beginning of the Korean War in June 1950 was incompetent and institutionally flawed. Its soldiers lacked battleground experience, their function having been largely limited to internal police action. It is therefore unsurprising that the KPA needed only three days to capture Seoul.

Given the exemplary performance of the KPA, Kim Il-sung could have unified the Korean Peninsula if the Americans had not intervened. But Kim lost control of the conflict following his army's defeat at Incheon, after which the KPA became a subsidiary fighting force to the Chinese 'People's Volunteer Army' (PVA), which had come to the rescue. The relationship between Kim and General Peng Dehuai, the Chinese commander of the PVA, was strained at best. This humiliating experience would motivate Kim to use the KPA as a key tool not only to consolidate his own power, but also to gain and maintain North Korea's sovereignty through the creation of a garrison state.

The Americans' strategic bombing campaign during the Korean War had traumatised the North Korean people by inflicting massive civilian casualties. Youngjun Kim writes that Kim Il-sung 'skillfully transformed the traumatization of the North Korean people stemming from the American bombing campaign into a community spirit of victimization' (p. ix). Importantly, this sense of victimisation was extended to the country's treatment by its allies as well. Thus North Korea, the aggressor in 1950, convinced itself of its own victimhood, a narrative that continues to underpin the country's embrace of *juche* (self-reliance). It is unsurprising that the country would pursue a nuclear deterrent given this mindset.

Closing Argument

Letter from a Young Muslim

Anonymous

In *Letters to a Young Muslim* (Picador, 2017), Omar Saif Ghobash, the United Arab Emirates' ambassador to Russia when the book was published and currently its ambassador to France, presents a series of extraordinarily candid and penetrating notional letters to his sons on the quandaries faced by Muslims in the twenty-first century. A precocious young Muslim interloper might respond as follows.

I

Habibi Omar,

How could I not respond to your heart-warming and thought-provoking letters? Although depicting Islam in a condensed way, your letters tackle a lot of issues with which our young generation will have to grapple. I wholeheartedly agree with your conviction that 'Islam is a religion in transition and in conflict with itself.' I would even go further to say that Islam as we see it in our contemporary world is overwhelmingly reactionary. It is a reaction to the technological superiority of a self-praising group of countries calling itself the 'West', a reaction to the humiliations of colonialism and a reaction to the loss of our global relevance.

European nations like France, the United Kingdom and Germany are suffering the rise of far-right ideologies as they lose their imagined global dominance. Their current misery is what we have known for more than two centuries. It was when faced by the rise of such countries that our

The author is an Iranian national living in Europe.

Survival | vol. 60 no. 4 | August–September | pp. 207–212   DOI 10.1080/00396338.2018.1495449

religious reformers sought to counteract the growing dereliction of Muslim rule. Their analysis was well founded; some famous, bright minds like Jamal al-Din al-Afghani, Muhammad Abduh and Rashid Rida handed us the primary tools for a religious rebirth. The lessons that our forefathers took from them were, however, wrong. An interest in reviving Islam gave way to an obsession with recreating the glory of the seventh century. Ignoring the probity of history, our forebears developed a destructive reading of it, akin to the view of fascists for whom some group must rule over others. Imbuing our myths with warriors and conquerors, we conflated political conquest with Islam and saw only in jihadis the actors able to bring Islam back to the fore.

We are still stuck in a besieged mindset

We forgot that we are first and foremost followers of God, and started behaving like a closed-off nation. As you rightfully state, 'Muslims [got] locked in a position of particularity rather than universality'. We not only clung to the appearances of our Prophet's lifetime (peace be upon him) instead of studying his heart and values; we also became stuck in a state of mind from the thirteenth century, when hordes of Mongols killed millions, nearly erasing our presence on earth by drowning Baghdad's dazzling libraries and starting an era of narrow parochialism and withdrawal from Islam's universal values. You note, aptly, that many of our co-religionists take cues from Ibn Taymiyyah's hateful and disgruntled writings, which shows that, despite the disappearance of Hulagu Khan's empire, we are still stuck in a besieged mindset imagining threats everywhere. Unfortunately, the real threat is not external but rather internal to our religion. Sectarianism is currently dividing the Middle East in novel ways. As sociologists would tell you, groups engage in a lot of internal strife when trying to oppose outside forces. A disaster in the making that you failed to sufficiently raise is the gradual disappearance of diversity inside our religion and the opposition to grey areas between each tradition. Although coming from a Sunni tradition, Sufism is the essence of the whole of Islam, tying our different communities together with the values of love, peace and moderation. However, scholastic guardians of the tradition and radical ideological innovators have gradually encroached upon the power of the state and managed to raise 'orthodox' Islam above the grey zones you are encouraging.

The ulema, our practitioners of jurisprudence and theology, take much of the blame in your letters, and rightly so. They have ruled my country, Iran, since 1979, and this class has greatly influenced its history, especially after the conversion to Shiism in the sixteenth century. It took me a long time to stop lumping all mullahs in the same category of archaism and bigotry. I share your view that most of them have a 'warped view of the world' and have failed to extend a theology of generosity and kindness, therefore missing out on the various ways a person can lead a worthy life. Instead of focusing on the most crucial and elementary questions of our time and using reason to make sense of the world in Islamic terms, the ulema have closed themselves off in a fortress of theology and dogma. Their interpretation of Islamic sources has given way to irrelevant and often outrageous concepts. Securing a monopoly over the faith, the Shia ulema in Iran have pushed the youth away from religion instead of being its well-meaning counsellors. For them, a Muslim is never Islamic enough to take part in a theological discussion. Only those dedicating their whole life to the Hawza or sacrificing their life in jihad are deemed to be true Muslims. The others are disdained and never knowledgeable enough. From whatever standpoint we take, we are deemed to be corrupted by the alien and nefarious 'Western' system of thought. This has led to a great impoverishment of Islamic debates; non-mainstream ideas embracing the world's complexity are rejected as alien and corrupted. The ulema have everything already sorted out for us, rules and behaviours that are to be accounted for on the day of judgement. The Muslim is turned into a rule-abiding robot without any capacity for reflection, which is considered an early sign of heresy. This vision of Islam is extremely potent. It is potent because it is professed loudly and structured clearly, identifying the good and the bad in a sentence and banishing complexity, uncertainty and fluidity from the lives and minds of believers.

Oddly enough, this view of Islam is shared by numerous Europeans I have met. Many Islamists and non-Muslims alike see Islam as a monolithic entity scheming for world domination, proud of its patriarchal structures and above all representing a totalitarian ideology. And here lies a problem that you certainly have felt: people like us, Muslims desiring a return to a more reasonable and peaceful Islam, are caught between often orientalist or even Islamophobic outsiders and our own fundamentalists. In consequence, we have deserted Islam, not as a faith but as a competitive market for ideas, and our fundamentalist opponents have managed to monopolise the religion, to the great service of far-right thinkers. Fundamentalists are not novel in religions. Islam itself has had different strands of them: from Kharijites to Hashashin and now jihadis influenced by Wahhabism. The celebrated Persian poet Hafiz himself lamented the obtuse and hateful behaviour of the religious figures of his time. As much as far-right thinkers claim that only they can define the authenticity of a nation, fundamentalists believe they alone can construe authenticity in Islam. In both groups, fluidity and questioning are signs of treason and to be forbidden. Being bi-national and brought up with insights into both Islamic and Christian theology, you and I are embodiments of the grey zones such groups want so much to erase. Yet it is not in spite of Islam but thanks to its rich tradition of tolerance and diversity that many Muslims can ably navigate this complex world.

II

From his Mogul court, Akbar the Great ruled one of the most diverse and complex countries in the world. Governing a majority of Hindus, experiencing the birth of a new religious movement called Sikhism and observing the activities of numerous Portuguese missionaries, this illiterate king is remembered for his tolerance and thirst for knowledge, be it drawn from Islamic or non-Islamic contexts. In hindsight, his rule is one in which you can truly see the universalist extent of our religion. Yet, this approach has been rejected for fear of a loss of unity among Muslims. Islam and its community, the umma, have been elevated as goals to accomplish instead of embraced as paths to follow. In lieu of servicing believers with values such as compassion, moderation and wisdom, too many religious leaders have required believers to serve Islam and the umma with violence, extremism and proselytism. This contradiction is inherent to any human system. Rousseau's social contract led people like Maximilien Robespierre to kill and maim in order to preserve the endangered unity of the vaunted 'general will' instead of using the ideals of the Enlightenment to further the French Revolution's goals. All of this leads me to ask everyone the question that you so rightfully raised: is it more ethical to have a strict Islamic system or a psychologically healthy Islamic community?

All too often, and just like you, I have observed among my relatives and friends the dull, monotonous movement of the pendulum. Another contradiction inherent to religions is the one pitting the plainness of the worldly against the sheer awe of the otherworldly. This has left many confused and unable to negotiate an equilibrium between these two worlds. Seeing two vastly different worlds has created two personalities in each of us: one seeking the pleasures on earth to the fullest, and the other spurning them. Since the two are diametrically opposed, people oscillate between them, shifting between episodes of excessive intemperance and periods of tormenting repentance. This oblivious alternation is even more flagrant in an age in which we chase intense and yet short-lived emotions, drinking through the night and dropping honest tears of worship and shame the next day at the mosque. At home we celebrate the worldly with a pinch of zealotry, while outside we adorn ourselves with the veil of modesty and religious devotion. The life of a Muslim is thus full of contradictions, but silence and censorship leadenly quell self-examination. Observable in many familial congregations, silence has become synonymous with wisdom and fulfilment, when it often represents ignorance and the repression of personality. Living intense emotional lives lurching between the sinful and the sacred, we have eschewed moderation and accepted to live permanently with a haunting emptiness.

There will always be external and internal 'threats' carrying our attention away from self-reflection. Given American imperialism, European Islamophobia and geostrategic competition among Islamic countries, there will always be excuses not to ask the many questions that could save us from contradictions, emptiness and deafening silences. As Akbar's legacy shows, however, it is by asking questions that we deepen our faith. Respecting and reviving Islam doesn't require fruitless time travel back to the so-called 'true Islam' of the seventh century. It rather means asking all the questions that our generation faces and providing us with adequate Islamic tools to make sense of the contemporary world without eschewing it. I am glad that your letters brought up all these questions, even going as far as demanding a deeper Islamic understanding of homosexuality. Given that the Shia ulema have developed a theological basis for accepting transgender identity as an assigned rather than a wilfully chosen 'illicit' sexual orientation, why shouldn't there be room for a similar dispensation for homosexuality?

III

Historiography until now has worked against the renewal of Islam. Indeed, Muslims themselves have misunderstood their history. Yet Islamic history is full of examples showing that our religion can be at the forefront of universalist values that make us human: from the strong female figures surrounding the Prophet (PBUH) to the philosophy of love developed by mystics like Rumi, there is abundant material to be used. The intertwining of our peoples' fate with others also teaches us not to recreate this warped view of the world demanding domination and clear boundaries.

Although far-right movements might relish their idea of a 'Judeo-Christian' civilisation, the more salient point is that they are as Eastern as we are Western. The fact that Europe and Islamic countries share the same misery of bigotry is representative of a broader shared history. We are bound by centuries of commerce and philosophical discussion. You might think that we are more indebted to them than they are to us because of the Industrial Revolution, but don't you remember that the core of their imagined 'Western' civilisation was transmitted through our elaboration of Greek philosophy?

I wish happiness and success to your sons, hoping that they will learn from their father.

Yours sincerely,
A young Muslim